THE NAYAKS OF TANJORE

THE NAYAKS OF TANJORE

V. VRIDDHAGIRISAN

EDITED, WITH AN INTRODUCTION, AND
SUPPLEMENTARY NOTES BY

C. S. SRINIVASACHARIAR

GYAN

Published by

GYAN

Gyan Publishing House
5, Ansari Road
Daryaganj, New Delhi-110002
Phone: 011-47034999, 9811692060
E-mail: books@gyanbooks.com

Distribution Network
gyanbooks.com
India, USA, Canada, UK, Australia, France

ISBN : 978-81-212-3811-3 (PB)
First Published, 1942

2nd Impression 2020

Printed at: Gyan Press, Delhi.

The Nayaks of Tanjore
Author: V. Vriddhagirisan

Annamalai University Historical Series No. 3

THE NAYAKS OF TANJORE

BY

V. VRIDDHAGIRISAN, M. A., M. LITT., L. T.

EDITED WITH INTRODUCTION
AND
SUPPLEMENTARY NOTES

BY

RAO BAHADUR PROFESSOR
C. S. SRINIVASACHARIAR, M. A.

PUBLISHED BY THE UNIVERSITY,
ANNAMALAINAGAR.
1942

CONTENTS

PREFACE

An attempt is made in the following pages to study the history of the Nayaks of Tanjore and this monograph embodies the results of investigations carried on by me as Senior Research Student in History in the Annamalai University during the years 1937–39. The Professor of History who kindly undertook to direct me, suggested that I should take up this subject as he was of the opinion that the rule of the Tanjore Nayaks has not so far received the much needed corrective as that of the Nayaks of Madura and Gingee has received and that there have been but few attempts at presenting a connected history of them. Till recently the *History of Tanjore Nayak Princes* by Mr. T. S. Kuppuswami Sastri in Tamil (1903) was the only attempt made to present a connected account of the Tanjore Nayaks. But his work contained very little information, as it was based mainly on the chronicles and other Sanskrit sources then available. The *Madura Manual*, the *Nayaks of Madura* and the *Aravidu Dynasty of Vijayanagara* contain more information about the Nayaks, as a result of the authors' close and critical study of the foreign sources embodied in the Jesuit letters and Portuguese chronicles. However the Nayaks of Tanjore received only a passing consideration from these authors, since they were more concerned with their chosen topics. The *Tanjore Andhra Nayak Charitam* by Mr. K. Sitaramayya Garu (1931) was the next attempt made so far, to present the history of the Tanjore Nayaks in a connected form and this author has given some additional information as a result of his study of the Telugu sources. But his treatment also is not full, and it is marked by the absence of references to the Nayaks' foreign relations. Besides, only a few epigraphs of the Nayaks were noticed. Hence a thorough and systematic study of all the available sources was undertaken to present the history of the Tanjore Nayaks in all its aspects. However, many an intricate problem still remains to be solved by future research into the still unearthed sources of epigraphy, numismatics and literature.

I wish to acknowledge my grateful thanks and indebtedness to my revered Professor, Rao Bahadur C. S. Srinivasacharyar, M.A., Head of the Department of History and Politics, Annamalai University, for his continued interest throughout the investigation. He was also kind enough to go through the manuscript and offer valuable suggestions both in regard to matter and manner. I am all gratitude to him for his encouragement, guidance and permission to make full use of his library.

I am also thankful to Rev. S. Gnânaprakâsar, O.M.I., President of the Jaffna Historical Society, Jaffna, for having kindly supplied me with extracts regarding the Nayaks' relations with Jaffna. Mr. Sistla Sathyanarayana Rajasekharam Garu, *Sangita Bhushana*, was kind enough to spare some of his leisure hours in reading some of the Telugu works for me. Pandit V. Ramakrishna Sarma, *Sahitya Siromani*, has put me under great an obligation by reading along with me some of the important and difficult portions of the Sanskrit sources. They have laid me under a deep debt of gratitude for their invaluable services rendered so ungrudgingly.

I also wish to record my thanks and gratitude to the authorities of the Annamalai University for awarding me a studentship which made this work possible.

V. VRIDDHAGIRISAN.

INTRODUCTION

The rule of the Nayaks of Tanjore which is the subject-matter of this book, written by Mr. V. Vriddhagirisan, M. A., M. Litt., L. T., a Senior Research Student in History at the University for some time, is a most important and a very significant period in the history of South India. It has left a permanent impress on the culture and institutions of that historic region and has likewise shown that a change of dynasties did not mean a rude break with the prevailing administrative institutions and cultural traditions, but, rather, their invigorated continuation. The Nayaks of Tanjore emerged as substantially independent rulers paying only formal allegiance to their Vijayanagar overlords, about the middle of the sixteenth century, when the system of governorships arranged for the government of their southern conquests displayed signs of weakening and disruption. The Tamil country had come under the control of the Vijayanagar Rayas shortly after the middle of the fourteenth century. Though we hear of recurring campaigns and victories of the generals of Vijayanagar, we know, from the testimony alike of literature and inscriptions, that the indigenous dynasties continued to rule for some time in their hereditary dominions. But with the accession of Krishnadeva Raya to the Vijayanagar throne, there began a new process of administrative reorganization of the southern districts, which inevitably led to the complete disappearance of the old ruling dynasties and to the establishment of powerful representatives of the central government in the different parts of the land.

The view is put forward in Chapter II of this treatise that the rebellion of Vira Narasinga Raya, who was in charge of the Chola and the Tondamandalam countries in part, in the early years of the reign of Achyuta Raya, and the revolt of governor Nagama Nayaka of Madura were not inter-related, as Nagama's rebellion had been already put an end to by Krishnadeva Raya himself before 1529, and that the foundation of the Tanjore Nayakship was the immediate and distinct result of the suppression of Vira Narasinga's rebellion, as well as of Achyuta Raya's perception that the whole of the Eastern Karnataka, *i.e.*, the Tamil country stretching from Chandragiri to the borders of the Tiruvadi Rajya, should not be entrusted safely to a single man, even though he might have been a personage of the stature and abilities of Visvanatha. The date of the beginning of the rule of S'evappa Nayaka, the founder of the Tanjore line, has been fixed in this book for the early part of the year 1532 A.D., since Achyuta Raya had finished his southern campaign and had proceeded against Seringapatam by July of that year, after making arrangements for the government of the Tanjore region.

Our author discusses, in the next chapter, the career of S'evappa (A.D. 1532-1580) from his youth and also his ancestry. He would hold the view that the exchange between S'evappa and Visvanatha of Trichinopoly and Vallam, respectively, was effected by Achyuta Raya himself, probably at the time when the former was appointed to the Nayakship. He also details the construction by him of the great tower at Tiruvannamalai and his other charities, his wide tolerance and patronage of all religions, including even Buddhism and Islam, and his encouragement of the Portuguese at Negapatam, testified to in an anonymous life of St. Francis Xavier; and at the end he discusses the duration of his active rule.

Mr. Vriddhagirisan takes up in Chapter IV the account of the rule of Achyutappa (A.D. 1560-1614) to whom he attributes a long rule of over 50 years. Achyutappa's loyalty to his suzerain was productive of a lasting bitterness between Tanjore and Madura. He tries to show that what Venkatapati Raya did to the cause of the Empire in the north, that Achyutappa did in the south. The campaign undertaken by Venkatapati against Virappa Nayaka of Madura (1572-95) in which the battle of Vallamprākāra was the most important event, has been generally ignored in the indigenous historical works.

In this connection, our author discusses the significance of the Pudukkottai Plates of *Saka* 1505, particularly that portion of them, which has been interpreted to imply that Achyutappa Nayaka fought in this campaign against his overlord, instead of for him, and arrives at the conclusion that Venkatapati Raya and his loyal ally of Tanjore defeated Virappa Nayaka of Madura and thus contrived to nip in the bud the earliest attempt at independence on the part of the Madura rulers who generally followed a policy of insubordination and non-co-operation and of positive disloyalty towards the suzerain power. We learn that Virappa attempted a second attack on Tanjore towards the close of his rule. His successor, Muttuvirappa Nayaka (1603-1623), was, however, generally considered to be the first ruler of Madura to exhibit open hostility towards Tanjore; he was also the real fore-runner and example of Tirumala Nayaka in the display of an attitude of open and active disloyalty to the suzerain. Some doubt prevails as to the waging of a war by Venkatapati against Madura and Tanjore in 1610, though there was an actual struggle raging between Tanjore and Madura during that period. The Jesuit letters, upon the evidence of which such an assumption has been made, are shown to contain nothing definite that would indicate either a war or even a refusal of the usual tribute either by Tanjore or by Madura now or even earlier, as those letters largely relate to statements and general observations made about the prevailing political situation. From an inscription of 1609 we learn that Venkatapati Raya made a gift of a village on the north bank of the Cauveri to some Brahmans at the request of Muttuvirappa Nayaka who was till then loyal; but the records of the next year, though they do not imply the continuance of friendly relations, yet reveal no open manifestation, as yet, of hostility to the emperor by the Madura Nayak. As to the war between Tanjore and Madura waged in 1610-11, there is also no definite information available as to how it came to a close. Attention is drawn by our author to the fact of Achyutappa's co-operation with Venkatapati Raya in the latter's wars with the Muhammadans, and to the Tanjore Crown Prince, Raghunatha, winning a victory over them at Penukonda in A.D. 1589. The evidence of Jesuit letters held to support the view that the Nayak of Tanjore had adopted an insurgent attitude, probably even as early as 1598-99, is well attempted to be countered on the basis of data gleaned from the indigenous chronicles that definitely point to a continued display of Tanjore's co-operation and loyalty. The letter of Coutinho, of 17th July 1600, is claimed to refer, in all probability, to the revolt of the Nayak of Gingee and not to that of the Tanjore ruler. Achyutappa Nayaka's victory over the Portuguese at Negapatam, described in the *Sāhityaratnākara*, cannot be ascertained in all its details, on account of lack of corroborating evidence; it was probably undertaken on behalf of the Jaffnese ruler and was the first of a series of wars that continued for several decades between the Nayaks and the Portuguese. The enemy against whom Achyutappa waged war cannot be held to mean the Dutch, because by the end of the first decade of the seventeenth century they had established themselves only in Tegnapatam in the kingdom of Gingee, and they were then negotiating from the Nayak of Tanjore for permission to settle at the port of Tirumalarajanpatnam.

The question of the date of the termination of Achyutappa's active rule is answered by the conclusion, arrived at on epigraphical evidence, that shows clearly that Raghunatha, his son, had become associated with the administration at least from A.D. 1600; and this inference is held to be strengthened by that gleaned from the Jesuit letters. We also learn that Achyutappa did not abdicate actually in or shortly before 1600 and die at Srirangam soon afterwards, as maintained, but probably abdicated only about 1614 and lived on till A.D. 1617. Our author attempts to reconcile the evidence of the *Sāhityaratnākara* and the work of Ramabhadramba on this matter and shows that these two works are not contradictory in their data in reality, but are only complementary to each other. Raghunatha had become the Yuvaraja sometime before A.D. 1589; but his actual coronation as ruler took place only about 1614; it was necessitated in view of the growing danger caused by the outbreak of the civil war of succession to the Chandragiri empire.

Raghunatha Nayaka (A.D. 1600-1634) was the most illustrious prince of his line; and he made Tanjore the Florence of South India. It has been rightly shown in Chapters V and VI of this book that but for him the history of the Nayaks of Tanjore would have been dull and comparatively lifeless. The famous War of Succession to the empire of the Rayas in the years 1614-17, in which Raghunatha greatly distinguished himself as the chief ally of the loyalist party, has been unravelled in this book clearly, in the historical sequence of its successive stages and incidents, from out of the discrepant and perplexing accounts of his military exploits as given by Ramabhadramba and Yagnanarayana Dikshita. The former's account is full regarding the battle of Tōppur and Raghunatha's part therein; while the latter stops with the Nayak leaving his capital for the campaign, but gives an almost epic description of the Tanjore army and its equipment. The historical sequence of the incidents of this momentous war is proved to be best understood only in the light of a careful and comparative evaluation of the evidence contained in the indigenous works and the letters of Barradas and Jesuit missionaries. Raghunatha's subjugation of the powerful and cruel of S'ōḻaga of Devikottai (Ṭivukotta) at the mouth of the Coleroon, who was one of the principal feudatories of Gingee and who was obviously helped by the Portuguese (termed *Pāraśikas* in the *Sāhityaratnākara* and as *Paraṅgis* in the *Ragunāthābhyudayam*) follows. As a consequence of Raghunatha's victory, Krishnappa, the Nayak of Gingee, who had sided his powerful feudatory, is said to have fled from the field of battle. The Tanjore Nayak immediately followed up this initial victory by a march along the coast to the Gulf of Mannar; and after crossing the sea by a chain of boats, he managed to land on the Jaffnese coast where he defeated the Portuguese who had usurped power, and installed the native ruler. A detailed treatment is given, in this connection, by our author, of the help rendered by Tanjore to the rulers of Jaffna from Achyutappa's time, *i.e.*, from about the middle of the 16th century. It deals, clearly and in some detail, with the many troubles that affected the politics of Jaffna in this period, and gives a connected narrative of the fortunes of the Jaffnese rulers on the basis of an examination o

Jaffnese accounts like the *Yālpāna Vaibhava Mālai* of Mayilvāhana Pulavar (of the early 17th century) and the Portuguese chronicles. Some confusion was entertained between Sangili, the Jaffnese ruler, who was helped by S'evappa Nayaka in 1547, against the Portuguese and the later Sangili Kumara, the usurper, who sought the assistance of Tanjore in 1616 A.D. and seems to have regained his kingdom with the aid of its forces under one Khem Nayak. The dates 1616 and 1617 for Raghunatha's intervention given by some recent writers on the history of Ceylon cannot be accepted as, according to more definite and reliable evidence, Raghunatha was on his march to Tōppur in August 1616 after having finished the Jaffnese campaign. It is however held to be a matter of uncertainty whether Raghunatha went over to Jaffna and led the campaign in person or whether the Tanjore forces were led by Khem Nayak, as has been described in some of the sources. Raghunatha's intervention in favour of Sangili Kumara did not settle the matter of the Jaffnese succession; and the Portuguese chronicles tell us of subsequent sporadic attempts made by the Tanjore Nayak to regain Jaffna from the Portuguese into whose hands it had definitely fallen about A. D. 1620. In view of the fact that the Dutch were then pursuing a policy of friendly relations with Venkatapati Raya and of the definite statement we have from their records that Hans de Haze who came to Masulipatam about the end of 1616 to improve the Dutch prospects on the Coromandel Coast, enjoined an attitude of strict non-intervention in all native affairs and in the War of Succession then raging in the land, it is justifiably held by our author that the Pārasīkas who composed a part of the Tanjore infantry could not have been the Dutch. Raghunatha's part in the War of Succession did not cease with the victory at Tōppur, but was prolonged into a subsequent campaign against Krishnappa Nayaka of Gingee who had to be driven from an advance position he held, back into his dominions to the north of the North Vellar river.

The consequences of these campaigns connected with the War of Succession, as regards the distribution of political power in the south were to make Raghunatha, supreme, for the time being, among his fellow Nayaks and the most powerful ruler in the Tamil country. Raghunatha's subsequent attempts to conquer the kingdom of Jaffna were made on behalf of his *protége*, the Prince of Ramanaçor (or Rameswaram), and these are also noticed as indicated above. Again, stress is properly laid on the policy of complete and unalloyed loyalty that Raghunatha displayed towards his suzerain; and an attempt is made here to prove that Raghunatha's attitude was one of complete co-operation and was not marked at any time either by any suspicion or by any actual exhibition of disloyalty as has been assumed by some historians, largely on the basis of the letters of the Jesuit Fathers, which have to be correlated with other available contemporary sources for enabling the student to come to final conclusions.

While Raghunatha's reign witnessed the advent of the Dutch, the Danes and the English in the Tanjore realm, it is remarked that the arrival of the Danes on the coast and their founding of a settlement at Tranquebar happened without any previous plan and the date of the settlement of their factory was not 1612, as mentioned in the *Imperial Gazetteer*. The English made an attempt to found a factory in the kingdom in 1624 at Karikal; but the Portuguese and the Danes were greatly opposed to this move and dissuaded the Nayak through presents and representations; and in consequence he made an outrageous demand that the English should pay an annual rent of 7,000 *rials of eight* for this privilege. Their failure was largely due to the intrigues of the Danes, who enjoyed a considerable amount of influence with the Nayak and who even went to the extent of influencing the governor of Pondicherry under the Nayak of Gingee to prevent the English from founding a factory there. It is interesting to learn, in connection with these events, some new details of the remarkable career of Mallaiya (*alias* Chinana Chetty) who played a very prominent part in the politics and trade of the coast for very many years and who set off, on several occasions, the decaying power of the Raya of Chandragiri against the Dutch and *vice versa*. He had in his service a large body of soldiers and frequently and freely changed sides in the kaleidoscopic shiftings of power between the European settlements, the struggling Raya and the advancing Muhammadans.

Raghunatha's epigraphs are found scattered from Tirukōshtiyur in the Ramnad district to Nedungunram, the home of his ancestors, and Narattampuṇdi, in the North Arcot district. His great minister, Govinda Dikshita, figures prominently in a number of these. A separate chapter is devoted by our author to the detailing of the career and achievements of this great minister. Raghunatha's numerous charities and impartial patronage of all the prevailing religious faiths, his learning, martial exploits and musical skill have been adequately dwelt upon. Stress is laid on the view that he was a great authority on the science of Carnatic Music and could even be 'deemed to be the founder of it', as he was the author of new *rāgas* and new *tāḷas*. The authorship of the *Sangīta Sudha* is also attributed to him, though his minister's second son, Venkatamakhi, refers to it as having been written by his father at the request of Raghunatha; and the view is here put forth that the work was very probably written by the Nayak in collaboration with his great minister. Among the great scholars that graced Raghunatha's court were Govinda Dikshita and his two sons, Yagnanarayana and Venkatamakhi, Raja Chudamani Dikshita, Bhaskara Dikshita and the well-known Lakshmi Kumara Tatacharya, who was Rajaguru to the Rayas and probably conducted the coronation of Venkata II in 1630, and whose active life extended for a number of years from about A. D. 1575 to about 1630, as evidenced by epigraphical references. Ramabhadrāmba was only one of the several accomplished ladies that graced the Nayak's court which also patronised theatricals and wherein the southern school of Telugu literature contributed to the growth of the *Yakshagana* type of drama.

Govinda Dikshita's career is sketched in brief compass, but in very good proportions, in the succeeding chapter. It is certain that the Dikshita was prominent at the Tanjore court only from the last years of S'evappa's rule. From an examination of the epigraphs, his active association with the government of Tanjore may be said to have lasted from A. D. 1588 to 1634; perhaps he had settled at Tanjore a few years prior to the demise of S'evappa. Apart from his numerous and magnificent charities and public works, the Dikshita devoted much attention to the promotion of learning; and there is sufficient evidence to show that, side by side with Sanskrit learning, Tamil literature also seems to have been fostered by him and that personally he was responsible for the translation of the *Tiruvaiyār Māhātmyam* into Tamil about A. D. 1605. The skill of the Dikshita as an author is illustrated by the title of *Advaita Vidyāchārya* attached to him; and his son, Venkatamakhi, says distinctly that his father re-established the Advaita School of Philosophy and was, in this respect, an elder contemporary of the great Appayya Dikshita. The minister's patronage of Carnatic Music was equally notable. He was believed to have been well versed in the science of astrology as well and to have written a treatise on it. The Dikshita's impartial justice is well-known and he was practically a court of arbitration in himself. We learn that the Dikshita was mainly responsible for the abundant patronage of the Saiva temples indulged in by the Nayaks, who were professed votaries of Vishnu.

The brilliant literary renaissance which marked the later years of Raghunatha's rule was largely inspired by the Dikshita. An apt parallel may be traced between the long ministerial career of this

Tanjore minister and the even more famous Aryanatha Mudaliar, the co-adjutor and *Dalavay* of Visvanatha Nayaka of Madura, who was for over fifty years the second in power in the Madura state and was especially responsible for the quasi-feudal organization of the Pālaiyam system in the Pandyan country—the poligars of the south continuing to be specially attached to his memory even at the present day. The absence of any mention of either the Dikshita or his son Yagnanarayana in the records and literature of the reign of Vijayaraghava Nayaka has led some writers to think that both of them must have died about the same time, *i. e.*, soon after the accession of this Nayak.

Vijayaraghava (A. D. 1633—1673) the last of the Nayak line, also known as Mannārudasa, has not left a rich epigraphical heritage, and we have to rely for his reign mostly on the indigenous chronicles and on Jesuit letters. A certain amount of uncertainty exists about the exact date of his assumption of power and about his relations with his brother, Ramabhadra. The available evidence is also discrepant as to the method by which he attained the throne, whether by violence or by peaceful means. Literary evidence gives no clue as to whether Ramabhadra, the other son of Raghunatha, who is said to have accompanied his father in the campaign leading to the Tōppur battle, was killed in the field, or returned home in safety. If Ramabhadra did survive, one cannot be definite why and how Vijayaraghava attained the throne in 1633 when his father was still alive; Raghunatha's death should be dated only in the following year, on the authority of his epigraphs. Vijayaraghava (Chapter VIII) continued to be devoted and loyal towards his suzerain as his predecessors had been, and this factor effectively kept the aggressions of Tirumala Nayaka out of range of Tanjore politics, at least in the early years of his rule. But as time went on and as Vijayaraghava came to be hard pressed by Tirumala on one side and the ever-threatening Muhammadan advance on the other, his attitude towards the last of the Rayas, Emperor Sriranga III (*acc.* 1642), became uncertain and vacillating. The political conditions of the land at the time were such that they offered only two alternatives to the Nayak, either to co-operate with Sriranga and thus to work out his own ruin at the hands of the Muslim enemies or to abandon the Raya and save himself from the prospect of immediate destruction.

With Mysore under Kanthīrava Narasa Raja Udayar practically independent, with Madura under Tirumala Nayak positively truculent.

and with Gingee always aiding Madura and, above all, with the Muhammadans both of Bijapur and Golkonda surging south into the neighbourhood of Vellore and Gingee, the political conditions were very unfavourable to Tanjore and greatly injurious to her traditional policy of loyalty to the empire. Soon after the accession of Sriranga III to the throne (1642), troubles began.

To explain the situation, we may be permitted to indulge in a little digression. Sriranga Raya who was the last emperor of Vijayanagar, succeeded to the throne in quite unpropitious circumstances. Even his very succession was opposed by the powerful Damarla Venkata, governor of Wandiwash and brother-in-law of the late Raya, and by several other chiefs. The Golkonda forces which had advanced to the neighbourhood of Pulicat and Venkatagiri, perhaps at the instigation of Damarla Venkata, now became more aggressive; and Sriranga, detecting the Nayak in intrigue with Golkonda, imprisoned him and deprived him of his territories; but he was soon forced to release him and restore him to his dominions, on account of the pressure brought to bear on him by the Nayak's brother and kinsmen. The Raya put up a bold front and attempted all means to preserve his state which had been already enfeebled by wars of succession, repeated rebellions of feudatories, the steady pressure of Bijapur in Western Karnatak and of Golkonda on Madras and Eastern Karnatak. In addition there were the kaleidoscopic changes in the relations of the Raya and his Nayaks, *inter se*, and in their alliances with the invaders and the further confusion caused by the European powers of the coast.

According to Jesuit evidence, Tirumala Nayak formed an alliance with both his brother rulers of Tanjore and Gingee; but the former of these two seems to have fallen off from that alliance as soon as he came to know of the aim of the confederates and to have actually betrayed the plans of the latter to Sriranga. The Raya is said to have thereupon attacked Gingee; but when his own capital was threatened with an invasion by the Muhammadans of Golkonda, he had to beat a hasty retreat from his objective back to his headquarters; but he contrived to gain a victory over the Muhammadan invaders with whom one of his own feudatories, Damarla Venkatappa, had been intriguing. Some time after 1645, the Raya's position had become strengthened and he even contrived to push back the advance of Golkonda for the time being. Soon, however, his ill-luck began to pursue him and we have in the Dutch records a reference to the defeat of the Raya under the walls of Vellore itself by the Bijapur army. This set-back of the Raya was brought about through the intrigues of Mir Jumla, the Golkonda general who, after the defeat that he suffered, negotiated both with Bijapur and with Kanthīrava Narasaraja Udaiyar of Mysore to bring about the combined attack on Vellore. Consequent upon Sriranga's withdrawal from Gingee, the position of Tanjore perhaps became worse in its relations towards Madura and Gingee, though we have no direct evidence on the point. Yet the claims made in Vijayaraghava's *Raghunāthābhyudayam* that he compelled the *Pandya* and *Tundira* to sue for peace when they opposed Sriranga and made them wait at his door, must have reference to this period. The turn that was given to the politics of the country by a renewal of the Muhammadan attack upon the Rāya has been carefully indicated. Sriranga, finding his position endangered at every turn, felt convinced that he must effect a concerted combination of all the Hindu forces and that he would have no chance of success unless he should secure the support of all the three Nayakas and according to Prōēnza, he spent more than a year trying to bring about a combination, during which the Muhammadan armies quietly achieved the conquest of the heart of his dominions. We read in this book that Tanjore was not opposed but, on the other hand, remained loyal to the Raya at the time of his attempted combination. The suspicion that was cast against Vijayaraghava for having allowed Sriranga to go to Western Karnataka for help and for having practically abandoned him in a crisis is countered by a stress laid on what was probably the real situation, namely, that Sriranga despaired of the prospects of a joint action on the part of the Nayaks, left Tanjore and Vijayaraghava to their fate and tried to secure the help of the powerful Sivappa Nayaka of Ikkeri, who had already helped him in raising the second siege of Vellore and was enjoying considerable reputation for power. The successful siege and capture of Gingee by the Muhammadans in the end of 1648 led to their advance on Tanjore itself and Vijayaraghava had to purchase peace from them at a very heavy cost. He is blamed severely for his cowardly submission, as well as for his abandonment of his suzerain in the latter's last attempt. It is clearly explained here that it was the continued determination of Madura not to join Tanjore and the proved ability of the Madura Nayak to prevent any likely alliance between Tanjore and Mysore that worsened Vijayaraghava's helplessness and brought about his impotent and ignominious surrender. What has elsewhere been called the fall of Hindu Karnatak into the hands of the Muhammadans was thus quietly accomplished by 1649. Sir J. N. Sarkar's view that all the three Nayaks considered the decline of their suzerain as a golden opportunity for gaining *Pūrṇa Swaraj* and accomplishing the extension of territory is perhaps somewhat unjust to Vijayaraghava. After the fall of Gingee, the Bijapur army, as we saw above, marched against the Nayaks of Tanjore and Madura and returned victorious with a great deal of treasure. But Sriranga seems to have shortly afterwards recovered a part of his former dominions with the help of Mysore and even repulsed a Golkonda army that had advanced to oppose him. But it was the fatal and persistent disunion among his two southern feudatories that prevented his getting any further victory. Tirumala Nayaka appealed to the Muslims, opened the mountain passes in the west of his dominions to them and enabled them to push forward into Mysore itself from a fresh vulnerable quarter. The Raya tried to reconquer the Vellore district, but was finally deprived of his royal capital by a Bijapur army after a long seige, and forced to content himself with Chandragiri.

Some time later, the war was renewed and the Bijapurians made their second invasion against the Raya in 1653. The practical destruction of the Raya's power led to the further weakening of Tanjore. Once again, Bijapur easily got the submission of Vijayaraghava. The Muhammadans had thus completely annexed Gingee, made Tanjore a vassal state and got annual tributes from Madura. After this time, Vijayaraghava's troubles chiefly came from Madura and in order to protect himself from this inveterate foe, he had to adopt a policy of total submission to the Muhammadans. Once again, according to Jesuit evidence, he was guilty of having obstinately maintained the family feud with Madura in the face of the Muhammadan advance, after Muttuvirappa had succeeded Tirumala. Encouraged by the lack of even a passing understanding between these two houses, the Bijapur ruler despatched a very large army against them. Vijayaraghava fled to Vallam, leaving Tanjore to be defended by his son-in-law. Both the forts fell and the Nayak became a fugitive. This disaster happened in the spring of 1659. Madura now played a better part and offered a stubborn resistance to the Muslim advance; and the Muhammadan army, finding a continuous occupation of the land difficult, owing to the continued prevalence of famine and the troubles from the Kallars who were adepts at plunder and cattle-lifting, departed while Vijayaraghava reoccupied his throne. But he was not to enjoy any peace; and there now began fresh troubles with Madura. The new Madura Nayak Chokkanatha, after suppressing a domestic revolution and freeing himself from the danger of supersession, declared war upon Tanjore for co-operating with his traitorous general Lingama, who had joined the Bijapur commander, Shahji Bhonsle. This invasion of Tanjore by

Madura took place in 1660-61 and the victory of Madura was easy and marked. On account of the prevailing confusion and famine in the Tanjore country, a large number of poor people were enticed by the Dutch to their settlement at Negapatam with promise of abundant food supplies and then heartlessly sold as slaves and transported to labour on their plantations in the Eastern Archipelago. Nor did the submission of Vijayaraghava bring about the longed-for peace for the unfortunate land. In 1663 when the Bijapur general, Vānamiyān (Bahlol Khan Miana ?) came south, he laid seige to Trichinopoly, plundered the surrounding region and went away after receiving a large sum from the Madura Nayak. Thereupon the indignant Chokkanatha turned on the faithless Tanjore Nayak, who had, in violation of the recent treaty between them, joined the Muhammadan invaders. He now marched on Tanjore for the second time, took the citadel of Vallam and left a garrison therein. Proenza speaks of Vijayaraghava having been decisively defeated and greatly fleeced by Chokkanatha on this occasion. Shortly afterwards, Vijayaraghava contrived to secure peace in the border country. But both sides remained prepared for war. Vijayaraghava fortified Tanjore, Arantangi, Pattukkottai and Tirupattur on his southern border, while Chokkanatha transferred his headquarters to Trichinopoly in 1665 and greatly strengthened its fortifications with a view to making it a base of operations against Tanjore. The impending storm broke out in 1673 over an apparently trivial cause, relating to Vijayaraghava's refusal to give his daughter in marriage to the Madura Nayak. But this was only a superficial excuse, as has been well pointed out by our author. The proposed marriage alliance, refusal of permission to which by Vijayaraghava was generally held to be the immediate cause of war, has been differently interpreted and even the fact of it has been questioned, particularly when the Madura chronicles make no mention either of this marriage proposal or of the earlier alleged marriage of Tirumala Nayaka with Raghunatha Nayaka's daughter.

According to Prof. R. Sathianathier, the author of the *Nayaks of Madura*, it was Tanjore's part in the struggle of Chokkanatha against the Mysore ruler, Devaraja Udayar, and the consequent disagreement between Tanjore and Madura as a result of their defeat at the battle of Erode (1670) that probably precipitated this war, though the fact of Vijayaraghava's sending his general to participate in the Erode battle at all would require to be supported by further evidence. The reconquest by Vijayaraghava of the territories lost to Madura in the previous war and the continuance of the old animosities between the two houses should have been the main causes of this momentous war of 1673. The advance of the victorious army of Madura to Vallam and thence to Tanjore, Vijayaraghava's plan to have the zenana blown up at a given moment and his perishing along with his son, Mannārudāsa, in the fatal fight, the resultant annexation of the Tanjore Raj by Madura and its government being entrusted to Aḻagiri Nayaka, a foster-brother of Chokkanatha—these are all detailed in cogent sequence. The Jesuit letter of 1673 which gave an account of this war is lost to us. But a subsequent letter, dated 1676, begins with a reference to this war and to the occupation of Tanjore by Aḻagiri Nayaka.

Vijayaraghava's relations with the Portuguese seem to have been generally friendly except for a short break. Their hold over Negapatam ceased in 1658 and when the Dutch first occupied it, Vijayaraghava did not acquiesce in their possession; but soon he gave them a charter, at the instance of the formidable Mallaiya (*alias* Chinana Chetty), confirming them in their acquisition and even supplementing it four years later with another, sanctioning the starting of a separate mint at that port, and further following it up with the grant of the port of Tirumalarajanpatnam. The Danish settlement at Tranquebar did not seem to have been very flourishing in Vijayaraghava's time. Chokkanatha after he became the master of Tanjore offered to cede both Negapatam and Tranquebar to François Martin, the French Captain and the Founder of Pondicherry, in return for his help in driving away the Dutch and the Danes from his kingdom. The English attempt to settle at Karikal and at the acquisition of Tranquebar from the Danes and their further attempt to found a factory at Devicottah—all proved to be failures.

The long reign of Vijayaraghava which thus ended in disaster was, however, marked, as in the case of all his predecessors, by considerable cultural activity. His court was graced by the great Vaishnava teacher, Kumāra Tātāchārya, and by numerous men of letters including several well-known poetesses like Rangājamma, as well as some musical composers. Vijayaraghava and his son Mannarudasa, were themselves authors of no mean repute. According to the high authority of Jayanti Ramiah Pantulu, the Telugu Prabhanda literature, inaugurated by Allasani Peddana, attained its glory under the careful nourishment and patronage of Vijayaraghava, who likewise gave an impetus to the development of the drama. His political ineptitude and military impotence were redeemed to some extent by his cultural brilliance.

Coming to the last days of the Tanjore Nayakship, the emergence of Chengamaladas (A.D. 1674–1675), either a son or grandson of

Vijayaraghava, the enmity between Aḷagiri Nayaka and his master Chokkanatha, the appeal of Rayasam Venkanna to Bijapur for help to place Chengamaladas on the Tanjore throne, the resultant march of Vyankaji (Ekoji Bhonsle) against Aḷagiri, his occupation of Arni and victory at Ayyampet over the usurper—these form the chief episodes in the first act of the drama of Maratha occupation of Tanjore and have been told in brief compass in chapter IX of this book.

The crowning of Chengamaladas by Vyankaji, the conspiracy between the latter and Rayasam Venkanna, the advance of Vyankaji from Kumbakonam upon Tanjore and the flight of Chengamaladas to Ariyalur —these constitute the main events in the second stage of this fateful drama. The Maratha usurpation of the Tanjore throne in the early part of 1675 has been severely condemned by an indigenous historian, Narayana Kone, who stresses the injustice and immorality of the action of Vyankaji and informs us that all his wealth was expended in a very short time in fighting against the chiefs who were alienated, forcing him to confiscate the wealth of the temples which roused the anger of his minister Raghunatha Narayan Hanumante, and brought about the subsequent invasion of the Carnatic by Sivaji. The fate of Chengamaladas and of his descendants can only be gleaned from traditional stories.

A general account of the features of the Nayak rule is given at the end of the book. One very advantageous feature that characterised the Tanjore kingdom was the relative absence of the Pāḷayam system, which had become so deep-rooted in the sister kingdom of Madura. The agents of the Nayak collected all the taxes; but village administration seems to have run very much in the old groove. Epigraphical evidence gives us details about the numerous and varied taxes levied, though we know little about their incidence. The army expenditure, in the absence of feudal levies, was very great, while public works like the construction of tanks and irrigation channels and temples were not neglected. We read that while learning and fine arts were patronised in an abundant measure, the government of the Nayaks did not take an active interest in extending facilities for education to the general public, but merely contented itself with allowing the indigenous institutions to continue their work. The progress of Carnatic Music and of fine arts such as sculpture and painting was very marked under the Nayaks. The rule of a Telugu dynasty over a Tamil kingdom with such cultural and other benefits to the land is indeed a most striking and creditable feature in the history of South India and forms a most pleasing epoch of vigorous and continuous cultural growth.

In introducing this useful treatise to the public in general and to the world of scholars in particular, I can confidently say that it has been carefully worked out by the author on the basis of data garnered as the fruit of patient study of the different sources,—indigenous literature epigraphs, notices of missionaries and foreign writers, and other supplementary material, traditional as well as literary. The documentation has been made as full as the necessities have required. I have no hesitation in saying that this carefully drawn up and clear account of the Nayaks of Tanjore has been made as authentic, impartial in its arguments and moderate in the conclusions as to disputed points, as has been possible. The book fills a long-standing gap in the historical literature bearing on the dynasties of the Tamil country and has been appropriately published under the auspices of the Annamalai University, one of whose aims is the resuscitation of the history of the Tamil land.

Annamalai University,
Annamalainagar,
30—8—1942.

C. S. SRINIVASACHARI.

CHAPTER I

INTRODUCTION

The rule of the Nayaks of Tanjore which comprises roughly a period of about a hundred and fifty years from the second quarter of the 16th century down to the third quarter of the 17th century, has not hitherto received sufficient attention at the hands of historians. The Nayaks of Tanjore who started their rule first as loyal feudatories under the patronage and authority of the mighty Vijayanagara Emperors, grew in course of time to be independent of the suzerain power; but they were never disloyal to their overlords as they were related to the Imperial house and it was only during the time of the last ruler that Tanjore lagged behind in extending her helping hand to the kings of Vijayanagar. Even this was largely due to her own internal weakness and degeneration. The Nayak rule came into existence when the suzerain power was in its palmy days and declined, undergoing all the vicissitudes of fortune so much characteristic of almost all our ancient dynasties. Unlike other dynasties that rose and fell and whose memory and achievements have become past history, the Nayaks have left deep and indelible marks of their rule and benevolence behind, and such monuments still remind the on-looker that their age was after all not far removed in tempo and culture from the modern times. The Chola country and its capital, Tanjore, became the centre of all their activities and it may be said that the period of their rule formed the connecting link between the epoch of Chola rule and the intrusion of foreign powers into the land. Thus the land after the decline of its indigenous Tamil rulers, passed on under the sway of Telugu chiefs coming from the north and after them of Marathas, before it came to be absorbed in the British dominion in the beginning of the 19th century.

Mr. J. H. Nelson (of the Madras Civil Service and author of *The Madura District, A Manual*: 1868) was the first writer to devote some attention to the rule of the Tanjore Nayaks in his well-known work; but his account is meagre and far from satisfactory. He had indeed made a careful study of the Tamil and Telugu chronicles besides the epigraphs then available and had also brought to bear upon his work foreign evidence contained in the letters of the Jesuits and other writers who had come to visit the land from as early as the 16th century. But Tanjore received only a passing and necessarily secondary consideration in his narrative as he was concerned mainly with the history of Madura; and so reference to Tanjore and its affairs was made only wherever and whenever she came into contact with Madura and her politics. However meagre the information might be, yet it contains a good account of one phase of the history of Tanjore under the Nayaks and furnishes a picture drawn with critical historical judgment based on historical facts. Moreover, his treatment served as the basis for others who followed him. 'The History of the Tanjore Nayaks' in Tamil by Mr. T. S. Kuppuswamy Sastri (1903) was the next attempt made to present a connected account of their work. But it was not meant to serve as an elaborate and exhaustive account and so it remains a meagre narrative based upon Nelson and some indigenous chronicles and accounts available in the Tanjore Palace Library. *The Tanjore Manual* by Mr. T. Venkasami Rao (1883) contains some information about the Nayaks; but much of the matter embodied in it is only an annotated version of what is contained in Mr. Nelson's and Dr. Caldwell's works (*The Madura Country, A Manual* and *A History of Tinnevelly*). The account given in the *Tanjore Gazetter* by Mr. Hemingway (1906) is largely based upon Nelson and Mr. Kuppuswamy Sastri with reference to the history of the period of the Nayak rule. 'The History of the Nayaks of Madura (1924)' by Prof. R. Sathianatha Aiyar, the 'Aravidu Dynasty of Vijayanagara' (1929) by the Rev. Father Henry Heras. S. J., and the 'Tanjore Andhra Nayaka Charitam' (1932) by Kuruganti Sitaramayya Garu are more recent publications; they embody valuable information regarding the Tanjore Nayaks; and their treatment bears ample testimony to the fruit of modern historical scholarship and criticism bearing on South Indian History in the 16th and 17th centuries. The greater portion of the available and necessary information pertaining to these Nayaks has been carefully collected, collated and made use of by them; but they are not unanimous in their views about affairs and in the sequence of events. Thanks are due to the indefatigable energy of the first two of the above mentioned scholars for their great service in getting translations from the French, of the contemporary Jesuit letters contained in 'La Mission de Madurē' and also the originals of the important letters written in the Portuguese language. Father Heras gives us valuable additional information as a result of his wide and intensive study of the letters of of the Jesuit missionaries. Mr. Sitaramayya's book in Telugu presents a connected account of the rulers of the dynasty; the author has studied carefully the available Telugu sources and made a good use of them. A historian needs to be dispassionate and disinterested in his treatment of historical material. This golden rule seems, however, to have been kept out of view by the author in his treatment of the dynasty generally and of the last Nayak in particular, when he grows extravagantly eloquent on the moral and ethical fruits of his reign and activity. Besides, the author's own parochial views are allowed full and free play. His conclusions are based only on Telugu sources and a few inscriptions and the category of foreign evidence has been largely ignored by him.

Sources.—The principal material for the history of the Tanjore Nayaks falls under two broad divisions, *viz.*, literary and epigraphical. Under the former we have the native chronicles and memoirs, most of which are however not strictly contemporary, but belong to later times. They contain the local traditions current at the time of their composition. The manuscripts collected by Colonel Colin Mackenzie (studied and classified in William Taylor's 'Oriental Historical Manuscripts' 1835, and his 'Catalogue Raisonnée of Oriental Manuscripts' in three volumes published in 1857, 1860 and 1862) belong to this category and supply us with varied information besides historical facts. The compilers of many of these chronicles did not display the necessary degree of discrimination in sifting the information obtained; and so they contain both historical as well as non-historical, and sometimes unreliable, details and accounts. However, their usefulness in some particulars cannot be ignored or underrated, as they form the main source of our history, especially for the 16th century, and are really helpful, in those places where other evidence is not available. A careful examination of these chronicles will afford a quantum of valuable facts and will certainly help the student; but he should proceed very cautiously in deducing conclusions from them. The 'Karnātaka Rājākkaḷ Śavistāra Chariṭam' composed under the direction of Col. William MacLeod early in 1803, by Narayan finds a place among these chronicles and can be instanced as a specimen of the more valuable class among them. The accuracy of these writings is obvious when they are corroborated by other sources of evidence. The *Tanjāvūri Andhra Rājulu Charitamu* and the *Tanjāvūri Vāri Charitam* (which contains in the main the same matter) belong, likewise, to this category of chronicles as they are not strictly contemporary to the events they portray. But these records are indispensable to the historian of the 16th century, as they give us a fairly connected account of the foundation of the Madura and Tanjore Nayakships. But their historical evaluation needs some corrective and the help of other evidence for balancing and modifying. Only facts common to them and other sources of information may be accepted by a process of searching internal and external criticism. These chronicles invest the bones of bare historical facts with a superfluity of flesh accretion, and fill up the gaps in our knowledge usefully in many points.

Besides these indigenous chronicles, we have a volume of literary evidence which is at once contemporary and native. Tanjore is particularly fortunate in possessing this kind of material in an abundant measure as the fruit of the enlightened literary patronage of the Nayak rulers. The importance of these works for the study of Tanjore history can hardly be disputed. They are, in one sense, documents of the kingdom and may be taken as authentic to a large extent, since their authors enjoyed the full liberty of knowing things at first hand. The *Sāhityaratnākara* of Yagnanārāyana Dikshita and the *Raghunāthābhyudayam* of Rāmabadrāmba, both of them in Sanskrit, the *Mannārudāsavilāsam* and the *Ushāpariṇayam* of Raṅgājamma and the *Vijayarāghava Vamśāvali* of Cheṇgalvaḷa Kāḷakavi in Telugu are all contemporary and so constitute very important sources of information among others. Besides these, we have another set of works that contain valuable and very direct information on the doings of the Nayaks as they have been handed to us in the form of *prabhandas* composed by the Nayaks themselves, who were noted for their versatile learning and scholarship as well as for their patronage of poets and of men of letters. The *Sangīta Sudha*[1] by Raghunātha Nāyaka along with the illuminating introduction to it by his well-known minister Gōvinda Dikshita and the *Raghunāthābhyudaya Nātakam* by Vijayarāghava Nayaka contain what may be regarded as the official version of the history of the Tanjore Nayaks; and their value is abundant and obvious, though they are not available to us in their complete form. Tanjore seems to have excelled in having her own historiographer-poets, and in this respect she far surpassed her neighbours like Madura and Gingee. All these works contain almost identical information about facts, expressed in varying diction; but they are not so full of historical facts as one would expect them to be and they contain no chronology. They do not constitute history in the true sense of the word as they are marked by elements of romance, imagination and praise of heroes that are the characteristics of a *kāvya*. Their authors did not aim at writing true and unvarnished history and so the narration of historical details was only incidental to their treatment. They were out to praise and please their patrons and in this they vied with one another, both in the use of pompous language and in the manner of treatment. Still they are historical or, at the least, quasi-historical, poems giving us fair and full ideas regarding the royal capital, the life of the people, the king and his army, his military achievements, his benefactions, his patronage of the different religions of the land, etc., and thus they amplify the truth that the culture and civilisation of an age are best seen reflected in its literature. Hence these are of some value; and a careful study and collation of the information contained in them are very necessary before one arrives at anything definite. There are surprising omissions of otherwise known important historical facts as well as additional information, whose

1. Published in the Journal of the Music Academy, Madras.

validity cannot be accepted without a dispassionate external criticism. For instance, the *Raghunāthābhyudayam* of Rāmabhadrāmba and the *Sāhityaratnākara* of Yagnanārāyana Dikshita, who was a pupil of Raghunātha Nayaka are strictly contemporary works, since both authors flourished in the same reign. Naturally one would expect from them first-hand and fully reliable information. But unfortunately there are some obvious omissions and several differences in narration which may appear to be negligible, but are very important from the point of view of the student. Rāmabhadrāmba refers to Raghunātha's victories in his early wars fought with the Muhammadans on behalf of his overlord, Venkatapathi Raya and to the release of the Gingee Nayak from imprisonment on his intervention. The *Sāhityaratnākara* does not contain, strangely enough, even a passing reference to these facts. Besides, they also differ from each other with regard to the date of the installation of Raghunātha as Yuvaraja. The former would put it before Raghunātha's march against the Muhammadans, while the latter would place it somewhat later. As regards the genealogy again these works give varying information. The Sanskrit books are not so full in their account as the Telugu works ; and the sifting of details of historical facts from them becomes difficult.

Herein comes to our aid the evidence embodied in the writings of foreign travellers and the Jesuit missionaries who visited South India as propagators of the Catholic faith. The Jesuits were primarily concerned with the growth and expansion of their missionary activity and their mission stations. They were obliged to send home periodical reports of their work and progress. In submitting such reports in long letters they gave a good picture of the prevailing political conditions of the land as also of the conditions precedent to the result of their labours. Extracts from such epistolary sources can be taken as a corrective to and a supplement of the local traditions and literary compositions since the letters were of cultured men who had wide experience. However, they, being foreigners by descent and missionaries by profession, had their own views of things Indian; and hence too much reliance placed on all their information may be rather unsafe, because they might not have had either the privilege of knowing incidents and facts at first hand or of consulting the state archives to which they had evidently no access. At best they can be held to be only secondary sources, though affording considerable material for the history of the 16th and 17th centuries. Besides, the records of the Portuguese and the Dutch factors on the Coromandel Coast contain a wealth of information, regarding the life of the people and the commerce of the land. But they contain, in many places, exaggerated and distorted accounts in vital respects. In such cases it may be possible to disentangle truth from overstated facts by a careful study of the environment, political and social, and the spirit of the age. The observations of the foreign travellers, like Nuniz, Barradas and others contained in "*Purchas: His Pilgrims*" shed welcome sidelights on many facts and events. Even though they are superfluous to the Jesuit letters in many respects, yet their value is seen in the absence of more reliable information. Barradas's account presents the events following the death of Venkatapathi Raya in all their significant aspects and agrees admirably, in the main, with the internal evidence furnished by the indigenous chronicles and literary works; and it fills up the gap very ably, throwing much light on those obscure facts which would otherwise need further elucidation. Passing references to the customs and manners of the people and other social institutions which these contain are remarkable in their own way and are very useful. The English Factory Records volumes embodying the letters written by the Factors of the trade centres in India to the Directors at home, contain a substantial amount of information about the internal and external trade of the land and also on the business carried on with towns and other centres of industrial or political interest. It was during the period of the Nayak rule that the European nations like the Portuguese, the Danes and the Dutch came and settled on the Coromandel coast and developed trading agencies between South India and other countries. The Nayak rule also witnessed the first attempt made by the English Company to share in the coastal trade of Tanjore. The starting and consolidation of these settlements marked the decline of the former traders of the land, like the Arabs and the Moors.

Epigraphy forms an indispensable aid to history and furnishes it with the substance of documents engraved on stones and other durable material. A good portion of these epigraphs approximately constitute contemporary evidence. They serve as mile-stones and the information contained in them can be said to constitute the skeleton of history. They help in settling questions of chronology and also give incidental insight into the details of the administration and other matters of importance, political and economic, religious and social, and are the most trustworthy records of all periods. Inscriptional evidence is preferable to literary and other information. The historical introductions of the epigraphs containing the genealogy of kings, the chronology of events and the distinguishing *birudas* of the rulers, are of much value, while the substance of the epigraphs throws side-lights upon the religious and social life of the people. The facts mentioned in them are rendered real and living by the literary accounts which form a useful supplement to them. In attaching the requisite value to this category of evidence, one needs to be discriminate and critical, and a note of caution has to be sounded against the acceptance of spurious and forged documents that claim to be genuine and would go forth for popular consumption. And the inscriptions of the Tanjore Nayaks present a peculiar difficulty in as much as they do not contain any reference to the regnal years and in many cases the Saka era and the cyclic year mentioned do not agree with each other. Almost all the epigraphical information now available has been collected in Robert Sewell's *List of Antiquities*, Madras; the volumes of *South Indian Inscriptions; the Annual Reports on South Indian Epigraphy* and *the Travancore Archæological Series* besides other minor publications.

Archæology is a hand-maid to a proper study of history and its remains are silent witnesses to the growth of historical forces as well as of the glorious past. They preserve the art and architecture of the past into the present. The archæological remains belonging to the Tanjore Nayaks are found chiefly in the city of Tanjore and its neighbourhood. The *Śeppanēri*, the feeding reservoir to the present Sivaganga Tank, the cracked fort ramparts, the almost unidentifiable and disappearing moat around it, the dilapidated palace walls, the temples at Mannārgudi and Kumbakōnam and the Vallam fort—all these supply us with much of antiquarian interest and have their own sad story to tell of their pristine glory. The names of villages and streets such as Ayyampēt, Ayyaṇkadai Street, Achyutamaṇgalam, Raghunāthapuram, Gōvindapuram and the Dikshitalingam at Pattīswaram trace their own associations with the Nayaks and their Brahman minister. The presence, even at the present day, of a large body of Telugu speaking people living in various places in the heart of the Tamil land is another instance of the steady migration that took place from the Telugu country during the period of the Vijayanagar and Nayak rule. The famous public library in the Tanjore Palace, called the Saraswati Mahal Library has been built upon the nucleus left by the Nayaks. The Editor of the 'Descriptive Catalogue of the Tanjore Saraswathi Mahal Library' says that the present library is the greatest of Oriental manuscripts libraries and its unique value lies in the fact that it has preserved the literary works of authors spread over three and a half centuries. The collections which were begun 'as early as the 15th century (about 1450) were continued both by the Nayaks and their successors in power, the Marathas. And the change of rule from the Nayaks to the Marathas did not, as is usual with alien invasions, produce any serious unsettlement in the existing social and other conditions of the people of the land. Military successes have always meant a full stop, for a temporary period at any rate, of all lines of progress, particularly in *belles letters*, art and other non-political activities of the vanquished. This was never the case with Tanjore; and the Maratha rulers seem to have been greater and more enthusiastic patrons of literature and art than their predecessors.'

Coins form another source, and their bearing upon the history of the Tanjore Nayaks has to be proved by future research. Vijayaraghava Nayak's grant to the Dutch postulates the existence of a mint at Tanjore and in some other places.

Apart from these original sources, we have the second hand information contained in the writings of modern historians to which reference has been made above.

Chapter II

THE FOUNDATION OF THE TANJORE NAYAKSHIP

Tradition says that the Tanjore Nayaks were first appointed to the regular charge of the Chola country by the Vijayanagar emperor, Achyutadēvarāya, (acc. 1529-30 A.D.).[1] This is confirmed by the evidence of Telugu literature like the *Tanjāvūri Andhra Rājulu Charitamu* which says that Śevappa Nayaka who married Mūrtimāmba, the sister of Tirumalāmba, a consort of Achyutadēvarāya, was appointed to the governorship of the Chola country which was given away as dowry to Mūrtimāmba. The Samskrit sources refer to the marriage of Śevappa to Mūrtimāmba, the sister-in-law of Achyutadēvarāya, but do not refer to the gift of *strīdhana*. Yagnanārāyana Dikshita says that Śevappa got Tanjore by his own prowess.[2] There is no inscriptional evidence to substantiate the traditional account which seems to be true and indisputable. The political circumstances of the times under the powerful emperors of Vijayanagar and their southern invasions, particularly by Krishnadēvarāya and his successor Achyutarāya, do not admit the possibility of Śevappa Nayaka's acquiring the principality of Tanjore by conquest or by usurpation. The already established powerful, loyal viceroyalty of Madura on the one hand and the empire on the other would certainly have put down any attempted insurrection or open hostility on the part of Śevappa. And hence his rise to position and power in Tanjore must have been due to the imperial favour and support; and the reference to Śevappa's marriage with Mūrtimāmba in the chronicles and his close relationship to Achyutadēvaraya only bear ample testimony to his rise under the royal patronage. But there is no unanimity among the various chronicles as regards the date of the actual appointment of Śevappa to the viceroyalty of the Tanjore territory.

Different dates are given by scholars for the foundation of tne Tanjore Nayakship. (1) There is a tradition which says that a Kannada Brahman of the name of Gōvinda Dīkshita, then a boy of seventeen, well versed in the Śāstras as well as in palmistry and astrology, migrated to the then flourishing city of Vijayanagara and there come

1. 40 of 1900 is dated in Virōdhi and in the month of Kārtika. 157 of 1924 from Kālahasti is dated in Saka 1452; also 200 of 1910.

2. "Sāhityaratnākara" by Yagnanārāyana Dikshita, edited by Dr. T. R. Chintamani, University of Madras, Canto III, Sloka 1.

into contact with Achyutarāya who invited that Brahman along with other astrologers, to predict the future of the son that had just been born to him. Admiring his knowledge of Jyōtisha Śāstra, the emperor is said to have honoured him. Shortly after this event, the Dikshita came across a Nayaka orphan, Śeva by name, whom he took into his service. Finding in him signs of future greatness, Gōvinda Dīkshita introduced him to Achyutarāya, who had him appointed as his Tāmbūla Karaṇḍavāhin (betel-bearer)—an office of importance in the court, which brought the holder into personal association with the Rāya. Soon, Śeva, the betel-page, distinguished himself in Achyutarāya's wars; and in due course, Mūrtimāmba, the sister of Rāya's consort Tirumalāmba, who fell in love with him was married to him. Achyutarāya appointed him to the governorship of Tanjore which was then in need of a strong ruler. Śeva, on going to Tanjore, took the Dīkshita along with him; and this is said to have happened in the year 1540 A.D.[3]

This account which is relied on by some, falls flat for want of confirmation; nor can it stand the test of intensive criticism. Inscriptional evidence shows that Śevappa belonged to a family of nobles who had for some time been ruling over the Toṇḍaimaṇḍalam country. Moreover, Gōvinda Dīkshita who is said to have been the minister of two kings in the Tanjore epigraphs of this period, is mentioned in a record dated 1634 A.D.,[4] and this is the latest year so far available for him. Beginning from 1528 A.D. when a son was born to Achyutarāya and ending with 1634 A.D.,[5] the latest known date for Gōvinda Dikshita, and adding seventeen years to which age he had attained when he first came to Vijayanagara, we find that Gōvinda Dīkshita must have lived for more than hundred and twenty years which is absolutely impossible. The inscriptions assign a period of thirteen years from 1529 to 1542 A.D. for the reign of Achyutarāya. In that case the traditional date, A.D. 1540 given above, would place the appointment of Śevappa towards the end of his reign. The *Tanjāvūri Andhra Rājula Charitamu*, the two Sanskrit contemporary poems and the epigraphs, all refer to Gōvinda Dikshita, the illustrious minister, as having flourished only in the last

3. "Gōvinda Dikshita and his times" by Mr. N. K. Venkatesam Pantulu, in the "Journal of the Andhra Historical Research Society," Vol. II, Part II. Also "Sāhityaratnākara," Introduction, page 2.

4. 290 of 1927 is dated S. 1553 Prajōtpatti. 257 of 1927, Bava corresponding to A.D. 1634.

5. "Sources of Vijayanagara History", edited by Dr. S. Krishnaswamy Aiyangar: p. 170 and Introduction, p. 12.

days of Śevappa and not in the earlier part of his reign. Hence this account is unreliable for want of confirmatory evidence.

Secondly, the year 1541 A.D. is assigned for the foundation of the Tanjore Nayakship by the Rev. Father Heras.[6] The learned Father arrives at this date on the ground that Viswanātha Nayaka, the founder of the Madura line of viceroys, was also appointed by Achyutarāya to the southern viceroyalty towards the end of his reign, *i.e.*, about 1541 A.D. And so Father Heras would assign the foundation of the Tanjore and Madura Nayakships to the same date. His arguments in support of this assumption are not conclusive and in one place positively weak. He says (on p. 124, Note 3) that after the execution of Vīraśēkhara Chōḷa, Viswanātha was appointed to be in charge of both Madura and Tanjore. He gives no authority for the execution of the Chola king, in spite of the fact that there is no evidence except tradition referring to the rule of a Chōḷa king at all.[7] The *Tanjāvūri Aṅdhra Rājula Charitamu'* is definite in assigning the foundation of the Madura Nayakship during the time of Krishnadēvarāya, and Prof. Sathianatha Aiyar[8] has dated the foundation of the Madura Nayak's rule in 1529 A.D. Again, the Telugu chronicle[9] says that soon after the death of Chandraśekhara Pāndya in whose life time itself Viswanātha Nayaka had been nominated to rule over Madura, the Pāṇḍyan having abdicated in his favour and retired into private life, Viswanātha Nayak began to rule over both the Pāṇdya and Chōḷa kingdoms. Nothing is known about the fate of the Chōḷa ruler, Vīraśēkhara. Mr. Venkasami Rao (*The Tanjore Manual*, p. 750) adds that, the fate of Vīraśēkhara Chōḷa is not clearly known. He either fell in battle with Nagama Nayaka or was subsequently put to death; and his issue, if he had any, probably shared the same fate; for nothing more is heard of the Chola race.' Thus he proves the impossiblity of a Chola ruling over Tanjore at the time of Viswanatha Nayak's accession to Madura after he defeated his father Nagama Nayaka in battle. Hence it becomes probable that there was no Chola king at the time of the appointment of Śevappa. Even the

6. 'The Aravidu dynasty of Vijayanagar' by Rev. H. Heras, p. 170 and p. 124 and Note 3.

7. Father Heras believes the first part of the traditional story but would not give his reasons for discarding the rest of it which refers to the establishment of the Madura Nayak by Krishnadēvarāya.

8. 'The Nayaks of Madura', Madras University Historical Series No. 2.

9. The 'Tanjāvūri Aṅdhra Rājulu Charitamu' edited by V. Prabhakara Sastri, Vavilla Press; also "Sources," Dr. S. K. Aiyangar.

Achyutarāyābhyŭdayam of Rājanātha Diṇḍima[10] which describes in detail the early conquests of Achyutarāya in the South, does not mention the existence of a Chōḻa king of Tanjore at the time. Tirumalāmba, in her *Varadāmbikaparinayam,* refers to the defeat and imprisonment of a Chōḷa at the hands of Achyutarāya's father, Narasa Nayaka, and says that the Chōḷa is said to have escaped for his life to the sea coast.[11] The name of this Chōḻa is not known. If there was any Chōḷa king at the time of Achyutraya's *digvijaya* in the south, the *Achyutarāyabhyudayam* would have at least made mention of him. It is only the *Tanjāvūri Andhra Rājula Charitamų* and the *Tanjāvūri Vāri Charitamu* that refer to Vīraśēkhara Chōḷa who was responsible for the coming of Nāgama Nayaka and Viswanātha Nayaka to the south.[12] The *Karnātaka Rājākkaḷ Śavistāra Charitam* says that Krishnadēvarāya who conquered eastern Karnātaka and derived therefrom a revenue of three crores of rupees, had to divide his empire into three parts and to appoint three viceroys over them. Thus, according to this chronicle, Tubāki Krishnappa Nayaka was placed in the administrative charge of that strip of land which is bounded by Nellore on the north and the river Coleroon in the south, with Gingee as the capital. Vijayarāghava Nayaka was appointed to rule the Chōḻa country from the capital city of Tanjore; and Venkatappa Nayaka was commissioned to administer the land further south.[13] This account would suggest that these three viceroyalties were founded about the year 1518 A.D., the date of Krishnadēvarāya's return from his northern conquests. There is no other internal or external evidence to support the *Karnātaka Rājakkal Savistara Charitam*; and if too much stress is laid on this statement then it would antedate the foundation of the Tanjore Nayakship and bring in other anachronisms and conflicts. Moreover, the inscriptions of Krishnadēvarāya in the south show that there was one Vira Narasingarāya who was in charge of the Toṇḍaimaṇḍalam and Chōḻa countries as the king's

10. Sources. P. 159. Achyutarāya is said to have entered the Chōḷa country unopposed. A Chōḷa king is mentioned on p. 164 and this was Śellappa, who rebelled against him.

11. The '*Varadāmbikaparinayam*" by Tirumalāmba. Edited by Mr. Lakshman Sarup, Lucknow. Also sources, p. 174.

12. 'The Nayaks of Madura,' Introduction, page 9. 'It is just possible that complaints reached head-quarters in some number and one complainant with more pretentious claims even waited upon Krishnarāya in person. The only flaw in the story as given in the chronicles is that we have so far come upon no epigraphical evidence of the existence of a Chandrasékhara Pāṇdya in Madura or of a Vīraśēkhara Chōḷa in the Chōḷa country though neither case is impossible.'

13. 'The Aravidu Dynasty', p. 112.

deputy.[14] Contemporary Telugu and Sanskrit literature and the traditional accounts recorded in the *Mackenzie Manuscripts* and in the *Tanjavūri Andhra Rājula Charitamu* and the *Tanjāvūri Vari Charitam* clearly show that the foundation of the Tanjore Nayakship took place only in the reign of Achyutarāya. The epigraphs also point to the same conclusion. As the internal evidence regarding the Tanjore Nayaks has been well established, we need not hesitate to subscribe to the view that Achyutarāya nominated Śevappa as governor over the Tanjore principality. If this is agreed upon, another date, 1549 A.D., given by Mr. Kuppuswamy Sastri in the *Tanjore Gazetteer* and accepted for the foundation of the Tanjore Nayakship will have to be abandoned, since the reign of Achyutarāya came to an end in 1542 A.D.[15] and there was Sadāsivarāya ruling over Vijayanagara in A.D. 1549. Mr. T. S. Kuppuswami Sastri tells us of Śevappa's appointment by Achyutarāya; but he is more inclined to believe the version of *Sāhityaratnākara* that Śevappa got Tanjore by the strength of his own arm. Relying on this evidence, he ascribes 1549 A.D. as the date of Śevappa's accession to power and adds support to it by saying that the Samasarupalli epigraph of this Nayaka which is dated in the year 1549 (S. 1471) is the earliest record issued by him. The *Tanjore Gazetteer* (1906), following Mr. Kuppu-Swami Sastri, assigns 1549 A.D.; and in support of this date it advances arguments that Achyutarāya died in A.D. 1542 and there was Rāmarāja Viṭhaladēva, the able co-adjutor and general of Sadāsiva, who remained in the south till 1544 A.D. So it is concluded that Śevappa must have come to power only after the retirement of Rāmaraja Viṭhala from the south. Following Nelson, the *District Gazetteer* would also assign A.D. 1559 as the date for the foundation of the Madura Nayakship. That this date is untenable is proved by Achyutarāya's inscription which refers to his gift made for the merit of his agent, Viswanātha Nayaka, as early as A.D. 1535.[16] This epigraph is important as it definitely proves that Madura was under Viswanātha Nayaka even in that year.[17] The *Tan-*

14. *'The Nayaks of Madura,'* Introd. 8. The period 1520-5 seems to be a period of activity in organisation and may be regarded as the time when he appointed Vīranarasimha as viceroy of the Chōḷa country and gave the commission to Nāgama to organise the province of Madura; and the appointment of Vīra Narasimha to the Chōḷa country would indicate the appointment of a similar officer of high standing for Madura.

15. 373 of 1911.

16. 113 of 1908 Tirupattur, Ramnad District.

17. *'The Nayaks of Madura,'* pp. 44 and 296, Appendix C. All that we know of Viswanātha Nayaka from inscriptions, chronicles and other sources further confirms our contention that the Nayakship of Madura under him was an accomplished fact

javūri Andhra Rājula Charitamu says that Viswanātha who was appointed by Krishnadēvarāya was for some time governing the Chōḷa country as well, after the death of Krishnadēvarāya until Śevappa was specially appointed to Tanjore by Achyutarāya.[18] This would prove that the foundation of the Tanjore Nayakship could not have been far removed from the date of the foundation of the Madura Nayakship. Prof. Sathianatha Aiyar has proved that 1529 A.D. must be the initial date of the Madura Nayakship and that it was created in the last days of Krishnadēvarāya. In this connection his remarks on the validity and reliability of the statements contained in the *Tanjāvūri Andhra Rājula Charitamu* may be quoted :—'The facts contained in this account which are capable of verification are so singularly correct that the whole narrative compels conviction as a faithful description of the transactions'. Equally apt is the observation made by William Taylor regarding the *Tanjāvūri Vāri Chaṛitam* when he says: 'I consider the document very valuable as a contribution towards the history of the Tanjore country during the whole of the fifteenth and sixteenth centuries.' According to these accounts the Tanjore Nayakship was founded by Achyutarāya shortly after the foundation of the Madura Nayakship, and it also proves the impossibility of a Chōḷa ruling just previous to the time of Śevappa's nomination to its charge, when it says that Viswanātha was then in charge of both the principalities. Mr. Venkasami Rao's[19] date, A.D. 1530 assigned for the foundation of the Tanjore Nayakship is a little early as it shows that the same had happened towards the end of Krishnadēvarāya's reign. The reason for his discountenancing the account of the chronicles in general and of the *Tanjāvūri Varī Charitam* in particular is given out to be that after the death of Krishnadēvarāya the empire began to sink and hence no intervention in the affairs of the south could

before the death of Krishnadēvarāya in 1530. John Nieuhoff also refers to the rule of the Madura Nayaks in the year 1533.

18. 'T. A. R. Charitam,' p. 17. Also 'Sources', p. 323.

19. *The Tanjore Manual*. 1883 p. 748-9. Mr. Venkasami Rao relying on Dr. Caldwell's List of Vijayanagar kings as is given in his History of the Tinnevelly District pp. 45-6 says that the "Varicharitra mentions the name of a Raya who appointed the first viceroy of Tanjore as Achyuta" and adds "that the intervention of Vijayanagar in the affairs of Madura and Tanjore took place during the reign of Krishnadēvarāya than that it took place after it when the power of Vijayanagar was sinking. At the same time the interval between Nāgama Nayaka's expedition and the appointment of the first viceroy to Tanjore by Achyuta assuming the latter to be a fact could not have been long. On the whole, in the absence of more satisfactory data, the date of the subversion of the Chola dynasty and the commencement of the Nayak rule in Tanjore may, it seems, be safely fixed about A.D. 1530." He would also assign a period of about 132 years for the Nayak's rule.

have been possible. He believed then that the accession of Achyutarāya saw only the beginning of the rapid decline and downfall of the empire. And so he concluded safely that all the changes that might have taken place in the politics of the south, must have happened only during the reign of Krishnadēvarāya and more probably about the time when he commissioned his general, Nāgama Nāyaka, to effect a complete conquest of the south with a view to reorganising it. But subsequent researches into the then unexplored fields of epigraphy and other literature, have brought to light that Achyutarāya was not after all the craven that he was supposed to be, but was as good and powerful a ruler as his predecessor, and also the fact that the empire did in fact survive for more than a century after the death of Krishnadēvarāya. The *Achyutarāyabhydayam* bears evidence to the successful *digvijaya* led by Achyutarāya into the south and also the victories won by his general Śalakam Tirumalarāja. And from other pieces of evidence it is quite possible to surmise that Tanjore was not under any separate governor or ruler at the time of Achyutarāya's invasion. Thus it becomes clear that the date does not seem to be quite settled and needs revision in the light of subsequent accumulation of material. The inscriptions of the period also refer to the same state of affairs.

South India came under the influence of Vijayanagar as early as 1358 when Kumara Kampana began his victorious campaign into the south.[20] The presence of numerous epigraphs that are found scattered all over the country bears ample testimony to the overlordship of Vijayanagar Empire from about the 3rd quarter of the 14th century. Narasa Nayaka's expedition to the south and his victories over the Chōḷa and Pāṇḍya kings were referred to already.[21] That South India continued under Vijayanagar for long without any interruption and the fact that the old principalities continued for some time under their old hereditary rulers like the Chōḷas and the Pāṇḍyas who became feudatories of the new power, are established by the testimony alike of literature and inscriptions.

With the accession of Krishnadēvarāya a new epoch began in the history of South India. Hitherto the Vijayanagara emperors could not devote much of their time to the consolidation of their authority and the organisation of their hold over the southern principalities, as their

20. Madhuravijayam or Kamparāya Charitam by Gaṅgādēvī edited by Pandit Srinivasachari, Trivandrum. Also 'Sources'.

21. The 'Varadāmbikāpariṇayam'.

Muhammadan enemies on the north were engaging much of their attention. Krishnadēvarāya, having defeated his enemies in the north completely, found the necessary leisure to reconstitute and reorganise the southern principalities; and he set himself to this task soon. According to the chronicles, Madura and Tanjore which were then ruled by scions of the old lines of the Pāṇḍyas and the Chōḻas respectively, caused some trouble, and a Chōḻa ruler is said to have risen in revolt and captured Madura, setting aside the claims of a Pāṇḍya and this led to the latter's appeal for help to Krishnadēvarāya, their overlord.[22] Nāgama Nayaka's southern expedition was the immediate result of this, and Nāgama claimed to have defeated the Chōḻa and reinstated the Pāṇḍya whose birth was found out to be illegitimate. About the same time parts of the Chōḻa and the Toṇḍaimaṇḍalam countries were put in charge of another great general who was called Vīra Narasingarāya Nayaka. His inscriptions are largely to be found in the south ranging in dates from 1510 to 1530 A.D.[23] 83 of 1923 of Achyutarāya, dated Saka 1451, gives the information

22. Dr. Caldwell (History of the Tinnevelly District) says that the Chola referred to in the Chronicles was perhaps Chennaya Bālaya who figures in an inscription coming from Srirangam and dated Saka 1453 (A.D. 1531). This view is incorrect since we find Viswanatha Nayaka to be the ruler of both Madura and Tanjore for sometime about this period and the presence of epigraphs of Viswanatha in Srirangam proves this. However, there are numerous epigraphs to show that there were scions of the Chola race ruling as governors over small principalities of the land, not independently of the Vijayanagar authority. Some of them even traced their descent from the Cholas of Uraiyūr; but none of them seems to have had or enjoyed power as became an independent ruler.

23. 91 and 92 of 1908 Tiruppattur, Ramnad S1432 give him the surname Śellappa with the honorary affix swami.

361 of 1908 Māṇgādu, Tanjore District S 1437 says that Vira Narasinga belonged to the Agastya *gōtra* and Bōdhāyanasūtra.

256 of 1910. Urattur Achyutarāya S. 1451 mentions Śellappa alias Vira Narasinga Sāluva Daṇṇāyakar.

83 of 1923 Chingleput district: Achyuta S 1451 gift for the merit of Vira Narasingarāya.

544 of 1919. Little Conjeevaram S 1454 Achyuta *i.e.*, two years after his coronation. Records that in the year Virodhi on the day of his coronation Achyuta directed Sāluva Nayaka to assign certain villages to Varadāraja and Ekambaranātha equally neither more or less. But as Sāluva Nayaka gave more to Ekambaranātha, Achyuta hearing this equalised the number of villages by redistribution.

545 of 1919. Same as 544 above. This inscription is very important.

390 of 1914 Tiruvarangulam 1515 A.D. gift of taxes for the merit of Vira Narasingarāya Nayakar.

that, that general was also known by the names of Śellappa and Sāḷuva Nayaka and another epigraph (182 of 1929-30) dated Saka 1431 in the reign of Krishnadēvarāya says that he was the son of one Taḷuvakkuḷaindān Bhattar, a dēvakanmi of the Kānchi (Conjeevaram) temple. Vira Narasingarāya Nayaka seems to have entered the Imperial service as early as 1509 A.D. The provenance of his records shows that he was ruling over the south-eastern portions of the Vijayanagara empire, comprising the modern districts of North and South Arcot, Chingleput and Tanjore and also part of Ramnad district. Vīra Narasingarāya Sāḷuva Nayaka of the epigraphs of Krishnadēvarāya and Achyutarāya is perhaps identical with the Sâlvanāyque of Nuniz[24] who says that "Sālvanāyque, the present minister; he has a revenue of a million and a hundred thousand pardaos. He is the lord of Coramandel (Charamaondel) and of Negapatam (Negapatao) and Tanjore (Tangore) and Bomgrin (Bhuvanagiri ?), Devipatnam (Depatao) and Truguel, (Sewell says Tirukkovilur) and Caullin and all of these are cities: their territories are all very large and border on Ceylon. He is obliged to give a third of his revenues to the king and two-thirds remain for him for the expenses of his lascarins and horses, which he is obliged to main-

233 of 1901 Achcharapākkam S. 1450 Virodhi, mentions Vira Narasingarāya Nayaka who is called a Ubhayapradhāni of the king.

63 of 1923 Chingleput District gift to Śellappar Taḷuvakkuḷaindān Bhattar alias Vira Narasingarāya Nayakkar.

225 of 1916 Sengamal. S. 1442 Śellappar Vira Narasingarāya Nayaka is called the son of Taḷuvakkuḷaindān Bhattar.

399 of 1906. Tirumayam, S. 1444 gift by Vira Narasingarāya Nayakar.

182 of 1929-30. Chingleput district S 1431 (1509 A.D.) Sāluva Nayakkar Śellappar, son of Taḷuvakkuḷaindān Bhattar who is called a Dēvakanmi of the Kānchi temple.

390 of 1912. Dēvikapuran. 1515 A.D. refers to Vira Narasingarāya Nayaka.

487 of 1920. Singaperumāl Koil 1531 A.D. Gift by Taḷuvakkuḷaindān Bhattar for the merit of Śellappa Sāluva Daṇṇāyakar.

Dr. S. K. Ayyangar's ('Nayaks of Madura' and 'Sources', Introduction) view that Vira Narasingarāya's rebellion and Nāgama's revolt are inter-related is not tenable since the latter happened in the last days of Krishnadēvarāya and the rebellion of Vira Narasinga took place in the early years of Achyutarāya when Madura was firmly established under Viswanatha Nayaka the son of Nāgama Nayaka. Nāgama's rebellion was put an end to by Krishnadēvarāya himself before 1529 which marks the beginning of the reign of Viswanātha Nayaka. Śellappa's rebellion took place in 1531 ie., two years after the final settlement of the Madura affairs.

24. 'A Forgotten Empire'—Sewell, p. 384. Nuniz speaks of the feudal lords of Krishnadēvarāya. Also on p. 281 he says that Krishnadēva had five kings as his subject lords. Nuniz calls Sālvanāyque 'the present minister.'

tain for the king, *viz.*, thirty thousand foot and three thousand horse and thirty elephants; so that he only gets the balance after deducting the expenses of this force, Nuniz calls him 'the present minister' of Krishnadēvarāya, and an inscription of the same king (233 of 1901) dated 1528 A.D. calls Vīra Narasingarāya as Ubhayapradhāni. The account of Nuniz and the epigraphical evidence taken together clearly show that Vīra Narasingarāya Sāluva Nayaka must have been a powerful feudatory and minister of Krishnadēvarāya and of Achyutarāya, enjoying a big territory and a large revenue and he also maintained a well equipped army composed of elephants and horses. Achyutarāya's gift for his merit in the year 1529 A.D. shows the supreme position which Vīra Narasingarāya held in the empire. Nuniz also confirms this when he says that Sālvanāyque became the minister of the kingdom and governed the country till the coming of Achetarao (Achyutarāya) from the fortress of Chandragery (Chandragiri) ".[25]

If Vira Narasingarāya Sāḷuva Nayaka was a powerful ruler of all the eastern parts including the Chola country in the time of Krishnadēvarāya till the end of his reign and also in the reign of Achyutarāya, then one may well ask, where was the necessity for Achyuta to appoint Śevappa Nayaka as the ruler of Tanjore or what were the circumstances that led to the foundation of the Tanjore Nayakship? This question is answered by the evidence of the epigraphs and also by the contemporary literary evidence contained in the *Achyutarāyābhyudayam.* Vīra Narasingarāya seems to have grown powerful enough to set at defiance the orders of Krishnadēvarāya in his last days.[26] The Tiruppanaṇgādu epigraph[27] says that he exacted the taxes of *jodi* (a kind of quit rent) and *sulavari* from the inhabitants of the village, contrary to the expressed order of Krishnadēvarāya, who made a remission of these taxes amounting to 10,000 pardaos in favour of the Siva and

25. 'A Forgotten Empire' by Sewell, p. 367.

26. Studies in the Third dynasty of Vijayanagara by Dr. N. Venkataramanayya, University of Madras. A good account of Vira Narasingarāya's activities is given in pages 22-32. Dr. N. V. Ramanayya, p. 23, says that it is not true to say that Vīra Narasingarāya rebelled in the very last years of Krishnadēvarāya. Dr. S. K. Ayyangar says that he rebelled against Krishnadēva in his last days (*'Nayaks of Madura',: Introduction*, p. 9). Even though the inscriptions and literature do not refer to any open rebellion of Vīra Narasinga still his aim at independence very early is supported by the epigraphs.

27. 253 of 1906 dated S. 1453 Khara. Records that Vīra Narasingarāya exacted *jodi* though this tax was given in favour of Tiruppanangādu temple under the orders of Sāluva Timma, the minister of Krishnadēva during the latter's time.

Vishnu temples of the south.[28] The Tirukkadaiyūr epigraph (246 of 1925) which records the remission of the same taxes by the king, when it was brought to his notice by the *bhattars* (priests) of the temple that the remission ordered earlier was not given effect to, perhaps has some reference to Vīra Narasingarāya's growing insubordination even from the year A.D. 1521. Krishnadēvarāya did not live long enough to bring back this insubordinate vassal to a sense of subordination, and so it fell to the lot of Achyutarāya, his successor. Vīra Narasingarāya continued to exhibit the same recalcitrant attitude towards Achyutarāya also, and this is mentioned in a record dated 1532 A.D. (544 of 1919) coming from Little Conjeevaram. The record refers to the rule of Sāḷuva Nāyaka and to a gift of a number of villages made by Achyutarāya at the time of his coronation. Vira Narasingarāya Sāḷuva Nāyaka who was directed by Achyuta to assign this gift of villages to the Varadarāja and Ēkāmbaranātha temples equally 'neither more or less' to either, appears to have broken the royal order by assigning more villages to the Siva temple. The record continues that King Achyuta on hearing this, equalised the gifts by effecting a redistribution in 1532 A.D. Deviation from the royal provision in the order was regarded a serious crime which might result in the loss of life sometimes. Achyuta was perhaps dissatisfied with his misconduct and stubborn character and had him removed from the high offices of *pradhāni* and viceroy in A.D. 1531. An inscription[29] from the same place refers to one Bōgayyadēva Mahārāja of the solar race and a descendant of the Chōḻas of Uraiyur who is said to have succeeded Vira Narasingarāya to the rulership of those parts and restored the gift of taxes such as *jodi*, etc., amounting to 50 *pon* to the temple in the same year (A.D. 1531).

Vīra Narasingarāya who fell in the estimate of Achyutarāya and who was driven out of office, found himself in a desperate situation and so turned a rebel, perhaps with the idea of opposing the king and setting up an independent rule. In this endeavour he was not able to enlist the co-operation of the powerful Madura ruler, Viswanātha Nayak, and so he advanced further south and sought the aid of the Tiruvadi king.[30]

28. 137 of 1927, 210 of 1917, 100 of 1931-32, 223 of 1927, 184 of 1925, 226, 235 and 251 of 1925.

29. 253 of 1906 dated S 1453 expired Khara.

30. Dr. N. Venkataramanayya, p. 27, says that the Chēra King mentioned must be the King of Quilon. Mr. T. A. Gopinatha Rao 'Travancore Archaeological Series,' Vol. I and Dr. Krishnaswamy Ayyangar 'Sources of the Vijayanagara History,' Introd. say that the king who joined the renegade rebel Śellappa was the king

He was joined by another rebel, Tumbichchi Nayaka, the ruler of Paramakkudi situated in the Madura country. The reason for his revolt is not known for certain; perhaps he was not in favour of Viswanātha's administration. Vira Narasingarāya *alias* Śellappa, soon gaining strength seems to have defeated the neighbouring Pāṇḍyas of Tenkāsi as a consequence of which the Pāṇḍyan king who was deprived of his kingdom sought the help of Achyutarāya for his restoration. The *Achyutarāyābhyudayam* which describes in great detail this victorious campaign of Achyutarāya in the south, and also the Pāṇḍyan restoration, does not mention either the causes for Vira Narasingarāya's revolt or the rise of Tumbichchi Nayaka but refers to the former's escape to the Chēra country and to his defeat of the Pāṇḍyas. The news of Śellappa's disorderly conduct and organised rebellion reached the king who started on an expedition with a large army under the leadership of his brother-in-law Salakarāju Tirumalarāya. Vīra Narasingarāya did not suffer any defeat at the hands of the Imperial army before his escape to the Tiruvadi country.[31] The *Achyutarāyābhyudayam* describes the marching of Achyutarāya's army and the route it took to reach Srirangam. Śalakarāju Tirumalarāya with the army started on the Tiruvadi campaign under the orders of the king who having despatched the troops stayed behind at Srirangam where he is said to have led a happy life in the company of its Pandits.

of Travancore. The latter view seems to be correct. The Travancore kings were called Tiruvadis. [Āditya Varma and his brother Bhūtala Vira Sri Vira Udaya Mārtānda Varma ruled the Travancore country in the early decades of the 16th century. The latter was followed in 1535 by Bhūtala Vira Kērala Varma. They were known as Tiruvadis and enjoyed dominion in South Tinnevelly. Thus Mārtānda Varma was the Senior Tiruvadi of Siraivoy and Kerala Varma was the Senior Tiruvadi of Jayasimhanād (*The Travancore Manual*: Vol. I, pp. 296-7).] [Ed.]

31. *Achyutarāyābhyudayam*; *Sources*, pp. 158 and 162, Slokas 47 to 59. Dr. S. K. Ayyangar says on p. 152, Śellappa who had revolted and after being defeated in battle escaped from his province and had taken refuge with the Travancore king. Also N. Venkataramanayya's "Third Dynasty of Vijayanagara,' p. 29. But a careful reading of the slokas 47-59 would show definitely that there is nothing in them to refer to Vira Narasingaraya's defeat before he fled to Travancore. One of them (sloka 46) says, चन्नविग्रहतया पलायित, चेल्लपो वसति चेरसीमणि। चन्नविग्रहतया- would simply mean 'under disguise.' The word पुन: which means 'again' in sloka 57 is perhaps understood by these scholars to mean a second fight. But a careful reading of that line would show that the word पुन: is an *Avyaya* (indeclinable) and does not connote its meaning but should be read along with the preceding word, मदवतां. The author who expatiates on the morals has put this word to lay emphasis and this interpretation is justified by the succeeding words ननु शज लक्षणम्.

Śalakam Tirumalarāya's defeat of the Chēra king and his victorious return to Srirangam taking Śellappa and the Chēra ruler as captives are all mentioned in the *Achyutarāyābhyudayam*. Achyuta punished the Chēra king and re-established the Pāṇḍyan king on the throne. But what happened to Vīra Narasingarāya and Tumbichchi Nayaka is not at all stated, but their complete defeat is evident from the Kālahasti and the Conjeevaram Inscriptions.[32] The Tiruvadi king who suffered this humiliation was Udayamārtāndavarman.[33] The inscriptions and the *Achyutarāyābhyudayam* definitely say that Vīra Narasingarāya who was in administrative control of the Chōḻadēśa besides others, rose in revolt and he suffered a crushing defeat at the hands of Śalakarāju Tirumalarāya the able general of Achyutarāya. We learn from the same sources that Vīra Narasingarāya was not reappointed to the governorship of the Chōḻa country. Then what became of Tanjore ? Did Tanjore pass under the powerful Madura Nayak, or did it remain independent of it ? Inscriptions, tradition and literary evidence prove that Tanjore remained independent of Madura and became the seat of a new government under one Śevappa Nayaka, appointed by Achyutarāya himself. The foundation of the Tanjore Nayakship was evidently the immediate result of the suppression of Vira Narasingarāya's rebellion. Tradition says that Viswanātha Nāyaka was ruling over Tanjore also for some time. Achyutarāya apprehending danger and suspecting the loyalty of Viswanātha Nāyaka who might rise in opposition to the Empire as his father Nāgama Nayaka did before if left supreme in the south, thought perhaps of making Tanjore independent of Madura and directly subordinate to himself. Besides, there was the Chōḻa ruler handy to be put in charge of it since Viswanātha Nayaka is said to have been then ruling Tanjore as well. Moreover, to put an end to the future troubles such as the rise of any rival Chōḻas—if there should be any of them—the need for a strong ruler was also felt by the king. And the dismissal and the defeat of Śellappa left Tanjore without a ruler. Achyuta also saw for himself the difficulties and dangers in having a single viceroy to administer a large territory comprising almost the whole of the Eastern Karnātaka empire. These causes combined together greatly emphasised the need for the appointment of a capable governor over Tanjore. To ensure proper and good government, to check other feudatories from transcending their limits and to have a loyal supporter of the empire behind, Achyutarāya made a new settlement according to which he

32. 157 of 1924 and 'Tirumalai Tirupati Devasthanam Epigraphical Report', p. 221. Also, 'Third Dynasty of Vijayanagara,' pp. 22-23.

33. 'Travancore Archaeological series,' Vol. I, p. 55.

reorganised his southern portions of his empire entirely on a new basis.[34] The southern territories excluding Madura were split up into two main divisions on the traditional basis, *viz.*, the Chōḻa and the Toṇḍai maṇḍalams. Tanjore became the seat of the government by virtue of its geographical position at the head of the delta system and other natural advantages it had. Śevappa Nayaka, the powerful general and a near relation of the king, was appointed to rule over Tanjore, as he was then considered to be the most loyal and efficient man on whom the empire can rely for its support and co-operation. The Tanjore Nayaks by their unflinching loyalty and timely co-operation with the empire amply justified their choice. Political circumstances, diplomacy and statesmanship were responsible for the appointment of Śevappa Nayaka as the viceroy of the Chōḻa country.[35] If this was the arrangement made by Achyuta, then what is the date of the foundation of the Tanjore Nayakship ?

Vira Narasingarāya, *alias* Śellappa's inscriptions range from 1510 to 1531 A.D. and so he must have rebelled in the year 1531 A.D.[36] the year following the coronation of Achyutarāya. The *Achyutarāyābhyudayam* gives no dates and regarding the rise of Śellappa it simply says that on one day after his coronation the matter was reported by the minister to the king. But there are epigraphs which come to our help in arriving at a satisfactory date. The Kālahasti and the Tirupati records of Achyuta say that his southern expedition was completed before July 27, 1532 A.D.,[37] as they note 'that he went on a war with the Tiruvadi and levied tribute from him, brought under subjection Tumbichchi Nayaka, Sāluva Nayaka, and also the Ummātur chiefs.' His northern conquests began about the middle of 1534 A.D. An epigraph from Little Conjeevaram belonging to Achyuta and dated Saka 1454, cyclic, Nandana, corresponding to

34. The exchange of Vallam for Trichinopoly which was effected according to the *T. A. R, Charitamu* by the Madura Nayaka, must have happened about this time and the transaction must have been made by the king himself.

35. There is no inscription to refer to Śevappa earlier than 1549 A.D. The epigraphs bearing the later dates show however, the establishment of Śevappa as the first ruler. *The T. A. R. Charitamu, T. V. Charitam, the Raghunāthābhyudaya Nātakam, Vijayavilāsam, Sangitā Sudha, Ushāparinayam* and *Rukmani Parinayam* refer to the rule of the Tanjore Nayaks beginning from Śevappa. The Maratha records, the Factory Records and the numerous letters written by the Portuguese and the Jesuit missionaries also refer to the Nayak rule.

36. Śellappa's rebellion in 1530 A.D. is confirmed by Ferishta who speaking of the success of Adil Shah at Raichur in 1530 A.D. says that 'against this prince (Ram Raj) rebellions were excited by several Rays (Rāyas) so that the Muhammadans met with no interruption to their progress. Briggs, Vol. III, p. 66.

37. 157 of 1924.

1532 A.D. says that he gave effect to his early orders issued to Śellappa and redistributed the villages equally to the Ēkāmbaranātha and Varadarāja temples.[38] The *Achyutarāyābhyudayam* says that Achyuta was staying at Srirangam till the return of Śalakarāju Tirumalarāya from the Tiruvadi expedition. From Srirangam Achyutarāya is said to have proceeded against the Ummattūr chiefs. Besides, Achyutarāya was able to finish his southern campaign by the end of 27th July, 1532 A.D. the date of the Kālahasti inscription. The Ummattūr campaign would have taken him at least a period of three or four months. If we can allow this period of four months, then we arrive at the beginning of the year 1532 A.D. when Achyuta must have been staying at Srirangam. The defeat of the Tiruvadi king and the submission of Śellappa in 1531-32 would have taken place earlier, i.e., in 1531-2 A.D. Perhaps Śellappa's reduction and defeat must have made Achyutarāya finally settle the problem of reorganising his southern territories before his departure for Seringapatam from Srirangam. His bitter experience of Śellappa's disloyalty would have naturally impressed on him the need of appointing a loyal and trusted man as his deputy in the Chōḻa country. Probably this was the reason that weighed with him in appointing Śevappa Nayaka his close relation as the ruler of Tanjore in the beginning of the year 1532 A.D. which then is in all probabilty the year of the foundation of the Tanjore Nayakship. This date is confirmed by the reliable traditional account contained in the *Tanjāvūri Āndhra Rājula Charitamu* which says that Viswanātha Nayaka who was appointed to rule over the Madura country by Krishnadēvarāya 'became the sole ruler of the Pāṇḍya and Chōḻa kingdom and Krishnadēvarāya died sometime after this and was succeeded by Achyutarāya.[39] Achyuta appointed this Śevappa as sole viceroy over the Chōḻa country which had till then continued along with the Pāṇḍya country'. Also, Prof. Sathianatha Aiyar has fixed the date of the foundation of the Madura Nayakship and the beginning of Viswanātha Nayaka's rule in 1529 A.D. He says: 'Shortly after, the Chōḻa country was separated from the viceroyalty of Madura and entrusted to Śevappa Nayaka.'[40] These foregoing statements clearly show that the foundation of the Tanjore Nayakship followed in quick succession the foundation of the Madura Nayakship and so 1532 A.D. marks the beginning of the establishment of the feudatory rule of the Tanjore Nayaks.

38. 544 of 1919. The inscription records his gift of villages made to these two temples at Kānchi which was under the rule of Vira Narasingarāya. Vira Narasingarāya set at defiance the royal order early in 1531 A.D.

39. 'Sources of Vijayanagar History,' p. 323.

40. 'The Nayaks of Madura,' p. 52.

Chapter III

ŚEVAPPA NAYAKA (CIR. 1532 TO 1580 A.D.)

Śevappa Nayaka also known as Chinna Śeva[1], Śevanṛpati and Śevabhūpa in Sanskrit and Siru Seva[2] in Tamil, was thus the founder of the Nayak dynasty of Tanjore in the year 1532 A.D.[3] He was the successor of Vira Narasingarāya *alias* Śellappa in the governorship of the Chōḷa country. Achyutarāya, the brother and successor of Krishnadēvarāya, was then the emperor of Vijayanagar. Śevappa was very closely related to the emperor Achyutarāya, as his wife Mūrtimāmba was the sister-in-law of the latter. The Telugu works and the *Tanjāvūri Añdhra Rājula Charitamu* and also the *Tānjāvūri Vāri Charitam* say that Śevappa got Tanjore from the emperor as *strīdhana* for his wife, while the *Sāhityaratnākara* mentions that Tanjore was acquired by Śevappa by his own valour. The latter view is upheld by Mr. T. S. Kuppusamy Sastri on the ground that the work is a contemporary one. Rāmabhadrāmba, the authoress of another contemporary work, the *Raghunāthābhyudayam,* and the *Vijayavilāsam* refer to the marriage of Śevappa with the sister of Achyutarāya's queen, but do not mention the subject of *stridhana.* So does the *Raghunāthābhyudayam* of Vijayarāghava Nayaka. All these statements are not mutually conflicting, but are helpful in arriving at the truth. Inscriptions[4] show that Śevappa belonged to a noble family of powerful generals, and he might have distinguished himself in the emperor's wars. Achyutarāya was very much impressed by his valour and permitted him to marry the sister of Tirumalāmba, one of his consorts.[5] When the question of appointing a new governor over Tanjore arose, he readily

1. 424 of 1928.
2. 259 of 1913.
3. 'Tanjore Añdhra Nāyaka Charitam' by K. Sitaramayya, M.A. The author assigns the date 1535 A.D. as marking the foundation of the Tanjore Nayakship, on the authority of an epigraph 271 of 1907 coming from Tiruvidaimarudur. The epigraph is said to be illegible but however, Mr. Sitaramayya says that it must refer to Śevappa. If this record should belong to him, then it will support the fact that he was established in Tanjore by the year 1532 A.D.
4. 145 of 1924 dated in the cyclic year Vikrama corresponding to A.D. 1522 registers a gift made on behalf of Tirumala Nayaka, the agent of Krisnadēvarāya by Dalaway (commander) Śevappa Nayaka. A. R. E. 1924, pp. 111 and 112.
5. *The Vijayavilāsam* says that Mūrtimāmba was the younger sister of Tirumalāmba. But Tirumalāmba in her 'Varadāmbikāparinayam', a kāvya full of romance, calls Varadāmbika as the queen of Achyutarāya and whose marriage is

thought of Śevappa, whom he deemed, by virtue of his close relationship and loyalty, as the fittest person for the post. Śevappa's rise was largely due to his own remarkable strength and to his marriage with Mūrtimāmba. Even the marriage of Śevappa with Mūrtimāmba is doubted by some scholars, who speak of the impossibility in those days of a Nayaka having marital relations with the royal house that claimed its descent from the kshatriyas. Mr. V. Prabhakara Sastri has laboured hard in his Introduction to the *Tanjāvūri Añdhra Rājula Charitam* on this question and comes to the conclusion that Tirumalāmba was not the queen consort of Achyutarāya, but only a courtesan, since the emperor a kshatriya could not marry a lady of a lower caste. A relatively lower caste status is ascribed to Tirumalāmba on the basis of her sister marrying Śevappa Nayaka who belonged to the fourth varṇa, *i.e.*, a Sūdra.[6] Unfortunately, these wrong assumptions regarding their caste status have no validity since the epigraphical[7] and literary evidences clearly show that Achyutarāya and his well-known ancestors, Īswara Nayaka and Narasa Nayaka, were all only Nayakas and not Kshatriyas.

Śevappa's parents were powerful nobles and they played a prominent part in the Vijayanagara wars with the Muhammadans. His epigraphs are few and far between and are also found outside the Chōḷa country proper. From a study of the provenance of his records he seems to have enjoyed jurisdiction over the whole of the present Tanjore district and part of the North Arcot district. His records are remark-

the theme of this work. The epigraphs also refer to Varadāmbika as his queen, and Kumāra Venkatādri was his son by this queen. Perhaps, Varadāmbika was the senior queen *Pattamahishi*. Tirumalāmba calls herself as the 'be all and end all of the deepest love of Achyutarāya.' (Introduction to '*Varadāmbikāparinayam*,'—Edited by Prof. Lakshman Sarup. Varadāmbika is called the daughter of one Salaka Kshitipa. (Mahishipadē Salaka Kshitīsaturvarajātmajāh sit Varadāmbikā Vadūh). Tirumalāmba therefore appears to have beeh one of his queens. राजाधिराजाच्युतराय सार्वभौम प्रेम सर्वस्व विश्वास भुवा. The *Vijayavilāsam* and the *Subhadrā Pariṇayam* call her a queen of Achyuta and a talented poetess.

6. The literary works trace his origin from the feet of Vishnu. The *Raghunāthābhyudaya Nāṭakam* and the *Vijayavilāsam* by Ch. Venkatakavi and the epigraphs say that Śevappa belonged to the fourth caste.

'Vanajākshu padamula varalu vāhiniki
Anujayai mintsu Nālava jāti jagati
Ajātilōs thāla, Ādikulainaṭṭi
Rājulu Kondaru Prakyātiganiri.'

Also *Vijayavilāsam*, Introduction, p. 8. Also 497 of 1907.

7. 195 of 1913. The *Varāhapurāṇam* by Mallayya refers to Iswara Nayaka and others as the ancestors of Krishnadēvarāya. Also of 497 of 1907 from Neduṇgunram. The *Achyutarāyābhyudayam* and the *Varadāmbikāpariṇayam* speak of Achyutarāya's ancestors.

able for the absence of the customary valuable historical introductions found in the Chōḷa and the Pāṇḍya inscriptions and also the indication of the regnal years of their issue. The absence of these two important aspects in the Tanjore Nayaks' epigraphs in general and of Śevappa Nayaka in particular, present insurmountable difficulties in our attempt to correctly understand the sequence of the events of his rule. They do not give us any clue as to when Śevappa began to rule or as to when his power came to an end. Such literary evidence as will help us in our understanding of the epigraphs in their true historical perspective, is unfortunately wanting in these particulars also. The contemporary works like the *Sāhityaratnākaram* and the *Raghunāthābhyudayam* and the other work of the same name by Vijayarāghava Nayaka also do not help us with regard to the chronology. Hence a study of the history of the Tanjore Nayaks is beset with innumerable difficulties in spite of an abundance of traditional accounts and chronicles. The literary evidence presents differing versions regarding the ancestors of Śevappa's family. The *Raghunāthābhyudayam* and the *Rukmaṇipariṇayam*[8] by Rājachūdāmani Dikshita say that Śevappa was the son of Timmappa Nayaka or Timmabhūpati by his wife Bayyāmbika. Vijayarāghava Nayaka in his Telugu *Raghunāthābhyudayam* gives a genealogical list which begins with one Krishna whose son was Timma, the husband of Bayyāmbika; and he had four sons, *viz.*, Peḍḍa (elder) Śeva, Chiṇṇa (younger) Śeva, Peḍḍa Malla and Chiṇṇa Malla. Raṅgājamma, a courtesan and a poetess of Vijayarāghava's court, in her *Maṇṇārudāsavilāsam* and *Ushāpariṇayam* introduces another Timmappa, with his wife Gōpamāmba, between Krishna and Timmappa Nayaka, the husband of Bayyāmbika. She says that the Nayak's belonged to the Maṇṇāru gōtra (Maṇṇanāru gōtra vibhudēndrunin Vijarāghava Chaṇḍruṇi).[9] Since all the works quoted above are contem-

8. *Raghunāthābhyudayam*, Canto VI, Sl. 1 to 10. Edited by Dr. T. R. Chintamani, Bulletins of the Sanskrit Department, Madras University.

It is said from the feet of Vishnu was born the Cauvery river. She had a sister who gave birth to many sons. One of them was Timmabhūpa whose wife was Bayyāmbika. Vide also *'Sources,'* p. 284. The translation reads 'In the śūdra caste born from the feet of Vishnu was born a king called Timma'.

9. *Rukmaṇipariṇayam*, since published by the Vani Vilas Press, Srirangam.

Raṅgājamma speaks of Vijayarāghava as belonging to the Maṇṇāru gōtra. This will mean that the presiding deity *Maṇṇāru* (Vishnu) of the Maṇṇārgudi temple (Tanjore district) was their Kula dēvata (family god) and not to any *gōtra*, since the śūdras cannot claim any such thing. The śūdras are even now called as belonging to Siva and Vishnu *gōtras* according to their religious persuasion.

porary it is difficult to say which is correct and which is not, until further light should be thrown on this question. But all of them say that Śevappa Nayaka was the son of Timmappa Nayaka by his wife Bayyāmbika. The inscriptions of Śevappa confirm this statement[10]; and it may not be improbable that he had three brothers for the existence of whom we have, however, no direct evidence from the epigraphs.[11]

Timmappa Nayaka, *alias* Timmabhūpatī, must have been a powerful noble and also a ruler of some importance as the epithet bhūpati would indicate. Perhaps, he was the ruler of the North Arcot District with his capital at Neduṇgunram, a place thirty miles north of Tiruvaṇṇāmalai. The epigraphs of all the Tanjore Nayaks show that they, belonged to Neduṇgunram[12] and indicate that they must have had some connection with it. This finds further confirmation from their records found at Tiruvaṇṇāmalai. One of Krishnadēvarāya's epigraphs mention a Timmappa who had the high privilege of serving him as his doorkeeper (vāśal) and who took part in the Raichur campaign.[13] Perhaps he was the father of Śevappa Nayak,[14] who himself is described in an epigraph as the emperor's *daḷavāy* (commander).[15] Thus we see that Śevappa and his father were both serving the Vijayanagar emperors, Krishnadēvarāya and Achyutarāya, before the former was appointed to Tanjore. Śevappa himself had the high honour of serving Achyutarāya

10. 497 of 1907 dated Saka 1495 expired. Kuttalam, Tanjore district. Śevappa Nayaka was the son of Timmappa Nayaka of the fourth caste (Chaturtha gōtra) and who was a native of Neduṇguṇrm in Toṇdaimaṇdalam. Also 424 of 1928 which says Chinna Chevva of the family of Timmabhūpa.

11. 376 of 1912 from Dēvikapuram and dated in the cyclic year Sārvari, refers to the arrangements made for the supply of ghee to the temple by Mallappa and Śevappa Nayaka for the merit of Achyutarāya. Sārvari would correspond to A.D. 1541-2. Also 383 of 1912 dated Saka 1464.

12. 497 of 1907 cited above and 75 of 1925 dated S. 1471. Śevappa Nayaka of Neduṇgunram.

13. 455 of 1906, Pirānmalai, Madura District, dated S. 144. 182 of 1932 dated S. 1436 from Kālahasti.

14. This Timmappa must be different from the other Timmappa Nayakas of the inscriptions of Krishnadēvarāya. 13 of 1927-28 refers to Timmappa Nayaningaru of Kundūrpisīme. Krishnadēvarāya's epigraphs refer to more than one Timmappa Nayaka. 404 of 1913 mentions a Timmappa Nayaka. The record is found at Salem. He is called the ruler of Nadunadu. 4 of 1030 mentions a Timmappa and is said to be the son of Eramānchi Chikka Timmappa Nayaka. 60 of 1934 from the North Arcot District dated 1526 A.D. refers to a Timmappa as the son of one Aṇṇāchi Nayaka.

15. 145 of 1924 dated S. 1433 from Neduṇgunram mentions one *dalavāy* Sevvappa Nayaka who is called an agent of Krishnadēvarāya cited before.

as his 'betel-bearer', equivalent to the office of Aḍappam in Tamil and Tāmbūla Karaṇḍavāhin in Sanskrit.[16]

Śevappa's rule was not marked by any notable event or wars; and his reign was one of peace and comparative prosperity and this is best seen in his works of charity and magnificent buildings. Śevappa remained a loyal feudatory of the emperor; and his epigraphs bear ample testimony to this fact. His inscriptions recording his gifts are dated in the reigns of his overlords, *viz.*, Achyutarāya, Sadāsivarāya and Tirumala. An epigraph of Śevappa from the Tanjore district is recorded in the reign of Sadāsivarāya.[17] The Vijayanagar kings had full control over their feudatory Nayaks, right from the beginning; and the presence of a number of epigraphs of Krishnadēvarāya and Achyutadēvarāya in the Chōḷa country confirms their supremacy.[18] The great minister Gōvinda Dikshita, in his introduction to the *Sangīta Sudhā,* speaks of Śevappa's loyalty and interest in the affairs of the empire when he gives him the *biruda—Karṅāta śimhāṣana kārya ḍuryaha.*[19] On account of his relationship with the emperor under whose patronage the Tanjore Nayakship was founded, Śevappa must have been held in high esteem and regard by the neighbouring Nayak rulers of Madura and Gingee; and there apparently existed happy and friendly relations between them.

One of the earliest features of Śevappa's reign was the transfer of Trichinopoly which was then comprehended in the Tanjore governorship, to the Madura Nayak, in exchange for Vallam.[20] Viswanātha Nayak is said to have fortified Trichinopoly by building a double-walled fort therein and by constructing a big tank inside it. The necessity for fortifying the place, it is said in the chronicles, was due to the predatory ravages and hardships from which the country suffered at the hands of robbers who swooped down on the pilgrims bound for Rāmēswaram and caused much injury to them, both bodily and materially. Taylor says that

16. 380 of 1919 from Little Conjeevaram. Achyutappa Nayaka is called the son of Aḍappam Chinna Śevappa Nayaka.

17. 72 of 1925 (Māṇdai, Tanjore District). The cyclic year Sādhārana will correspond to 1549 A.D. and another from Tiruvaṇṇamalai 427 of 1928 dated 1569 A.D. refers to the same overlord.

18. 39 of 40 of 1897 of Achyutarāya are found in the Tōppūr Pillayar temple at Tanjore and are dated S. 1454 and S. 1401 respectively. 271 of 1907 from Tiruvadamarudur is dated S. 1456. 261 of 1917 from Tirumakkōttai. 116 of 1931-32 is dated S. 1459, Paṇdanallūr, Tanjore District.

19. 'Sangīta Sudhā' Introduction, sloka 28. Published in the Journal of the Madras Music Academy.

20. Taylor, 'Oriental Historical' Mss.,' Vol. II, p. 109.

Viswanâtha Nayaka effected this transfer by giving over Vallam to the king of Tanjore. He was the ruler of Tanjore also besides Madura before the establishment of Śevappa Nayaka as the governor of the Tanjore country. Hence the ruler of Tanjore mentioned in the chronicles was no other than Śevappa himself, whose rule began in 1532 A.D. Both Viswanatha and Śevappa were feudatories of Achyutarāya. Śevappa who was just then appointed to Tanjore could not have effected this arrangement of his own accord. Evidently, the transfer was arranged by Achyutarāya himself while he was staying at Srirangam and also before he appointed Śevappa to Tanjore. This looks probable since the emperor reconstituted his southern territories and put them on an enduring basis needed for making full arrangements.[21]

Śevappa continued the same loyal and friendly attitude towards Sadāsivarāya, the Vijayanagara emperor and his general Rāmarāja Viṭhaladēva Mahārāya, when the latter came to the South on an expedition against the Tiruvaḍi Raja about the year 1545 A.D. and remained for about a decade at Trichinopoly as the viceroy of the south. Śevappa in all probability might have offered his help to Rāmarāja Viṭhala in his wars against the Tiruvaḍi king as well as against the Paravas of the Fishery Coast.[22]

21. *'Nayaks of Madura"* p. 52. Prof. Sathianatha Aiyar says that 'this must have been an imperial arrangement, for the empire was yet too strong to allow so much independence to the provinces.' The transfer of Vallam has been given different dates. *The Tanjore District Gazetteer,* p. 38 gives 1623 A.D. *The Tanjore Manual,* p. 751, has 1560 A.D. Mr. K. Sitharamayya Garu, 'Tanjore Andhra Nayaka Charitamu, p. 95 says, that the whole transaction must have been made during the time of a Chōla king and strangely enough, he speaks at the same time also of the possibility of Achyutarāya making this arrangement. Father Heras, *Aravidu Dynasty,* p. 129, says that this happened after 1539 A.D. 1532 A.D. satisfies all the circumstances and is also supported by evidence. We need not go into an examination and criticism of the various discrepant dates mentioned above. That Vallam and Trichinopoly were exchanged between Tanjore and Madura by Achyutarāya looks fairly satisfactory.

22. Rāmarāja Viṭhala's imposing expedition into the south was due to two causes which were of vital importance to the empire. The efforts of Udaya Mārṭhānda Varma, the king of Travancore to extend his dominion in the east and the appointment of a viceroy by him over the newly acquired territories in the present Tinnevelly District asked for the imperial intervention. "Udaya Mārtānda Varma, whose surname according to epigraphs was Maṇkonda Bhūtala Vīra Sri Vīra Udaya Mārtānda Varma, was a famous warrior who conquerred almost the whole of the Tinnevelly District. He married a princess, known as Chōḷakulavalli, who brought with her the district of Kalakād as dowry. The king made Kalakād his capital and built in it a new palace, called Vīra Mārtānda Chaturvēdimangalam Pudumāḷigai. He was the first of the three Bhutala Viras whose names occur in

Viṭhaladēva's viceroyalty did not contribute anything mateially to the rule of the Tanjore Nayaks and his authority was above those of the Nayaks in general.[23] It was during this period that the famous battle of Talikota was fought between the armies of Rāmarāja on the one side and the Muhammadans on the other.[24] We read from Ferishta that Rāmarāja on the eve of this war issued an order summoning all his dependents and rāyas from the banks of the Krishna as far as the island of Ceylon.[25] Muthukrishnappa Nayaka of Madura (1564-72) is said to have despatched an army under the captainship of Ariyanātha Mudaliar.[26] But there is nothing to refer to the part played by Tanjore

the coins of Tinnevelly. He gave grants of land as paḷḷichchandam to the god of the temple of Nagercoil at the special request of Guṇavīra Panditan and Kamalavāhana Panditan, probably Jainas. He protected the Christian Paravas of Kumarimuttam near Cape Comorin from being harassed by taxation at the hands of their Hindu brethren (Pillar Inscription of 20th Minam 701 M.E.=1526 A.D.). The Christians were evidently those converted by Father Miguel Vaz. The Travancore ruler was described by St. Francis Xavier in one of his letters of 1544, as "the great king having authority all over South India." [Ed.]

The more important cause seems to be the growth of a powerful influence as a result of missionary enterprise in the Fishery Coast. 'The coast region was open to Portuguese enterprise and the chief ports of the south contained Portuguese factories'. 'The advent of Francis Xavier in the southern region created a new and powerful influence the political aspects of which have not received adequate attention among the historians of this period. The Paravas, the fisherfolk along the coast were being rapidly converted to Christianity, and such conversion was interpreted as involving a change of allegiance of the inhabitants from their Indian rulers to the king of Portugal. This wholesale conversion of a class of industrious inhabitants of the coast, including among them those engaged in the valuable pearl-fishing, made them ipso facto subjects of the king of Portugal.' The Empire could not look on with indifference this transference of territory from his allegiance to that of the king of Portugal by the peaceful efforts of Portuguese missionaries. Rāmarāja Viṭhala's invasion resulted in the reduction of the Parava Coast 'to its normal sense of political allegiance.' See '*Nayaks of Madura,*' Introduction, pp. 13-14. Also p. 90 foot-note. Father Heras gives a detailed account of this invasion in his '*Aravidu Dynasty of Vijayanagara,*' pp. 159-162.

23. 140 of 1895 from Tiruvadamarudur belongs to Sadāsiva Rāya and it records a gift of two villages by Rāmarāja Viṭhaladēva. The record was issued by Rāmarāja in the Tanjore country while Śevappa was the ruler. 104 of 1911 from the Tanjore country dated S. 1482 (1560 A.D.) refers to a settlement made by Krishnamarājayyan the son of Aliya Rāmarāja. He appointed a certain Gñānaprakāsar Paṇḍāram of Tiruvārur as the supervisor of the temples at Sikkil, Vadagudi and Vōdachēri. The epigraphist says that 'Krishnamarājayyan was evidently a ruler of some portion of Tanjore.' A.R.E., 1911.

24. For an account of the battle, see Heras, Chapter IX.

25. Briggs, Ferishta, Vol. III, pp. 413-4.

26. 431 of 1928 from Tiruvaṇṇāmalai, records Śevappa Nayak's loyalty to Tirumalarāya I in 1570 A.D., a few years after the battle of Talikota 1565 A.D.

in this war. The chronicles do not mention Śevappa's help rendered to the empire, but all of them speak of his loyalty and faithfulness. As a loyal subordinate, Śevappa Nayaka must have helped the emperor in this hour of need, along with the ruler of Madura and others.

Nothing more is known of Śevappa's reign except his works of charity and public utility. He constructed temples, repaired numerous tanks and founded agraharas. He repaired the Sivagaṅgā tank at Tanjore and to ensure full supply of water he caused to be dug a feeder tank which was called after him. Even to-day the tank goes by the name of Śeppanēri a contracted form for Śevappanēri. The Sivagaṅgā fort also was repaired by him.[27] He also built the magnificent tower (gōpura) composed of eleven storeys of the Arunāchalēswara temple at Tiruvaṇṇā-malai. 419 of 1928 from Tiruvaṇṇāmalai says that in the year 1572 A.D. the gōpura was built at the request of one Sivanēsa and his brother Lōkanātha.[28] This great achievement of Śevappa Nayak was much appreciated and extolled by the people who recorded their praise in beautiful verses which are still to be found.[29] The *Raghunāthābhyudayam* and the *Sangīta Sudhā*, besides mentioning his building the Tiruvaṇṇāmalai gopura, refer to his other works.[30] Śevappa is said to have constructed the massive prākāras in the temples at Vriddhāchalam and Conjeevaram and covered the vimānas of both the Tirupati and Srīsailam temples with gold. In the Chōḷa country his benefactions impartially extended to both the Siva and Vishnu temples situated on either side of the holy river Cauvery. Besides, he made gifts of villages[31] and precious jewels to the gods and provided for the feeding of the Brahmans. The *Vijayavilāsam* and the *Rājagōpalavilāsam* refer to these gifts and speak of his pious deeds. *The Tanjāvūri Āndhra Rājula Charitamu* also mentions his building of the gōpura and the prākāras of the Tiruvaṇṇāmalai and Vriddhāchalam temples, respectively. The gifts made to these temples and the large contributions made to Siva and Vishnu temples show Śevap-

27. Of the two forts at Tanjore the small fort is said to have been built by Śevappa and the bigger by Vijayarāghava. *Annual Report of Archaeological Department, S. Circle,* 1912-13.

28. 419 of 1928. Śevappa is called Timmappa Chinnaśevvanṛpati

29. The verses are said to have been composed by one Srinivasa Dikshita of Satyamangalam, A. R. E., 1928, Pt. II. An account of this composer is also given.

30. Raghunāthābhyudayam, Canto VI, Sl. 7-10. Sangīta Sudhā, Introd., Sl. 28-33.

31. 421 of 1928 registers a gift of villages to the temple at Tiruvaṇṇāmalai. 27 of 1925 dated S. 1497 comes from Mūvalūr in the Tanjore district. It records a *sarvamānya* gift of land ten *vēlis*, for the maintenance of a choultry attached to the temple.

pa's patronage of these two leading religions. A spirit of toleration was largely developed by the Tanjore Nayaks who were Vaishṇavas by religious persuasion. His benefactions were extended to the other religious faiths such as Buddhism and Muhammadanism. An epigraph coming from the Kumbakōnam Taluk (292 of 1927) and dated 1579 A.D. refers to a Buddhist temple to which lands were allotted by the people in exchange of lands that belonged to the temple and which were used by them for other purposes.[32] An inscription (425 of 1924) found on the wall of the Samuśarupalli mosque in Tanjore registers a grant of seven *vēlis* of land made to the faqirs of the mosque by five Maṇṇaiyārs of Naṇjikkōttai at the instance of Śevappa in the year 1550 A.D. The patronage given by him to the Mādhvā religion is also seen in his grants made. In 1574 A.D. the great Mādhvā teacher, Vijayīndra Tirtha Sripāda, received a grant of a village from the Nayaka.[33] Śevappa also

32. The record states that the people of Tirumalairājapuram having had to cut a channel through the land that belonged to the Buddhist temple at Tiruviḷandurai, they made compensation by assigning 2¾ *velis* of land in Tirumalairājapuram. 'The Leyden grant refers to a Buddhist temple at Negapatam as early as the 18th century. The Buddha images within a radius of five miles of Kumbakōnam, one at the entrance into the Tiruvaḷaṇjuli temple and another within the temple at Pattīswaram and a third miscalled Bhārgavarishi in a Ganēsa shrine in Kumbakōnam itself testify to the prevalence of the Buddhist religion though perhaps in a fugitive condition in the heart of the Tanjore district in mediaeval times. The present record is of interest in that it mentions a Buddha temple in the Kumbakōnam taluk till so late as the time of Śevappa Nayaka. A. R. E. 1927, part II, p. 116.

33. The Arivīḷimaṇgalam plates. *Epigraphia Indica*, Vol. XII, p. 357. Śevappa Nayaka was also responsible for another grant made to the same maṭha by Srirangaraya. (Mysore Archaeological Report, 1917, p. 17). Here the king is called Vīrachevva Bhūpa and he is described as 'a moon to the ocean of Timmappa.' The record which is dated in A.D. 1575 registers the gift of Nāvalūr and Pūkkudi villages to the great teacher Surēndra Tīrtha, the spiritual guru of Vijayīndra Tīrtha. Besides, these two grants, the Rāghavēndraswāmi maṭha at Naṇjangūd is in possession of three copper plate grants referring to the Tanjore Nayak's benefactions. One of them, dated 1580 A.D. belongs to Śevappa and records a grant of villages in the Mayavaram Taluk, made to Vijayīndra Tīrtha at Kumbakōnam. The record bears the emblem of a boar which was the *lāṇchana* of the Vijayanagar kings and is signed Sri Rājagōpāla. The plates give an account of Śevappa's ancestors beginning from Vishnu, Ganga, Earth and Dēvaraja. The last mentioned person is said to have been a minister of Krishnadēvarāya and to have captured the fort of Udayagiri. His son was Chiṇṇarāja by his wife Maṇgalāmbika ; and Chiṇṇarāja was Rāmarāja's minister. He had two sons Śevappa and Chiṇṇa Śevappa. The plates say that Chiṇṇarāja was the founder of the Tanjore Nayaks. He was succeeded by Śevappa whom his brother Chiṇṇaśevappa regarded as his father. The record says that Vijayīndra and Tātāchārya, the great Vaishnava scholar and Appayya

made provision for the celebration of festivals. One Kālāttināthа Mudaliar who appears as the signatory of a record (245 of 1927) of Śevappa which relates to a gift of lands, must have been an officer of the king.

Śevappa Nayaka's patronage extended even to Europeans like the Portuguese who had then captured the maritime trade of South India from the Arabs. The Portuguese came to India and landed on the west coast towards the close of the 15th century. Soon their power increased and this was made possible by the complete absence of European rivalry and the impotence of the Mussalmans to resist their guns and ships. They carried on a large volume of trade with Ceylon, having established themselves both on the west coast as well as in the neighbourhood of the Fishery Coast. Their missionaries converted the Paravas of the Fishery Coast of Tinnevelly and soon grew powerful. It was their objectionable activities and mass conversions that stimulated the expedition of Rāmarāja Viṭhaladēva. The Portuguese soon came to possess factories on the Coromandel Coast the earliest being those of San Thome de Meliapur and Negapatam. Ferishta, speaking of the Christians in the year 963 A.H. (1556 A.D.), says 'that the Christians held the ports of Mangalore and Negapatam in the extreme south of the Peninsula.[34] By 1586 A.D. Negapatam had become a flourishing centre and came to possess a governor of its own.' Diogo Fernandez Penoa from Negapatam is said to have helped the Portuguese against the attacks of the Ceylonese king Rājasimha.[35] The Portuguese, either in the beginning of Śevappa's reign or even a little earlier, had settled at Negapatam and carried on trade between the outside world and the kingdom of Tanjore. An anonymous life of St. Xavier says that the Portuguese 'were greatly favoured by the lord of that country who is a very powerful captain of the king of Bisnaga.' Soon the Portuguese

Dikshita, the Advaita scholar used to meet in the court of Śevappa. The other two records dated 1614 A.D. in the reign of Chinnaśeva refer to further grants made to the same Vijayīndra Tīrtha. Śevappa, the brother of Chinnaśeva, is said to have been residing at Kumbakonam leaving the kingdom in the hands of the latter. The records in question were prepared at the instance of the king by his minister whose name is not mentioned. It is said that Chinnaśeva may be identified with Achyutappa ('Sāhityaratnākara' Canto III, Sl. 28). This view is not correct since the verse referred to speaks of him as Chinnaśeva Achyuta and not Chinnaśeva as is surmised. However, the genealogy contained in these plates differ in all essential respects from that of the literary and epigraphical evidence. One would like to know more about these plates and their paleography in particular before giving them their due importance and proper consideration. Already a note of warning is sounded in the same report regarding the authenticity of the grants of Sriranga given to the matha.

34. Briggs, Ferishta, Vol. IV, p. 534.

35. F. C. Danvers, *The Portuguese in India*, Vol. II, p. 32 and 76.

acquired royal favour in the Nayak's court. The Portuguese fortified the place and erected a fort and two churches, one dedicated to St. Francis of Assisi and the other to Our Lady of Health. It is recorded that in the very first year of the Portuguese occupation of Negapatam about 300 Hindus were baptized. Cesare Federici wrote of Negapatam in 1567 A.D. 'as a very great city and very populous of Christians of the country and partly gentile.[36] St. Xavier visited the town about 1550 A.D. Śevappa appears to have given them protection and permitted them to trade in his land. The erection of buildings could not have been possible but for the royal favour.[37]

Śevappa Nayaka, had a long reign and lived to a ripe age, having spent the major part of his life in his newly acquired kingdom. An inscription of his from Kumbakonam (Tanjore District) mentions A.D. 1579-80 and it is the latest date so far known.[38] The *Sāhityaratnākara*[39] says that he appointed his son Achyutappa Nayaka as Yuvarāja and put him in charge of the administration. Achyutappa's earliest epigraph is dated in the year 1560 A.D.[40] Śevappa ruled for about twenty-one years from A.D. 1532 to A.D. 1563 as king and spent the rest of his life in performing acts of piety,[41] till his death in 1580 A.D.[42] In his last days he appointed one Gōvinda Dikshita as his minister who later on became famous as a good administrator and a wise counsellor. Gōvinda Dikshita's name is still remembered by the people of the Tanjore country. 422 of 1928 from Tiruvaṇṇāmalai dated Saka 1502 (1580 A.D.) contains two verses by one Gōvindasūri who styling himself as a dependent of Śevappa Bhūpa expresses gratitude for favours received, by composing verses in praise of him. In all probability the author is identical with Gōvinda Dikshita who became the minister of Śevappa's successors.[43] Mr. Sitaramayya speaks of two images of Śevappa, one in the big Temple at Tanjore and the other in the Venkataramaṇaswāmi temple. However, they are not labelled Śevappa and Mr. Sitaramayya himself says that nothing definite could be said about them.

36. Heras *'The Aravidu Dynasty'*, pp. 174-175.

37. 'Tanjore Gazetteer' p. 244 says that Śevappa was opposed to the Portuguese.

38. 292 of 1927 contains the cyclic year Vikrama, Ādi. It corresponds to 1579-80 A.D.

39. Canto III, Sloka 17.

40. 536 of 1904. The cyclic year Rudrōdgāri and the Saka year 1480 do not agree. The cyclic year must be Raudri.

41. His epigraphs from Tiruvaṇṇāmalai and other places recording his works of building gōpuras, etc., are dated only after 1563 A.D.

42. Mr. K. Sitaramayya supposes that Śevappa must have lived till 1580 A.D. T. S. Kuppuswami Sastri assigns 1572 A.D. as his last known date.

43. A.R.E. 1928, Part II, p. 86.

CHAPTER IV.

ACHYUTAPPA NAYAKA (A.D. 1560, A.D. 1614)

Achyutappa Nayaka,[1] the son of Śevappa Nayaka, ascended the throne in A.D. 1580 on the death of his father. But his early connection with the administration of the kingdom and his joint rule as co-regent with his father which must have started, at least, from A.D. 1560 are best seen in his epigraphs; and the literary evidence records that he was appointed as Yuvaraja by his father in the latter part of his rule. He seems to have been named after Achyutarāya, the Vijayanagara emperor, by Śevappa, in gratitude to the Raya who was responsible for the foundation of the Tanjore Nayak line. Achyutappa Nayaka was also known as Chiṇṇa Śeva Achyuta[2] and Śevappa Achyuta.[3] His queen was also called Mūrtimāmba. He had for his minister the famous Gōvinda Dīkshita who had been appointed to that high office by his father in his last years. Gōvinda Dīkshita played a prominent part in the administration of the country during the reigns of both Achyutappa and his son; and it may be said that his achievement was similar in character and effect to that of Mādhava Vidyāraṇya, in shaping and laying the foundations of the internal and foreign policies of the Tanjore Nayaks.

Achyutappa Nayaka had a long reign of fifty-three years including the period of his joint rule with his father which lasted for about twenty years. In his last days, following the foot-steps of his father, he also abdicated the throne in favour of his son; but this time the abdication and retirement were largely due to the advice of his minister. Achyutappa was a powerful ruler endowed with a keen intellect and a faculty for quick decision. He was ably assisted in his administrative work by his minister who was equally noted for his deep learning, wise diplomacy and statesmanship. If Achyutappa was a past-master in the art of warfare and in the use of weapons (śaṣtra) his great minister was equally so in his knowledge of the śāṣtras and when the

1. The inscriptions call him Achyutappa Nayaka with the epithet Ayya added to it, while the literary evidence refer to him as Achyuta.

2. *Sāhityaratnākara*, Canto III, Sl. 38.

3. 425 of 1928.

former won a name by his success in wars, the latter attained renown by his performance of sacrifices.[4]

The Nayak was deeply religious; and the *Sangīta Sudhā* says that even from his boyhood he had been a great devotee of Lord Raṅganātha; and he had become the ruler even in his youth.[5] However, this single-hearted devotion to Raṅganātha did not deter him from extending a liberal measure of his patronage to other creeds; and his numerous gifts made to Śiva and Viṣṇu temples and to the Madhwa teacher, Vijayīndra Tīrtha, are remarkable instances of the catholicity of his religious outlook and his broadmindedness.

Achyutappa's reign was not one of continued peace, as his later years were marked by internal troubles and by wars with his neighbours and foreigners. The *Sāhityaratnākara* and the *Raghunāthābhyudayam* refer indirectly to his wars against the Muhammadans and the Portuguese which he waged on behalf of his overlord, Venkatapati Raya (1584-1614), and the chief of Jaffna respectively.[6] His epigraphs do not throw much light on his military achievements; but his reign on the whole seems to have been an eventful one. Achyutappa came to the throne when there prevailed peace and calm around, but abdicated at a critical time, when the land became involved in the throes of the great war of succession to the imperial throne, that broke out on the death of Venkatapati Raya.

Achyutappa continued the loyal policy of Śevappa Nayaka and maintained an attitude of unflinching loyalty to and co-operation with the Vijayanagara Emperors, *viz.*, Śadāsivarāya, Tirumalarāya and his successors Srīranga and Venkatapati Raya.[7] And it was this staunch

4. The *Tanjāvūri Añdhra Rājalu Charitamu*, edited by Mr. V. Prabhakara Sastri, Vavilla Press. In the Introduction it is said

त्रीणामाद्यन्तनुमाणौ महीक्षिद्दीक्षितावुभौ ।
शस्त्रे शास्त्रे.च निपुणौ आहवेषुहवेषु च ॥

Achyutappa the king, and Gōvinda Dīkshita the first and the last names of Trinãma, *i.e.*, Achuta, Anaṇta and Gōvinda were noted for their knowledge of the śaṣtra and the śāstras.

5. *Sangīta Sudhā.* Introduction by Gōvinda Dīkshita.

आरम्यबाल्यादतिभक्तिशाली मुदासदाऽसेवतरङ्गनाथम् ।
अवाप्यतञ्जापुरमप्रदीपः कौमारयेवाहृतराज्यभारः ॥

6. *Raghunāthābhyudayam*, VII, Sl. 49 and 50; *Sāhityaratnākara*, VII, Sl. 68-74.

7. 567 of 1902 dated 1567 A.D. and coming from Tiruvaṇṇāmalai records a gift made by Achyutappa Nayaka in the reign of Sadāsivarāya.

loyalty of Achyutappa towards his suzerains and his active co-operation with them in their wars that were responsible for the future hatred, enmity and warfare between Tanjore and Madura. He was mainly responsible for thwarting the schemes of the disloyal Madura and Gingee Nayaks and preventing their combination against the Raya. But for Achyutappa Nayak's hearty co-operation with Venkatapati Raya in the latter's war with Madura, while he was the viceroy of the South under Śrīrangarāya, the southern viceroyalty would have broken away altogether from the Vijayanagara overlordship. Achutappa was the mainstay of the integrity of the Vijayanagara Empire in the south; and the Raya largely relied upon the resources of the Tanjore Nayak for help at times of need. After the battle of Talikōta (Rakhastagdi) in A.D. 1565 which shattered the strength of the Hindu Empire, the southern feudatories took advantage of the crisis to aim at independence, withdrew their allegiance and withheld their tribute.[8] However epoch-making the battle of Talikota was, it did not mark the end of the empire as assumed by Mr. Sewell and others, but indicated only the beginning of a long process of decline. It took roughly another fifty years for the empire to be totally disintegrated; and in this period of decay sporadic attempts were made by the Rayas to recover their lost dominion and prestige and also to check the steady Muhammadan advance into South India. The Raichur Doab was no more the bone of contention between the Muhammadan and Hindu powers and the scene of action now shifted to the territories lying immediately to the north of the North Pennar river.[9] The success of the Hindus in this period was mainly due to the exertions of Venkatapati Raya I. In the extreme south, however, the battle of Talikōta encouraged the Nayaks to entertain ideas of independence. Tanjore alone remained firm and unflinching in her loyal attitude throughout this period and she contributed in a large measure to the military successes of Venkatapati Raya. What Venkatapati Raya did to the cause of the Vijayanagara Empire in the north, that Achyutappa did in the south, in maintaining the unity and supremacy of that Empire. Both Venkatapati and Achyutappa ruled at a critical time and contributed to the maintenance of the strength of the empire, postponing the days of its disruption and the spread of Muham-

8. Dr. S. K. Ayyangar, "*The Nayaks of Madura*," Introduction.

9. *The Climacteric of Talikota* by Prof. R. Sathianatha Aiyar, *Journal of Indian History*, Vol. VI (1927). The Muhammadan authorities support the view that the post-Talikōta history of Vijayanagar for half a century was not fundamentally different from its history before 1565.

madan dominance into the south. In all these wars, Achyutappa had the co-operation of his able minister, Gōvinda Dīkshita; and in his later struggles he had also the willing assistance of his illustrious son, Raghunātha Nayaka.

Achyutappa Nayaka's early years of rule did not witness any Imperial expedition to the southward, nor the superimposition of a viceroy like Rāmarāja Viṭhaladēva Maharaya. Since the Raya was intensively engaged with the Muhammadan armies of Bijapur and Golkonda, the South was practically left without any serious intervention till the appointment of Venkatapati Raya as its Viceroy by Srīrangarāya.

Venkatapati had his capital at Chandragiri. In the north, Srīrangarāya was carrying on the struggle for Hindu independence against great odds from Penukoṇda (the Ghanagiri of the epigraphs), which had then become the capital. The powerful viceroy of Madura, it appears, did not send any help to the Emperor; and evidence is not wanting to prove his attempts at independence following the siege of Penukoṇda by the Muhammadan armies in A.D. 1579.[10]

It was the Adil Shah that first marched against Penukonda and blockaded it for three months in 1577. He was then forced to retire from the siege, though the Raya himself had retreated for safety to Chandragiri. In 1579 he advanced for a second time against Penukonda and began its siege. But he failed owing to a combination of the armies of Srīranga and Golkonda.[11] Tanjore's part in this imperial struggle is not known in detail; and in the absence of any contradictory evidence, we can safely conclude that her moral support at least was extended to the Raya at the time.

Achyutappa Nayaka had no difficulties to encounter so long as his father was alive. The first important event of his independent rule

10. *The Climacteric of Talikota.* This was the second time when Penukonda was besieged by the Muhammadans. The first took place in 1577; and the third in 1587.—Ed.

11. The Raya had deputed an envoy with magnificent presents to the Kutb Shah, 'soliciting his aid against their common enemy'; and it had always been "an understood principle with the Mahomedan Kings of the Deccan, not to invade the Beejanugger territories without the general consort of the whole." The Kutb Shah sent a general to skirmish and plunder the borders of the Bijapur territory and himself moved to the southward to the support of the Raya: "Their junction induced Ally Adil Shah to raise the siege of Beejanugger (Penukonda) and return to Bijapur." (Brigg's *Ferishta,* Vol. III, p. 435).

was the part, which he played in the war of Venkatapati Raya[12] in the battle of Vallamprākāra (the modern Vallam near Tanjore) against the Madura ruler, Virappa Nayaka (1572-1595). However, none of the records of Achyutappa Nayaka nor the literary evidence of the *Raghunāthābhyudayam* and the *Sāhityaratnākara,* refer to this important war except the Pudukottai (Srīvilliputtūr, Ramnad District) plates of Ativīrarāma Srīvallabha and his cousin Varatuṇgarāma.[13] The omission of this important battle in the Tanjore literature was perhaps due to the fact that both the *Raghunāthābhyudayam* and the *Sāhityaratnākara* which give an account of the Tanjore Nayaks, were written during the reign of Raghunātha only and in obvious praise of his victorious wars.[14] Moreover, Tanjore's part in this war was not due to any hatred or personal grudge between her and the Madura ruler, Virappa Nayaka, but was only necessitated by the fact, that Tanjore being loyal to the Raya, she had to assist her imperial overlord in the latter's war upon another disloyal feudatory. And Tanjore could not but join Venkatapati I against Madura, as her own dominions were imperilled, and the battle at Vallam suggests the possibility of the Madura Nayak's attempts made to get possession of that place, as it was of strategic importance to Tanjore. The causes for this imperial invasion under Venkatapati Raya are not known; but it may be opined that Virappa Nayaka's victories over the Mābalivānāḍirāya chieftains of the extreme south, which might have excited in him a desire for independence, and his consequent refusal to pay the usual tribute to the Emperor Srīrangaraya consequent on the siege of Penukonda by the Bijapurians in A.D. 1579, were sufficient causes for the Raya's attempt to restore his authority over the south.[15] Virappa Nayaka's epigraphs point to his early subordination to Srīrangarāya only till the year A.D. 1578[16] and his inscriptions upto the year A.D. 1586 do

12. Venkatapati Raya I is called the II by some on the ground that Achyuta rāya's son also was called Venkatādri. But others call him the I, since he was the first man of that name to assume the crown of the Empire and to have ruled as emperor.

13. 7 of Appendix A, 1906. *Report on South Indian Epigraphy* and *The Travancore Archaeological Series,* Vol. I, pp. 61-68.

14. Both Rāmabhadrāmba and Yagnanārāyana Dikshita were concerned in extolling the qualities and achievements of Raghunātha Nayaka who was their hero. However, a passing and indirect reference to the help rendered by Achyutappa is made by Rāmabhadrāmba when she speaks of Tanjore's early help to Venkatapati Raya, (Canto VII, Sl. 49).

15. *The Nayaks of Madura,* pp. 78-79 and foot notes No. 100 and 103. Also *The Aravidu Dynasty of Vijayanagara,* pp. 285-6.

16. 663 of 1916.

not refer to his recognition of any overlord at all, as they were issued in his own name.[17] Also, the battle itself being fought on the outskirts of the kingdom of Madura, suggests the open insubordination on the part of Madura Nayak and his consequent attack upon Tanjore.

The Pudukottai plates, dated Saka 1505, and the cyclic year Subhānu, corresponding to A.D. 1583, refer to a gift of villages made by Ativīrarāma Srīvallabha and Varatuṇgarāma at the request of one Tirumala Nayaka, an agent of Vīrappa Nayaka, after obtaining the latter's permission.[18] Towards the end, the plates contain a reference to Tirumala Nayaka's achievements of killing à Basavarāja, a former refugee of his, and of his capturing the horses and elephants that fought on the battle field of Vallamprākāra. In this war the armies of Venkatapati, Vīraraja and Achyutaraja are mentioned, and Venkatapati must undoubtedly refer to Venkatapati Raya since, in the preceding lines, the great Alīya Rāmarāja, the *de facto* ruler of Vijayanagar under Śadāsivarāya, and who had died on the battle-field of Talikōta is mentioned. Besides, there was no other person called Venkatapati except this member, who had then been appointed by Tiruṃalarāya as the viceroy of the south. His contemporaries were Vīrappa Nayaka of Madura and Achyutappa Nayaka of Tanjore and the mention of these two, lend support to the assumption that the reference is to Venkatapati and to his victory over the Madura Nayaka. The validity of the plates has been questioned by some on the ground that, in A.D. 1583 —the date of the plates under reference—there was no Venkatapati Raya on the Vijayanagar throne as his accession took place only in A.D. 1586. This argument is untenable since we find Venkatapati Raya ruling from Chaṇdragiri as the viceroy of the south in A.D. 1583, and the Pudukottai Plates themselves contain references to this fact, when they call Alīya Rāmarāja of Talikota fame, as Emperor and Venkatapati by his simple name alone without any royal attribute.[19] This ordinary reference to

17. Absence of the name of overlords in the epigraphs of subordinates cannot be taken *ipso facto* to mean the independence of the latter. For instance the Tanjore epigraphs of Raghunātha Nayaka and his successor Vijayarāghava do not mention their overlords. But at the same time Tanjore's loyalty cannot be doubted as internal and external evidence are agreed on this point.

18. The Pudukottai plates: T. A. S. Vol. I. Virappa is called 'Virappa Kshōnipāla' here. Tirumala Nayaka calls himself as the right hand of Virappa. Verses 65 to 68.

19. The verses have विख्यादलिय रामराजनृपतौ व्यापादिते etc., and ऋद्धेयोधकुलेन वेङ्कटपतेर्युद्धे etc.

Venkatapati shows that at the time of Vallam battle, he was not the Emperor, but only a viceroy.

Since the plates[20] are dated in the beginning of (Chitrai) April A.D. 1583, the events referred to, must have happened in the previous cyclic year Chitrabānu, *i.e.*, in the beginning of the year A.D. 1583. The record referring to the death of one Basavarāja, who was perhaps a commander of Venkatapati, says that in that battle of Vallamprākāra, the armies of Vīraraja were destroyed, while those of Achyutappa Nayaka (Achyuta Dharaṇīpati) fled from the field out of fear. Naturally the question would arise as to why Achyutappa's army should have taken to its heels while there was present, on the field of battle, Venkatapati, the victor. This is explained in the succeeding lines of the verse 164 which refer to Tirumala Nayaka's capture of the horses and elephants. The plates suggest that both Vīrappa Nayaka and Tirumala Nayaka were engaged in the battle and the latter must have

20. The Pudukottai Plates are dated Saka 1505 (Subhānu, Chitrai). See *Madras Report on South Indian Epigraphy* 1906, p. 54. 1909, p. 84. 1910, p. 91. 1012, p 66. *The Nayaks of Madura*, pp. 101-2 and footnote on p. 101. *The Pāṇdyan Kingdom* by Prof. K. A. Nilakanta Sastri, p. 251. *The Aravidu Dynasty of Vijayanagara* by H. Heras, pp. 285-6. The plates contain some discrepancies. Verses 19 and 20 say that Srivallabha was crowned after the death of his brother Ativīrarāma and V. 42 mentions that the gift was made in the 21st year of Ativīrarāma Srivallaba which corresponded to Saka 1503. Ativīrarāma is identified with Ativīrarāma Srivallabha of the Teṇkāsi Inscriptions which give him A.D. 1561 for his accession. But in A. D. 1583 there was no Varatungarāma, his cousin as his accession took place in A.D. 1586. Prof. Sathianatha Aiyar, *Nayaks of Madura*, p. 101, says that these plates must belong to Muttu Vīrappa Nayaka I (1603-1623) and not to Virappa Nayaka (1572-1595) as the latter continued the policy of subordination and loyalty towards the Vijayanagara emperors ......' On page 81, he says in connection with Vīrappa's supremacy over the Teṇkāsi Pāṇdyas, 'If the Pudukkottai Plates of Sri Vallabha were issued in 1583, his relation towards the Pāṇdyas as overlord is clear.' But he is inclined to assign the plates to Muthu Virappa Nayaka when he says (page 101) 'Perhaps the expression armies of Vira Raja and Achyuta Raja' were loosely used for the forces of the loyalist party and of Raghunātha Nayaka. 'If the date (1583) is correct it is difficult to explain such a combination of contending parties in 1583 or before. Thus he would take the Vallam battle to refer to the Tōppūr engagement, in which the loyalists fought against Jaggarāya and the Madura ruler. However, casting doubt on the date of the Plates, he has assigned them to the reign of Virappa Nayaka, p. 344, No. 76. That the battle of Toppūr is distinctly different from the Vallam battle is proved by the literary and internal evidence and Dr. S. K. Ayyangar's view that 'it is clear from this that the battle of Vallamprākāra referred to in the Pudukottai plates (of date 1582-3) cannot be taken to refer to the battle of Toppūr' (p. 102, Note) will hold good until it is proved to the contrary by future research.

put up a strong and valiant fight. When Vīrappa's army was completely destroyed and when victory was won by Venkatapati, the Tanjore army must have retreated instead of advancing upon the enemy that might have escaped the disaster, and Tirumala Nayaka would have taken possession of the horses left behind. Otherwise, the flight of the Tanjore forces will mean that they must have also opposed Venkatapati along with Madura. For such an interpretation there is nothing to support even in the traditional accounts.

These foregoing facts show that there was a battle at Vallamprākāra in which Venkatapati and the Tanjore Nayaka took part against Vīrappa Nayaka, whom they defeated in the end. Thus the earliest attempt at independence on the part of the Madura Nayak was nipped in the bud with the hearty co-operation and timely help rendered by the loyal Tanjore ruler, Achyutappa Nayaka, but for whom, it may be said that the south would have had a different history in the 17th century. Perhaps it was to this timely help of Achyutappa, reference has been made in the work of Rāmabhadrāmba.[21] Achyutappa continued the same loyalty and co-operated with Venkatapati in all his wars waged against Madura. It appears that Venkatapati had to teach the recalcitrant Nayak of Madura the salutary lesson of subordination and allegiance at least on two occasions.[22] The exact nature of the part played by Tanjore

21. *Raghunāthābhyudayam*, cited before. Canto VII, Sl. 49.

बहुप्रकारैर्नृपतिप्रवेक प्रत्यर्थिपृथ्वीपतयो मदीयाः ।
संग्रामभूमीषु जगत्प्रसिद्धं खण्डीकृतास्ते खरखड्गवल्ल्या ॥

This verse is addressed to Achyutappa Nayaka by Venkatapati.

22. Prof. Sathiayanatha Aiyar (*The Nayaks of Madura*) says that there is nothing to doubt regarding the loyalty of Vīrappa Nayaka and his successors till the accession of Muthu Virappa Nayaka in A.D. 1609 and all the Vijayanagara wars must have happened in his reign *i.e.*, 1609-1623. Dr. S. K. Aiyangar says that there were two more Vijayanagara invasions upon Madura besides the Vallam campaign in the reign of Venkaṭapati and in one of them, Venkatapati himself took the command in person. (*Sources of Vijayanagar History*, Introduction, p. 19 and *Chikkadēvarāya Vamśāvali* of Tirumalarāya, p. 302 and *Sources*, 248). According to him the second campaign was led by himself. (*The Nayaks of Madura*, Introduction, p. 17). He would place the victory of Mātla Ananta mentioned in the Sidhout Inscription dated A.D. 1605 either in A.D. 1583 or a little later (Sources p. 248 and foot note 2). Father Heras discountenances the value of the *Chikkadēvarāya Vamśāvali* and says that there were three invasions of Venkatapati, (1) Before 1595 (2) about 1599 when Venkata marched personally and another (3) about 1610 when Mātla Ananta defeated the Madura ruler. Father Heras quotes evidence from the letters of Anquetil du Perron, Father Du Jarric, Father Pimenta, Father Vico and Father Laerzio. (*Aravidu Dynasty of Vijayanagar*, Chapter XVII).

on these occasions is not known for certain, but there can possibly be no doubt as regards Achyutappa Nayaka's co-operation with the imperial forces. And this co-operation developed the germs of mutual distrust and hostility, growing between Tanjore and Madura; and evidently the latter was looking out for an opportunity to wreak vengeance upon Tanjore. But Vīrappa Nayaka could not effect any harm to his rival, so long as there was Venkatapati Raya to take up her cause. And so, even the second attempt made by Vīrappa in his last days (*circa* 1595) proved fruitless.[23] These two defeats sustained by Vīrappa had their natural consequences and for about a decade following his death, there occurred no open hostilities between Madura and Tanjore. Krishnappa Nayaka II (1595-1601) the successor of Vīrappa, and Muthu Krishnappa Nayaka (1601-1609) of Madura remained loyal to the empire; and besides, they had their own troubles in the Travancore and Marava countries respectively; and the reorganisation of the Marava country under the Śētupatis was made by Muthu Krishnappa Nayaka after bringing that territory to subjection and allegiance. Since troubles nearer home demanded their continued attention, it was not possible for the Madura Nayaks to indulge in hostile manifestations against Tanjore and the Empire. Two Jesuit letters, dated A.D. 1606 and A.D. 1608, refer to Muthu Krishnappa Nayaka's loyalty to the Empire and to his remittance of the usual tribute.[24]

Muthu Vīrappa Nayaka, the son and successor of Muthu Krishnappa Nayaka, was the first ruler to exhibit his hostility towards Tanjore openly. He was a powerful ruler;[25] and he was the forerunner of Tirumala Nayaka in his policy of defying the imperial suzerain. He also appears to have pursued the aggressive policy of independence right from the beginning, since a Jesuit letter dated 25th November 1611[25] refers to a war which he waged with Tanjore. The letter says that Father Alberto Laerzio, in his tour on an inspection of the missionary centres of the

23. Father Heras (*Aravidu Dynasty of Vijayanagar*, p. 342) says that this war was the result of Virappa Nayaka's refusal to pay the tribute as mentioned by Anquetil du Perron.

24. *The Aravidu Dynasty*, p. 358. 'Moreover in September, 1604, Venkata II received in audience a special envoy of the Nayak of Madura, as a Jesuit letter of the year 1006 (mistake for 1606) tells us.' The letter of Father Coutinho dated October 11th, 1608 refers to the tribute paid by both Madura and Tanjore.

25. Father Vico's letter speaks of him as the powerful prince of the country. Bertrand: *La Mission*, Vol. II, 254, quoted in the *Nayaks of Madura*, p. 111.

26. Bertrand: *La Mission du Madure* II, p. 108. Letter from Father A. Laerzio to Father C. Aquaviva, Cochin, December 25th A.D. 1011. Also Father Heras, p. 361.

land, was at San Thomē on the 22nd September 1611. When he was about to leave that place, the letter says that he was prevented from going, the reason being that there was a war then raging between the Nayaks of Madura and Tanjore. Since the letter is dated the 25th of November 1611, it is probable that the war also must have come to an end sometime earlier, as otherwise, it is difficult to explain how he could have reached Cochin in full safety. We have no other evidence to refer to this war, in which Tanjore was directly involved. Neither the causes nor the results of this war are noticed or indicated in any of the Tanjore literature. Father Heras suggests, on the evidence of two Jesuit letters, that Achyutappa Nayaka's help to the Emperor in the previous year, i.e., A.D 1610, against Madura must have been the cause for this feud between the two houses.[27] He thus notes the significance of this war:—"We

27. Father Heras says that Venkatapati's last war upon Madura took place in A.D. 1610 when Mātla Ananta might have held the supreme command, (*Aravidu Dynasty of Vijayanagara*, p. 360) as the latter is called 'the conqueror of the territory called Panchapāṇdya, *i.e.*, the kingdom of Madura in an Inscription dated A.D. 1612-13 (Butterworth and Venugopaul Chetty): *Inscriptions of the Nellore District*: Vol. I, p. 246). From the Sidhout Inscription of Mātla Ananta, (*Sources*), we know that his victory over the Nayak of Madura must have happened sometime earlier than A.D. 1605 the date of the epigraph. And so this inscription dated A.D. 1612-13, on which reliance is made by Father Heras must also refer to the same battle fought sometime before A.D. 1605 as there is no evidence to prove another war upon Madura by Venkatapati Raya in his last days. Moreover even the evidence contained in the Jesuit letters on which Father Heras bases his views, is not definite and conclusive if careful attention is bestowed upon their general meaning. Father Heras places two letters as evidence in support of a war in A.D. 1610. One of the letters written by Robert de Nobili is dated 12th December, A.D. 1610 (*Aravidu Dynasty of Vijayanagara*, p. 361) and it says 'A certain notable Pandāra said to one of my Christians *these last days* that the coming of the king of Bisnage was the destruction of the Naiche, just as my stay in this country was the destruction of the Pandaras.' Father Heras says that 'the saying referred to in his letter proves evidently both that the war was over at the end of the same year, and that its result was satisfactory to the Vijayanagara Emperor,' and in support of this he quotes Father Vico's letter dated 30th August A.D. 1611. (Bertrand's *La Mission du Madure*, Vol. II, p. 124 and the *Nayaks of Madura*, p. 293). Again this letter says "The great Nayak of Madura and those of Tanjore and Gingee are themselves tributaries of Bisnagar, to whom they pay or have to pay each an annual tribute of six to ten million francs. But they are not punctual in paying it; *often they postpone the payment; sometimes they even refuse* it with insolence. *In that case* (the king of) Bisnagar comes or sends one of his generals, at the head of hundred thousand men, to make them pay all the arrears with interest. *On these occasions which are frequent*, it is again the poor people who pay for the fault of their princes; all the country is devastated, and the people are plundered or massacred." Father Heras concludes from this letter that 'the same (war) is meant by Father Vico' and quotes the last portion of the letter in support of his argument.

shall see that this feud between the two houses, that came to a head and burst in Venkata's reign, continued unabated till the extinction of one of them; and that very soon, just after the death of the Emperor, the Madura and Tanjore Nayaks again came to blows."

A careful and critical reading of the Jesuit letters quoted by Father Heras and the epigraphs[28] of the Madura Nayaks would clearly prove the impossibility of an imperial war with Madura in A.D. 1610 and so Achyutappa Nayaka's part in that war and against Madura as mentioned by Father Heras, is very highly improbable. Hence it is clear that the causes for a war between Tanjore and Madura mentioned in Father Laerzio's letter A.D. 1611 are to be traced somewhere else.

But a close reading of the contents of these two letters will show that the conclusions based upon them are not warranted and are baseless. They do not contain anything definite to show either a war or the refusal of the tribute by Madura in A.D. 1611 or even earlier. The *italicised* words clearly show that the statements made therein are only general observations made regarding the political situation. Father Nobili's letter embodies the observations made by a native to one of Nobili's followers regarding the general state of affairs then prevalent in the land. And Father Vico's letter contains his own personal observations and the loose words 'often' and 'sometimes' clearly indicate the possibility of only this interpretation. The phrases that 'they (the Nayaks of Madura, Tanjore and Gingee) are not punctual in paying it' and 'they postpone the payment' speak of the attitude of these Nayaks in general and they lend support only to this interpretation. Apart from this, too much stress cannot be laid upon the validity of these statements as they cannot withstand internal criticism. If Father Vico's letter is to be considered an authentic summary of the political history of the country, then it will mean that all the Nayaks were opposed to the Emperor in that year and not Madura alone as is surmised by Father Heras. And Prof. Sathianatha Aiyar's view, (*Nayaks of Madura*, p. 99) that Vico's letter refers to the Madura Nayak's withholding the tribute in that year, needs revision. The literary evidence proves the loyalty of Tanjore to the Empire and Tanjore's part in the Toppūr battle fought a few years after, only confirms their loyalty. The foregoing explanation shows that there could not have been any war between Venkatapati Raya and the Madura ruler in or about A.D. 1610.

[Father Heras says that Muttu Vīrappa of Madura, who succeeded Muttu Krishnappa in 1609, continued on good terms with Venkata II during the first years of his rule. An inscription of 1609 records that Venkatapati Raya made a gift of the village of Nagenalluru, on the north bank of the Kāveri, to Brahmans, at the request of Muttu Vīrappa and that in the records of the next year (1610) these friendly relations do not seem to have continued. This however, cannot mean that there was any open manifestation of hostility by the Madura Nayak towards his suzerain.—[*Ed.*]

28. Muthukrishnappa Nayaka's epigraphs show his loyalty to the Empire till his death in A.D. 1609 and "two records of Venkata I prove his authority in the Nayak dominions.'

Muthu Vīrappa Nayaka's earliest attempt at independence probably began in the year A.D. 1610; and his first measure towards this aim was directed against Tanjore, the immediate neighbour, as she had always supported the cause of the empire to the detriment of the particular interests of the Madura Nayaks. Achyutappa Nayaka's part in the Vallam battle in A.D. 1583, in co-operation with Venkatapati Raya and against Madura, and his continued rancour must have been sufficient causes for this outbreak of hostilities. Perhaps Erumaikatti Nayaka's capture of some fortress and his victorious return to Madura, mentioned in a Jesuit letter dated 12th June, 1610, has reference to this note of a war.[29] The letter shows that Erumaikatti must have been a feudatory or subordinate of Muthu Vīrappa, and he must have captured some of the forts that belonged most probably to Tanjore. And it is said, that for this act he was shown favours by the Madura Nayaka. Since the capture of the forts and the consequent reduction of the Tanjore territories happened in A.D. 1610, there was evidently enough reason for Tanjore to enter into war with Madura in the following year, and it must have ended about October, A.D. 1611[30]. But it is not known how the war was brought to a close. Dr. S. K. Aiyangar says that in this war 'the Empire government had taken no part, probably because it was involved in one of those periodical struggles against the aggressions of the Muhammadans from the North.'[31] Achyutappa Nayak's plan to conquer the lands held by various rulers through his son, as mentioned by Yagnanārāyana Dīkshita[32] perhaps has a reference to this war.

Achyutappa's loyalty towards and co-operation with the Emperor have been mentioned already. The *Raghunāthābhyudayam* confirms this, and refers to the help given by Achyutappa's son, Raghunātha to

29. The letter says (*Nayaks of Madura*, p. 100) 'that Hermecatti (Erumaikatti Nayaka)........distinguished himself by his bravery took some fortress by assault and returned victorious from the war. The great Nayak (of Madura) loaded him with honours and new favours.'

30. The letter is dated 25th November, A.D. 1611 and it refers to the stay of Father Laerzio in the College at San Thomé in September, on account of this war (also quoted above).

31. '*The Nayaks of Madura*', p. 102, Note.

32. *Sāhityaratnākara*, Canto VI, Sloka 63.

जातुक्षमामथ विजापयितुं समस्तां नाना नरेन्द्रविधृतां निजनन्दनेन ।
संचिन्तयन्सन्नृपतिः श्रवसोरतानीत् कोलाहलं भूपकुलाङ्गनानाम् ॥

Venkatapati Raya, in the latter's wars with the Muhammadans.[33] The authoress refers to the marching of the Tanjore army and to Raghunātha's arrival at Penukoṇda, visiting on his way the capital city, Chandragiri. Raghunātha won the battle and the Muhammadan army was completely routed. Venkata is said to have acknowledged his services in open court and praised him for his great valour and courage, presenting him with numerous gifts.[34] This account is confirmed by the accounts of the Muhammadan historians, which refer to Venkatapati Raya's

33. Venkatapati appeared to have in breach of the treaties existing between his predecessor and the Sultan of Golkonda, removed according to Ferishta, his seat of Government from Chandragiri to Penukonda "situated on the Kootb Shahy frontier" and likewise made incursions into the latter territory. The Raya deputed Goparaj Timma, his minister, and Pavia Chetty his general, to the Kutb Shah, who had commenced a siege of Penukonda and now consented to an armistice. The Hindus took advantage of the consequent absence of the Muhammadans from the vicinity of the fort and contrived to introduce into it a large quantity of supplies and a large number of troops, horse, foot and musketeers under the famous Jadev Rao, Gulrang Chetty, Manup Raj and Papiah Samywar. The subsequent siege operations of the Mussalmans were not effective and the Kutb Shah raised the siege and retreated to Golconda leaving his garrisons in Gandikotta, Nandyal and other places (1589). Venkatapati took advantage of this situation to keep the Raja of Udayagiri to make an incursion into the realms of the enemy and to plunder all the neighbouring districts as far as Kondavīdu and the Krishna river. After some desultory operations, Venkatapati sent his whole army, amounting to about 100,000 troops under Yeltum Raj, Gulrang Chetty, Manup Raj, and others to recover Gandikotta from Sanjar Khan. Meanwhile a Golconda army under Murtaza Khan advanced to Cuddapah sacked the town and destroyed its temple. He defeated Yeltum Raj and Manup Raj in a severe action and forced them to fly. But the Hindus gathered up their forces once again and the Muslims found it impossible to engage them in a regular battle. At last, taking advantage of the encampment of the Muslim army in a black clayey soil (noted as lying between Cuddapah and Cumbum by J. Briggs, the translator of Ferishta) and of a momentary panic that seized them completely defeated them and destroyed their cavalry almost to a man; and only the bravery of Murtaza Khan could cover the retreat of the Mussalman army. In revenge the Kutb Shah despatched a large force under Etibar Khaṇ Yezdy, the Governor of Kondavidu (hereafter called Murtazanagar) to advance against Penukoṇda. He was opposed by Narasa Naṇdaraj of Anantagiri (one of the most famous hill forts) but the latter had to retire from the field with a considerable loss. The Muslims advanced to Kālahasti and plundered its shrine and ordered prayers to be read in its halls. Venkatapati, nothing daunted, invited the jaghirdars of the country around Kondavidu to revolt, while the Kutb Shahi Court was shaken by the appearance of a pretender. This is the gist of the narrative of the operations of the Mussalmans against Venkatapati Raya. On the whole the Hindu resistance proved itself to be well organised, formidable and successful.—[Ed.]

34. *Raghunāthābhyudayam,* Canto VIII, Sl. 43-70.

invasion of the Golkonda territories and the siege of Penukonda in A. D. 1589. The Muhammadan armies under Muhammad Kuli Qutb Shah is said to have suffered a defeat and the Muhammadan historian himself notes that the Hindu forces became so numerous that the Muhammadan armies 'found it impossible to give them battle but confined their operations to plundering and cutting off supplies.'[35] The *Raghunāthabhyudayam* says[36] that the Muhammadan armies on hearing the news of the coming of Raghunatha, got terrified and fled into the jungles; and it[37] also notes that the losses on the Muhammadan side were great. Raghunātha besides this, claims victory over a Murasa King, who was in possession of numerous forts like Baḷḷāḷapura.[38] This decisive victory over the Muhammadans was so important as it gave the much needed relief for the Hindus, and for about a decade to come, the Hindu Empire was enjoying comparative peace under Venkatapati Raya, the last great monarch of Vijayanagar. It is not known whether Tanjore took any part in the subsequent invasions of the Emperor against Kondavīdu which is held to have taken place in the period between A.D. 1591 and A.D. 1603.

Raghunātha Nayaka before his return to Tanjore, is said to have performed a meritorious act of chivalry in securing the release of Krishnappa Nayaka of Gingee from imprisonment with the sanction of the Emperor.[39] Krishnappa Nayaka is said to have given away his daughter in marriage to Raghunātha in appreciation of his services and out of gratitude.[40] Raghunātha's co-operation in this war of Venkatapati is clear proof of Tanjore's loyalty and she must have pursued the same policy throughout. But some of the letters of the Jesuit missionaries say that Tanjore was vacillating in her policy towards the empire, and she was not also punctual in her payment of tribute. Anquetil du Per-

35. Briggs' *Ferishta*, Vol. III, p. 454. Also '*Aravidu Dynasty of Vijayanagara*', p. 327.

36. *Raghunāthābhyudayam*, Canto VII, Sl. 63.

37. *Raghunāthābhyudayam*, Canto VII, Sl. 65. It is curious to note that the *Sāhityaratnākara* does not mention this event at all.

38. *Sources*, p. 285. Dr. S. K. Aiyangar says 'the people of Morasanādu the district embracing the northern side of the North Arcot and the adjacent parts of the neighbouring districts. Can it be Bellary ? Golkonda by the end of A.D. 1580 had conquered Guntur and parts of Bellary, Kurnool, Cuddapah and Nellore. *Climacteric of Talikota.*

39. *Raghunāthābhyudayam*, Canto VII, Sl. 72 and 73.

40. Subsequent events however, do not show that this marriage alliance could have been possible.

ron[41] says:—"Before 1595 the Naique of Tanjore, Madura and Gingi gave up all allegiance as they did not want to acknowledge as their sovereign one who had dethroned the legitimate king of Bisnaga." Father Coutinho in a letter dated 11th October, A.D. 1608 says that "the Naiques of Tangior and Madura sent their tribute consisting of 500 thousand cruzados and many sorts of presents to the king. In order to receive these the king dressed himself as on the days of great celebration with many ornaments of gold and precious stones." Father Coutinho says that he was present at the capital and witnessed this ceremony. He again mentions in another letter the insurgent attitude of Achyutappa Nayaka and says "that the rumour was that the king warred upon the Naichus of Tangaor, called Astapanaichus, (Achyutappa)" and the original says that "Venkata has a large army with many good generals in order to reconquer Kanchipuram, which city along with all the country around had surrendered to Astapanaichus the king of Tangior."[42] This letter is dated 17th July, A.D. 1600 and it again says that there was no war and adds that "It is quite certain that the King does not think of that expedition any more, and Venkata's designs were checked by the death of Achyutappa Nayaka."[43] Father Heras says that since this letter is dated in A.D. 1600, the quarrel mentioned therein, must have taken place in A.D. 1598-9. Again Father Vico's letter dated A.D. 1611 speaks in general terms of the unpunctual remittances of the tribute of the Nayakas. The validity and faithfulness of these letters cannot be taken without adequate proof, since all the internal evidence supports Tanjore's loyalty.[44] The Jesuit letters, some of which were probably written by persons with a superficial knowledge of the political affairs, must be utilised only as a corrective to the internal evidence and not as superseding the latter since they were written by men who could not

41. *'Aravidu Dynasty of Vijayanagara,'* p. 308.

42. Purchas, *'His Pilgrims,'* Vol. X, p. 222.

43. Purchas, *'His Pilgrims,'* Vol. X, *Ibid.*

44. *'The Aravidu Dynasty'*, p. 398. Father Heras says that Perron's reference to a war is misplaced. Tanjore's co-operation with the Emperor, Venkatapati, has been established fully by the literature of the Tanjore Nayaks and her prominent part in the war of succession that took place soon after the death of Venkatapati, also proves the same. Such being the circumstances, it is not possible to speak of Tanjore as obstinate and disobedient in the interim period. Father Coutinho's letter must in all probability refer to the revolt of the Nayak of Gingee and not to that of Tanjore (*The Aravidu Dynasty*, pp. 404-408) as there is nothing in the Tanjore literature to support the conquest of Kānchi which never belonged to Tanjore. However, Father Heras, who speaks of Tanjore's disloyalty on the basis of these Jesuit letters, produces the same evidence to prove the disloyalty of the Gingee Nayak as well.

have been, in all circumstances fully conversant with the inner politics and intrigues of the state. However, Venkatapati Raya's supremacy and hold over his southern viceroys are established by the numerous epigraphs found in the South.[45]

The *Sāhityaratnākara* speaks of Achyutappa's victory over the Pārasīkas at Negapatam.[46] The *Raghunāthābhyudayam* does not mention this war with the Portuguese, but refers to the later wars waged by Achyutappa Nayaka's son, Raghunātha against these Pārasīkas. Nothing more is known about this event from the Tanjore literature, and the epigraphs of this ruler. What were the circumstances that led to this war upon the Pārasīkas, who are called Paraṅgis by Rāmabhadrāmba and who could have been no other than the Portuguese. The Pārasīkas cannot be taken to mean Muhammadans or Moors since, the subsequent happenings that took place at Jaffna show that it was the Portuguese, who suffered a defeat at the hands of the Tanjore Nayak. The Portuguese were the first European settlers in India and they undertook missionary and proselytising work comparatively early in their Indian career. The conversion of the Paravas of the Fishery Coast to Catholicism by St. Francis Xavier, was their great achievement in this direction on the east coast. They had to encounter strong and continued opposition from the Vijayanagara rulers and their representatives, who disliked their missionary zeal. They also indulged in political intrigues and sometimes made use of their missionaries for this purpose. On the Coromandel Coast, San Thomē was next occupied, about the middle of the 16th century. San Thomē was for long associated with early Christianity and with the tradition of the activities of the Apostle Thomas in the Coromandel Coast. The Portuguese formed a settlement at the place in 1522, first with the object of rebuilding the chapel. Ferishta writing of the Portuguese says that in the year 963 A.H. (A.D. 1556) the Christians (Tarsas) were in possession of the forts of Hormuz, Muskat, Sumatra, Malacca, Mangalore, Negapatam, Barcelore, Ceylon and Bengal to the borders of China. They had also forts.[47] The settlement of Negapatam was an accomplished fact by the time of Śevappa Nayaka. The Portuguese, who had grown to considerable strength on

45. 334 of 1913 from Chidambaram, 91 of 1928 from Aḷagarkōil (Madura District), 36 of 1908 from Madura, 389 of 1918 from Shiyali (Tanjore District), 258 of 1916 from Srīmuṣhnam (South Arcot District) and 177 of 1926 from Pattukōttai. Robert Sewell says that Tanjore became independent in A.D. 1602.

46. *Sāhityaratnākara,* Canto X, Sloka 68.

47. Briggs, Vol. IV, p. 584.

the Malabar Coast, and who had captured all the ports of Ceylon and Jaffna, had Negapatam as a halting place on their way to San Thomē. By the year A.D. 1586 the Portuguese had gained in strength and power and was put in charge of a separate governor. In that year Diogo Fernandez Penoa, the chief of that place, sent men and provisions to the help of his countrymen, who were then waging a war in Ceylon.[48] Father Pimenta, who visited Negapatam in A.D. 1597, says that 'many Portugals dwell there and many winter there, which come from the Coast of China, Bengala, Pegu and Malacca.' Du Jarric, another missionary, notes that Father Pimenta was invited by Achyutappa Nayaka and was given permission to build a church at Negapatam 'while another one was already started at Tranquebar'. Father Pimenta himself says that while he was at Negapatam, 'a place for five hundred ducats for a new residence of ours was purchased;' and he is said to have sent priests to Negapatam which was situated 'by the river side, having the sea to the west and was fitter for the functions of the Society.[49] This information contained in the Jesuit letters and the internal evidence, though very meagre, make it clear that Negapatam was under effective Portuguese authority during the rule of the Nayaks. Achyutappa Nayak's victory over them has been referred to already but no detail is known about the war and the Portuguese sources do not give us any date. The Portuguese records refer to their interference into the affairs of Jaffna, whose king was opposed to them and their religion. The Portuguese became rulers of Ceylon on the death of Don Juan Dharmapala in A.D. 1597[50], who bequeathed to them by a deed executed in their favour, the whole island except Jaffna, whose ruler was not only opposed to, but inflicted much injury on the Christians. The Portuguese had to war with the Jaffnese ruler on a number of occasions till A.D. 1617 when the place finally passed into their hands. The *Sāhityaratnākara* and the *Raghunāthābhyudayam* refer to the Tanjore intervention on behalf of the Jaffnese ruler and against the Portuguese during the reign of Raghunātha Nayaka. And Achyutappa Nayaka's war with the Portuguese was in all probability undertaken on behalf of the Jaffnese in the

48. *'The Portuguese in India'* F. C. Danvers, Vol. II, p. 76.

49. *The Aravidu Dynasty of Vijayanagara*, pp. 397 and 398.

50. A convention of Sinhalese delegates met after Dharmapala's death and agreed to recognise Philip II as the king of Ceylon, provided the Portuguese would guarantee on his behalf that the laws and customs of the Sinhalese should be maintained inviolable for ever"—*Ed.*

beginning of the 17th century; and the Pārasīkas'[51] defeat at Negapatam perhaps refers to the beginning of the hostilities between the Nayaks and the Portuguese. The methods adopted by them in converting the people of the country to Christianity, and their generally bad treatment of the natives had made them very unpopular. The Dutch records show that both the rulers of Ceylon and Tanjore sought their help to drive away the Portuguese from the land.[52] The Dutch in the beginning of the 17th century had established themselves at Tegnapatam between the mouths of the Gadilam and the Pennar rivers (*circa*, A.D. 1610) situated in the kingdom of the Nayak of Gingee; and the Dutch had made a request even earlier for the port of Triminipatam from the Nayak of Tanjore to which no reply was received upto 7th April, A.D. 1609.[53] However, the Dutch were rapidly growing in their strength and resources and their records prove their friendly attitude towards the Emperor, Venkatapati Raya from A.D. 1612 onwards.

The provenance of his epigraphs shows that Achyutappa kept intact his hold over the kingdom, as it was left to him by his father. His records are also found at other places as Tiru-uṭṭarakōśamangai (Ramnad District) and Tiruvaṇṇāmalai and Neduṇguṇram (North Arcot District). We have seen already that Śevappa's epigraphs also, are found both at Tiruvaṇṇāmalai and Neduṇguṇram. The presence of the records

51. Father Heras says that the defeat was sustained by the Dutch. Mr. Sitaramayya, 'Tanjore Andhra Nayaka Charitramu' says that Raghunatha was sent against the Portuguese by Achyutappa Nayaka even on this occasion also.

52. However, Negapatam was held by the Portuguese till 1658 A.D.

53. The Dutch were carrying on negotiations with the Nayak of Tanjore seeking permission to carry on trade with Tanjore and to settle at Triminipatam (the modern Tirumalairajānpattanam) and the Portuguese maps (*Aravidu Dynasty of Vijayanagara*) also locate this port between Negapatam and Tranquebar. The Dutch wanted to get hold of this port since 'much was expected of the cloth trade of this place.' (Poonen, 'Dutch Beginnings,' Chapter VII). [The Dutch sought the permission of Krishnappa Nayaka of Gingee to build a fort at Dēvanampatnam; and the necessary order was granted in 1608 (30th November). On receipt of the Nayaka's *olla* (cadjan leaf embodying the grant) the Dutch began to build a small fort. The Portuguese persuaded Venkatapati Raya to send a messenger to the Nayak ordering him to expel the Dutch from his territory. Undaunted by this failure, the Dutch again sought permission from Krishnappa Nayaka to settle at Dēvanampatanam and at Krishnapuram (Porto Novo) then recently founded by the Nayaka. Again they were refused permission on account of the dissuasions of the Portuguese. Venkata had always ordered the Nayaka to act according to the demands of the Fathers and expel from his territories "the foes of the Portuguese who are better friends than the Dutch."]—[*Ed.*]

of these two Nayaks at these places, and particularly at Nedungunram show that there must have existed some connection between the Nayaks and the latter place the exact nature of which is not known. The epigraphs of Śevappa Nayaka show that Nedungunram was their native place and the epigraphs point to their close associations and love for the place of their birth, and the temple there was enriched by their large gifts. 567 of 1902 from Tiruvaṇṇāmalai records the remission of some taxes in the villages belonging to the temple by the order of Achyutappa during the reign of Sadāsivarāya in A.D. 1567. The Tiru-uttarakōśamangai inscription which records a gift[54] made to the temple, must have been issued by the king in commemoration of his holy pilgrimage to Rāmēswaram. The ruler is said to have made a gift of a village in the Chōḷa country while he was at Rāmēswaram, and the Tanjore literature speaks of Achyutappa Nayaka's annual visits to Rameswaram (Sētu).

Achyutappa Nayaka's reign was one of comparative peace in spite of wars. The country, it appears, did not suffer either from the bad effects of prolonged warfare or from the evil consequences of invasion from outside. He seems to have been a patron of learning and devoted much of his resources to works of public utility, besides the building and repairing numerous temples. Achyutappa added to the gifts of his father made to the Tiruvaṇṇāmalai temple by setting up golden kaḷaśās on the gōpura built by his father.[55] The Siva temple at Tiruvidaimarudūr received a gift of a village, the income from which was to be utilised in celebrating the car festival of the goddess on the Ādippūram day[56]. The Mārgasahāyēswarar temple at Mūvalūr (Mayavaram Taluk) where Śevappa made a gift of lands for the maintenance of a choultry, was also a recipient of a gift of lands from Achyutappa, the proceeds of which were to be spent in burning lamps in its shrine. Private benefactions also were encouraged and a record from Viḷanagar (Mayavaram Taluk) refers to the building of the *arḍha* and the *mukha maṇtapas* (the central hall and the hall adjacent to the *sanctum sanctorum*) in stone, the expenses of which were met partly out of the palace funds and partly by private contributions.[57] This record is of interest as it refers to the Nayak's subsidy granted in favour of the temple. Another record dated in the year A.D. 1566[58] mentions a gift by Achyutappa

54. 84 of 1905, dated A.D. 1583.
55. 425 of 1928.
56. 84 of 1905 dated A.D. 1583.
57. 259 of 1913 dated Saka 1488.
58. 416 and 423 of 1918.

Nayaka of the village called Tiruvēṭkaḷam.[58a] (South Arcot District) to the Tirumūlasthāna temple at Chidambaram, for the merit of the Vijayanagara king Tirumalarāya. · The same temple received further endowments during his own life time; and two other epigraphs[59] refer to a gift of land and taxes accruing from the village called Perumaṇgalam, made by one Aḷagapperumāl Pillai to Chidambarēswara for the merit of Achyutappa. Another record registers a gift of five villages made for the merit of the same Nayaka called here as the son of Aḍappam Chinna Śevappa Nayaka, to the temple at Little Conjeevaram during the reign of Srirangarāya.[60] 389 of 1928 dated A.D. 1588 refers to another gift of land made to the Panaipākkam temple (North Arcot District) by one Sēshagiri Ayyan, son of Giriyappayyan who calls himself an agent of Achyutappa Nayaka.

Besides these royal gifts, the famous minister, Gōvinda Dīkshita (called Dīkshitarayyan, out of respect in the epigraphs), also made large gifts and additions to temples. He is said to have constructed the Turaikāṭṭuvār maṇtapa in Viḷanagar temple in the year A.D. 1608.[61] The intimate and happy relations between the minister and the king and the high regard which the latter had for the former are best seen in two epigraphs[62] which record a gift in money for the merit of Gōvinda Dīkshita made by Achyutappa himself.

Inscriptions also refer to the gifts made to communities apart from the temples. 22 of 1897 is the record of a charter given by the king to the community of goldsmiths in Tanjore exempting them from the payment of certain taxes in A.D. 1577. 426 of 1928 from Tiruvaṇṇāmalai dated A.D. 1590 registers the taxes fixed on the maṉrādi living in the eastern street of that place at the rate of two *paṇams* for each taḷaikkaṭṭu (groups of men) and one *paṇam* as *kudippaṇam* per annum on them. These inscriptions mention Venkatapati Raya.

Of all the temples that received large benefactions and gifts from him, the great Vishṇu temple at Srirangam stands first and foremost. Gōvinda Dīkshita in the *Sangīta Sudhā*, Yagnanārāyana Dikshita and Rāmabhadrāmba, all speak in glowing terms of Achyutappa's lavish gifts to Srirangam. He is said to have constructed the golden *vimāna* of the inmost shrine and presented the image of the god with a golden

58a. Part of the site of the village is now occupied by Annamalai University.

59. 380 of 1919 dated Saka 1493.

60. 380 of 1919 dated S. 1493.

61. 164 of 1925.

62. 119 of 1930 and 710 of 1904 dated A.D. 1588 and A.D. 1596 respectively.

crown studded with precious stones, a jewelled armour and a golden *simhāsana*. He is also said to have added to the gōpuras on the east, west and north of the temple, along with the construction of the 8th prākāra and several maṇtapas. The flight of steps leading to the Cauvery and the garden attached to the temple were his other gifts. His inscriptions also confirm these presents.[63] He performed the great ceremony of gifts known as *Tulāpurushas* and *Hiraṇyagarbha dānas*[64] every year. He is said to have paid annual visits to Rāmēśwaram and built the gopuras of that temple. He claims to have fed a thousand Brahmans everyday. He built the Pushyamaṇtapas, with steps leading to the Cauvery at Mayavaram, Tiruvidaimarudur, Kumbakonam and Tiruvādi. He also founded numerous agrahāras.[65] One remarkable act of public utility by which the Tanjore country has benefitted largely was the construction of a dam across the Cauvery near Tiruvādi[66] by which the irrigation facilities of the neighbourhood were largely improved. The *Raghunāthābhyudayam* and the *Sāhityaratnākaram*

63. 410 of 1924 refers to a gift of a garden to Srirangam.

64. 426 of 1924 refers to his several gifts. Also *Sangita Sudhā*, Slokas 38-44. It refers to his alms given to Gorayis (Bairagis) and to his gifts made to the temples at Kālahasti and Tirupati.

65. Rājachūdāmani Dikshita in his *Rukmaniparinayam* says:—

मायूरमध्यार्जुन कुम्भघोण श्रीचंपकारण्य मुखस्थलेषु ।
महत्तरं मण्डपमाततान मतयामहत्या परमच्चुतेन्द्रः ॥
अग्रियाननेकानपि चाग्रहारनसौ व्यतारीदवणी सुरेभ्यः ।
शौर्ये च धैर्येपि च दानकेल्यां समेनकश्चिधरणी भृतस्य ॥

quoted by Mr. V. Prabhakara Sastri.

Raṇgājamma in her *Maṇṇārudāsa Vilāsa* refers to his gifts to Srirangam, Rāmasētu and Śrīmushnam. 'Srimushṇa mukhya Visēsha sthalambula śakala vaibavamula sagamjēse.' and mentions his charitable acts done to all the Vishnu temples of the Pāṇdya and Tundira countries as well.

66. 426 of 1924 dated cyclic Manmatha corresponding to A.D. 1596:—

कैंकर्याणि कृतानियेन सकलान्यासंश्च रङ्गेशितु-
भूयः सह्यमहीधरेन्द्रतनया सेतुश्च येनोद्धृतः ।
कृत्वा मन्मथवत्सरे वृषभगे सितद्वादशी तिथ्यां
येन हिरण्यगर्भमवनौ श्रेष्ठत्वमासं महत् ॥
तत्ताद्दक्षगुणोयमच्युत विभुः चेवप्प भूपात्मजः
श्रीमण्विष्णु विरिञ्जितीर्थे महिते कल्याणसिन्धोस्तटे ।
बागेपल्लनदी.........

(Inscription in the Pushyamantapa, Tiruvadi).

devote special chapters to the description of the land and its fertility under him, the land being termed a paddy forest (Śālivanam).

Achyutappa's patronage was impartially and generously extended to the three prominent faiths of the land, *viz.*, the Saiva, Vaishnava and the Madhwa, and this is mentioned in the epigraphs and in the literature as well. The gift made to Vijayīndra Tīrtha by Srirangarāya on the request of Śevappa Nayaka appears to have been made by Achyutappa himself very early, perhaps soon after his appointment as Yuvarāja.[67]

Achyutappa's last years saw the beginning of troubles caused by the rise of a powerful chief, Sōḻaga, who was a subordinate of the Gingee Nayak and the ruler of Kōttaitīvu situated at the mouth of the Coleroon and also by the Portuguese settlers on the coast. The king of Jaffna, who was opposed to the Portuguese was driven out of his country and he had to take refuge at the Nayak's court. To crown all, the great Emperor of Vijayanagara, Venkatapati Raya-died leaving the throne to be disputed by two parties in a terrible civil war; and in this struggle, the loyalist party supporting the cause of

67. The Aruvīḻimangalam plates. *Epigraphia Indica, Vol.* 12, p. 342. The plates record a gift of the village called Arivīḻimangalam (also known as Achyutasamudram and situated in the Nannilam Taluk of the Tanjore District) to the great Madhwa teacher Vijayīndra Tīrtha. Verses 40 to 45 say that this gift which was made by Achyutappa Nayaka earlier, was now ratified by the Vijayanagara Emperor, Srirangarāya at the request of Śevappa Nayaka, the father of Achyutappa. Vijayīndra, the donee is said to have given away this village which was composed of sixty *vrittis* to Brahmans for his own merit and for the merit of Śevappa and Achyutappa. Vijayīndra Tīrtha is said to have occupied the pontifical seat 'for fifty-five years, five months and sixteen days, *i.e.*, from Saka 1461 to Saka 1517 (A.D. 1539 to 1595). His death in the cyclic year Manmatha would correspond to A.D. 1595-6. The importance of these plates consists in the fact that Achyutappa was closely associated with the administration of the government of his father and both of them were loyal feudatories of the Vijayanagara Empire. They also explain the royal patronage extended to the Madhwa religion. Vijayīndra is said to have been a contemporary of the great Advaita scholar, Appayya Dikshita. The plates are dated in the cyclic year Dhātri and in the month of Āshāda. The chronogram Ratna, griha, payōdhiṇdu ganitē Sakavastarē is taken to mean Saka 1499 equal to A.D. 1577-8 by Mr. T. A. Gopinatha Rao and Mr. T. S. Kuppuswamy Sastri (*Epigraphia Indica*, Vol. XII, p. 342).

Sl. 40. कुमाराच्युतभूपेन दत्तपूर्वं विशेषतः ।

Sl. 41. वीर श्रीचेव्वभूपस्य विज्ञप्तिमनुपालयन् ।

Achyutappa is called here Kumāra Achyuta Bhūpa.

Chikkadēvarāya, the emperor's nephew who was nominated by Venkatapati himself, and the other taking up the cause of a putative son of Venkatapati. The former was led by Yāchama Nayaka, while Gobburi Jaggarāya, the Emperor's brother-in-law became the organiser and head of the disloyal group of chieftains. And the Tanjore Nayak, as a loyal feudatory was naturally drawn into this struggle. All the Tanjore literary evidence are unanimous in mentioning that Achyutappa, who was then old, thought it proper and best to leave the administration in the hands of his son Raghunātha, who had already won fame as a warrior in the Penukonda campaign and so he abdicated the throne in favour of his son so that he might take part in the campaign as a faithful vassal. It is also known that in this course the king was well advised by his minister, Gōvinda Dīkshita, who played a prominent part in the administration of the country.

Achyutappa's abdication and Raghunātha's consequent assumption of the rulership of Tanjore are well established facts; but the question of the exact date of these events remains to be settled. The two historical poems of *Sāhityaratnākara* and the *Raghunāthābhyudayam* written during the reign of Raghunātha Nayaka contain different versions and so present us with some difficulty. Rāmabhadrāmba would place the installation of Raghunātha as the Yuvarāja sometime before his participation in the campaign against the Kutub Shah, made on behalf of Venkatapati Raya, *i.e.*, before A.D. 1589.[68] But her speaking about Raghunātha Nayaka's holding a war council at the capital soon after his return[69] would make us believe that Raghunātha was then the ruler. The *Sāhityaratnākara* would place the same appointment of Raghunātha as Yuvarāja some years later, *i.e*, about A.D. 1614 since its author says that this installation was made by Achyutappa Nayaka only on his hearing the news of the death of Venkatapati Raya and the war of succession.[70] All are agreed that Achyutappa lived on in retirement for sometime after this event. To add to these there are the Jesuit letters, which are definite in their assertions, regarding this question. Anquetil du Perron records that Achyutappa had resigned and given up the affairs some years before A.D. 1600.[71] Father Pimenta who passed through the Tanjore country a little earlier (A.D. 1597 says that Achyutappa 'has lately renounced the world and prepared himself for death.'[72] Father Heras concludes there-

68. *Raghunāthābhyudayam*, Canto VII.
69. *Raghunāthābhyudayam*, Canto VIII, Sloka 1
70. *Sāhityaratnākara*, Canto XII, Slokas 45-47.
71. *The Aravidu Dynasty of Vijayanagara*, p. 399.
72. *The Aravidu Dynasty of Vijayanagara*, p. 399 and Purchas X, p. 219.

from thus :—" Hence there can be no longer any doubt about the date of Achyutappa's renunciation and the year 1597 witnessed the coronation of Raghunātha "; and he tells the reader further that the account given in the *Raghunāthābhyudayam* agrees fairly with that given by Father Pimenta and Anquetil du Perron, and 'according to this poem, Raghunātha was crowned Yuvarāja long before the civil war and the war with Ceylon.' Both Father Pimenta and Father du Jarric say that Achyutappa Nayaka retired to Srirangam " accompanied in that devotion by his seventy wives, all which were to be burned in the same fire with his Carkasee ". And Father Coutinho writing from Chandragiri on July 17th, A.D. 1600 reports:—'This (Achyutappa Nayaka) died lately. His corpse, along with 370 wives still alive, was burnt in a big fire of sandalwood '.[73] Father Heras relying exclusively on the evidence of these letters and denouncing the facts mentioned by Yagnanārāyana Dikshita says that in order ' to give some dramatic interest to his poem, he placed the renunciation of Achyutappa after the outbreak of the civil war, and the death of Venkata. Nothing could be farther from the truth '.[74]

Turning to the evidence of epigraphy, we find that Raghunātha Nayaka had been associated with the administration of the kingdom at least from A.D. 1600. The Achyutamaṇgalam inscription (Tanjore District)[75] dated in the cyclic year Śārvari and corresponding to A.D. 1600 is the earliest record which mentions Raghunātha Nayaka. Another record from Lālgudi bearing the same date refers to a gift made for the merit of Raghunātha Nayaka and Gōvinda Dikshita.[76] These two epigraphs show that the commencement of Raghunātha's part in the administration of the land must be placed in A.D. 1600. This date seems to be fairly settled since one of the epigraphs of Achyutappa bears the latest date A.D. 1596[77] and moreover the *Raghunāthābhyudayam* says that Raghunātha was installed as Yuvarāja before the Penukonda war, that is, before A.D. 1589; and it is also mentioned that Achyutappa received him on his victorious return, in great pomp and splendour. The epigraphical evidence confirms the testimony of the Jesuit letters that Raghunātha took charge of the government in A.D. 1600. But the epigraphs do not throw full light with regard to

73. *The Aravidu Dynasty of Vijayanagara*, p. 400.
Father Coutinho says that the Nayaka went to Srirangam followed by 370 wives, while Father Pimenta mentions that they numbered only 70.

74. *The Aravidu Dynasty*, p. 400.

75. 412 of 1925.

76. 151 of 1928.

77. 426 of 1924.

the abdication of Achyutappa. The Jesuit evidence that he abdicated in or before A.D. 1600 and died at Srirangam, cannot be accepted in the light of authentic contemporary indigenous evidence contained in the *Raghunāthābhyudayam* and the *Sāhityaratnākara,* which definitely say that Achyutappa lived long after the installation of Raghunātha as the Yuvarāja. The *Raghunāthābhyudayam* says that Raghunātha was made Yuvarāja (canto VII, slokas 34 and 40); but it does not speak of Achyutappa's abdication nor is there any implication that he died shortly afterwards. In fact a careful reading of a passage would show that Achyutappa must have lived on till A.D. 1617, since the passage refers to Raghunātha's paying his respects to his father after his return from the Tōppūr battle.[78] The *Sāhityaratnākara* contains no reference to Raghunātha's help given to Venkatapati Raya in his Penukoṇda campaign, but it records that Achyutappa's abdication was necessitated by the political circumstances of the times, such as the outbreak of a civil war following the death of Venkatapati in A.D. 1614 and the rise of Sōḻaga and the Portuguese on the eastern coast. Achyutappa it is said here, was advised by his minister Gōvinda Dikshita to raise Raghunātha to the throne and the appointment of Raghunātha as the ruler must have taken place about A.D. 1614, when Achyutappa abdicated, on the receipt of the news of the death of the Vijayanagara emperor and its immediate consequences.[79] The *Sāhityaratnākara* says that Achyutappa retired after his abdication to Srirangam where he spent the rest of his days in the company of pandits.[80] These two different versions of the two contemporary works offer some difficulty. Mr. K. Sitaramayya says that these two versions are contradictory and in order to get over the difficulty he has glibly assumed that the account of *Sāhityaratnākara* is the more correct and reliable of the two. He says that the account given by Rāmabhadrāmba is not accurate and adds that she, being a mere courtesan of Raghunātha's court, might not have had the opportunity of knowing things in their correct historical sequence.[81]

78. *Raghuāthābhyudayam*, Canto XII, Sloka 83.

इति वादिनीषु हरिणेक्षणामणीष्वथ रामभद्रमभिपूज्यमानसे ।
विनतिं तदाच्युत विभोः प्रकल्पयन्नुदतिष्ठदेष शयनादुदारधीः ॥

If Achyutappa was dead the authoress would not have made menti[illegible] his name.

79. *Sāhityaratnākara,* Canto X, Sloka 55. The news was com[illegible]unicated to Achyutappa while he was holding a war council with his minister and son in order to punish Sōḻaga.

80. *Sāhityaratnākara,* Canto XII, Sloka 94. The reference to his retiring to Srirangam in the Jesuit letters earlier than this date, might refer to his annual visits made to Srirangam and Rāmēswaram.

81. *The Tanjore Andhra Nayaka Charitam*, p. 174.

If this view should be correct then one will have to leave out of account the part played by Raghunātha in the Penukonda campaign and which is confirmed even by the Muhammadan historians, on the ground that it is mentioned only by Rāmabhadrāmba and not by Yagna nārāyana Dikshita. And so his preference of the *Sāhityaratnākara* as the better source does not seem to be well established and so requires modification.

The facts mentioned in these two historical poems are not contradictory in reality, but on the other hand may be seen to be only complementary to each other, and the gaps left by the one are ably filled up by the other. Taking these two accounts together, it is possible to suggest that Raghunātha was made a Yuvarāja very early and that he ascended the throne only soon after the declaration of the war of succession to the Karnātaka throne. Rāmabhadrāmba referring to Raghunātha's appointment as Yuvarāja does not speak of Achyutappa's retirement. The *Sāhityaratnākara* refers to Achyutappa's desire early in his reign[82] to appoint Raghunātha as the Yuvarāja; but the actual celebrations took place after the lapse of a number of years and just before Raghunātha Nayaka's starting on his *digvijaya.*[83] Achyutappa's retirement seems to have taken place immediately after that. But Rāmabhadrāmba does not refer at all to Achyutappa's retirement following the Yauvarājyābhishēka whereas Yagnanārāyana Dīkshita places this immediately after the celebration. The aged king's retirement would be possible only after Raghunātha's coronation as king and not before that. Yagnanārāyana's mention of Raghunātha's great gifts like *Tulāpurushadāna* and *Mahābhūtadāna* said to have been performed in connection with this ceremony and the absence of any reference to the same in Rāmabhadrāmba's account, show clearly that the former speaks of his actual coronation alone, while the latter mentions his appointment as Yuvarāja and then passes on in silence, only without making any reference to his coronation.[84] Hence the reference to

82. *Sāhityaratnākara,* Canto V, Sl. 49. The actual ceremony is mentioned only in Chapter XII.

83. Raghunātha's invasion against Sōḷaga is mentioned only after his coronation, *i.e.,* after A.D. 1614 and *Sāhityaratnākara,* Canto X, Slokas 61 and 62 show Achyutappa's determination to appoint Raghunātha, as his successor on the receipt of the Karnātaka news.

84. These discrepancies are easily understood if one thinks of the authors and their purposes in writing these poems. It was not their object to chronicle the events, but both of them were bent upon pleasing their hero and patron, the famous Raghunātha Nayaka.

Raghunātha's coronation in the *Sāhityaratnākara* is loosely worded and miscalled *Yuvarājyābhishēkam* instead of *Pattābishēka*. Subsequent events, like the invasion of the Sōḷaga's territory and of Jaffna mentioned in these two works, support this conclusion. The way in which both have treated these two events, again gives support to the view already taken, that Rāmabhadrāmba and Yagnanārāyana speak of Raghunātha's installation as Yuvarāja and his coronation respectively.[85] As the other particulars agree in the main, and since the foreign policy of Achyutappa mentioned in them is confirmed by the Muhammadan historians like Ferishta, and the foreign evidence of Barradas, it is impossible either to overlook their importance or to accept the one at the expense of the other. The two, taken together give us a clear picture of the state of affairs then prevalent, and in the light of that evidence, it is not possible to give weight to the Jesuit letters. Since the internal evidence is well based with regard to the coronation of Raghunātha and the abdication of Achyutappa in or about A.D. 1614; the reference to Achyutappa's death in A.D. 1600 in the Jesuit letters stands condemned and cannot be taken seriously in the absence of further support.

Thus, it becomes clear that Raghunātha became Yuvarāja (heir-apparent) sometime before A.D. 1589; but his coronation which was accelerated by the political circumstances of the revolution after Venkata's death, took place about A.D. 1614 and this would prove that Achyutappa remained at Tanjore at least till the outbreak of hostilities between the loyalists and the rebel factions.

85. *Raghunāthābhyudayam* describes his appointment as Yuvarāja in 5 slokas (Canto VII, Sloka 35 to 40) while Yagnanārāyana devotes two full chapters (Cantos XI and XII).

Chapter V.

RAGHUNĀTHA NAYAKA, A.D. 1600 TO A.D. 1634 (I)

Raghunātha Nayaka was the most illustrious of the Tanjore line of Nayaks, as well as the main prop of their fame and glory. His rule was one of peace as it marked the revival and development of the many-sided, cultural activities for which Tanjore had been famous through the ages. Literature and art flourished side by side; and Tanjore became under him the greatest seat of learning and culture of the time in South India and as well as the home of Carnatic music. The Nayak himself was a great scholar and the author of numerous works in Telugu and also a musician of high repute. He was given the distinguishing epithet of Abhinava Bhōja.[1] Several poets flourished at Tanjore under his royal patronage. His victories in war brought him great renown and honour and much prominence to Tanjore. Yagnanārāyana Dīkshita, eulogising his reign, says that poverty left the country and Tanjore became the abode of Lakshmi (the goddess of wealth). The poets of the age have left behind glowing accounts of his rule and it is from them that we get incidentally some information about his ancestors also. It is certainly not an overstatement if it is said, that but for him, the history of the Tanjore Nayaks would have remained obscure and insignificant. But for him and his patronage of learning, the period of the Nayak rule in Tanjore would have been as mediocre as it was in Gingee. All the same, these accounts of Raghunātha's rule are not full and do not detail all the events of his reign, as they mostly stop with the description of his early conquests. He is called the establisher of the Karnāta and the Nēpāla (Jaffna) kings,[2] and a *Nēo Dāśaratī* (Rama) in building a bridge of boats across the ocean between the mainland of India and the Jaffnese coast of Ceylon, in his expedition against his Portuguese enemies.

Raghunātha by virtue of his victories and benefactions fully justified the high expectations of his grandfather, Śevappa. Gōvinda Dīkshita says that Śevappa on seeing Raghunātha, then a boy, playing, expressed the idea that he was the fittest person to rule and it was through

1. *Vijayavilāsam*; padyam 53 has Abiṇava Bhōja birudānkudu.

2. *Sāhityaratnākara*: Canto II, Sloka 71.
Vijayavilāsam; Padyam 62 has 'Nēpāla Nripāla sthāpana.'

him the fame of the Nayak's rule would be established.[3] The same high praise is given to him by Achyutappa also, his father. The latter says that by his (Raghunātha's) birth alone he himself had attained to great honour and adds that his own birth did not bring anything of that kind to his own parents.[4] The literary celebrities of his time also speak of Raghunātha in the same praiseful strain. These remarks and the sketches of his personal beauty and charm, given in their works, go to show that Raghunātha was a great and powerful ruler who may be favourably compared with the great Emperor of Vijayanagar, Krishnadēva Rāya.

Achyutappa appointed his son Raghunātha as Yuvarāja even early in his own reign, as he was fully convinced of his intelligence and capacity. It is sometimes held that Achyutappa had two sons and that Raghunātha, the more favoured of the two, got the throne by having his brother murdered.[5] Father Heras, relying too much on the Portuguese letters and at the same time underrating the internal evidence, adduces some arguments to prove, not only the existence of a brother of Raghunātha Nayaka; but also the treacherous part played by him, in getting the throne. He says further, that 'Govinda Dikshita implies that Raghunātha was the eldest son of Achyutappa Nayaka', and cites Anquetil du Perron and Father Coutinho for additional support. Of these two, the former says 'that the eldest son of Achyutappa had been imprisoned by order of his father,' and this information is confirmed by Father Coutinho in his letter of July 17th, A.D. 1600 addressed to Father Pimenta. Father Heras adds that 'no reason for such an imprisonment is given; what is clear is the extreme predilection of Achyutappa for Raghunātha.'[6] He also draws instances from the *Raghunāthābhyudayam* and the *Sāhityaratnākara* to prove this extreme predilection of Achyutappa and Śevappa for Raghunātha, but he does not cite the authority from which he drew the conclusion, that 'Gōvinda Dikshita implies that he (Raghunātha) was the eldest son.' This view is untenable in the light of a critical study of the contemporary works; and the information contained in the Jesuit letters is rather curious and comes almost a surprise. There is no evidence to show either that Achyutappa had two sons or Raghunātha had his brother murdered just before or after his accession to the throne. Father Heras, however, holds that both Rāmabhadrāmba and Yagnanārāyana Dikshita had concealed

3. *Sangīta Sudhā*:—"This child will become great and rule the whole kingdom and we shall become famous on his account."

4. *Sāhityaratnākara*; Canto VI, Sloka 34.

5. *The Aravīdu Dynasty*; Heras, p. 402.

6. *Ibid*, p. 401.

this fact. Nothing could be farther from the truth; and it is here that the full value of contemporary internal and external evidence which lies buried, becomes obvious. *The Raghunāthābhyudayam* and the *Sāhityaratnākara* alike say that Achyutappa was for long, without a child and add that he even did penance before Raghunātha was born to him and to Mūrtimāmba.[7] Gōvinda Dīkshita, in his introduction to the *Sangīta Sudhā*, speaks of Raghunātha only, as the son of Achyutappa and there is nothing even in the Telugu works as well, to imply or indicate that he had a brother. Vijayaraghava Nayaka in the genealogy given in his work, makes no reference to the existence of another son of Achyutappa, besides Raghunātha. Even the traditional accounts do not mention at all any brother of Raghunātha; and hence, in the face of these hard facts, the reference to Raghunatha's brother in the Jesuit letters is wholly misleading and unreliable and should have been based on a misconception.

The *Raghunāthābhyudayam* and the *Sāhityaratnākara* devote special chapters to detail his early life and education in the Sāstras, in Rājanīti, in the art of warfare, and in the use of various weapons. They give also a good pen—picture of the king's person, his broad forehead, long arms, broad chest, piercing eyes, pearl-like teeth and long moustaches (śmaśru) as dark as the clouds.[8] Rāmabhadrāmba says that he was married to a Pāṇdyan princess,[9] while the *Sāhityaratnākara* says that he married a number of princesses. The *Ushāpariṇayam*. says that his queens were Chencha Lakshmamma and Kaḷāvati. Vijayarāghava Nayaka was his

7. *Raghunāthābhyudayam*; Canto VI, Sloka 29 to 51. *Sāhityaratnākara*; Canto IV. Achyutappa Nayaka's pilgrimage to Rāmēswaram perhaps has reference to this.

8. *Raghunāthābhyudayam*; Canto VII, Slokas 1 to 33: *Sāhityaratnākara*; Canto VI, Sloka 39 to 69.

9. The reference to Raghunātha's marriage with a Pāṇdyan princess is given much weight in the *Tanjore Gazetteer*, as it tries to connect this marriage with a Pāṇdyan war in A.D. 1610. The Pāndya who waged a war with Tanjore is said to have been Ativīrarāma, the feudatory of Virappa Nayaka of Madura. The *Gazetteer* (page 39) says that Tanjore suffered a defeat; and the Pāṇdya in order to commemorate his victory named a port on the sea coast after him, and called it Adirāmpatnam (Ativīrarāmanpatnam) in the south-east corner of the Tanjore district. The Pāṇdyan victory over Tanjore is not possible in the face of Tanjore's victory over Vīrappa Nayaka at Vallamprākāra; and besides, there was Venkatapati Rāya on the Vijayanagar throne wielding the strong arm of his suzerainty over all his vassals. Even assuming a Pāṇdyan victory one cannot adequately explain the marriage of the Pāṇdyan princess with the defeated Tanjore Nayak. The *District Gazetteer* speaks definitely of a defeat and not even of a peace. Mr. K. Sitaramayya rejects this and says that Adirāmpatnam must be the shortened name of Adi-

son by his chief queen Kaḷāvati. The *Raghunāthābhyudaya Nātakam* by Vijayarāghava Nayaka calls Kaḷāvati as Pattampurāṇi. That Raghunātha had a number of wives, is mentioned in all the literary works and Rāmabhadrāmba calls herself as one of his numerous consorts. The reference to Kalāvati as the senior queen would imply the possibility of only one wife being the chief consort, while the rest must have been attached to the royal harem, and Rāmabhadrāmba perhaps means this, when she speaks of his other wives as *Kāṇta* and not *Mahishi* or Rāni.[10]

Raghunātha Nayaka's appointment as Yuvarāja, even while he was a youth, has been noticed already, and he was the joint ruler of the kingdom, along with his father, for a number of years. In that period, he distinguished himself in the wars of the Emperor, Venkatapati against Golkonda (1589), and even obtained laurels and high praise from the Raya, for the valuable help rendered to him. Raghunātha's fame as a great warrior came to be established soon after his victory at Penukonda. In the subsequent wars of Tanjore with Madura (*circa* A.D. 1611), Raghunātha should have played a prominent part; but of these we have no direct or detailed evidence. And Achyutappa's nomination of Raghunātha, as his successor and co-ruler, was the direct result of the troubles that were happening then. The *Raghunathābhyudayam* and the *Sāhityaratnākara* both refer to the atrocities committed by one Sōḷaga and the troubles caused by the Portuguese, besides describing the war of suc-

rājēndrapatnam. The Pāṇḍyan marriage must evidently be taken as nothing but poetic.

[*Further Note by the Editor.*]

F. R. Hemingway, the editor of the *Gazetteer* says that the Pāṇḍyan king destroyed the Cauvery dam at the western end of the Tanjore dominion and that his power seems to have extended some distance into the south of the Tanjore district at this time. The attack was manifested on two flanks, one near the dam, and the other on the coast country round Point Calimere. He accepts the view that the war was followed by a marriage between Raghunātha and a Pāṇḍyan princess. Ativīrarāma Pāṇḍya, surnamed Śrīvallabha (1563—1605) and his cousin, Varatunga Rama (1588—1609?) were in subordinate alliance generally with the Nayaks of Madura and seem to have acknowledged the suzerainty of the Aravīdu Rayas as well. Their jurisdiction seems to have been more in the southern part of the Madura Nayak dominion; and their active operations on the northern frontier of Madura should require more evidence before deserving acceptance. Achutarāya seems also to have married a Pāṇḍyan princess. The marriage of Raghunātha to a Pāṇḍyan princess is at the best doubtful.

10. *Raghunāthābhyudayam*; Canto III, Sloka 5. Raghunātha is described as Krishna in the company of a thousand wives. *'Sahasra Kāntājana.'*

cession consequent on the death of Venkatapati in A.D. 1614. And so, Raghunātha's association with his father and his subsequent coronation on the latter's abdication, were the outcome of political factors, but for which, Achyutappa might have continued on the throne for some time more. Moreover, Achyutappa having been in power from about A.D. 1560, should have also become feeble and so resigned the administrative charge of the land in the hands of his son.

Raghunātha, when he assumed the reins of government directly, had to face some difficulties that demanded his immediate attention, and the literary evidence shows that he set himself to this task without any delay. Good, but slightly discrepant, accounts of his military exploits are given both by Rāmabhadrāmba and Yagnanārāyana Dīkshita; and to understand the sequence of the events aright, a close study of their conflicting accounts is useful. Rāmabhadrāmba says that a war council for concerting measures for immediate action was held by Raghunātha himself.[11] She further says that Raghunātha was informed of the atrocities committed by Sōḻaga, by the Brahmans who had then assembled at his court, of the affairs of the Nēpāḷa kingdom by the Nēpāḷa ruler himself, who, it is said, had just then arrived at Tanjore and lastly of the Karnātaka war of succession by some loyal feudatory nobles (*Karnāta bhūpa srayībhihi*) of the deceased Raya, Venkatapati.[12] Raghunātha, it is again said, promising his help to the Karnāta nobles, started at once on his campaign against the Sōḻaga and other enemies, who were nearer home. Reference is made to his march first towards Kumbakonam on his way to the island fortress of Sōḻaga at the mouth of the Coleroon; from there to the town of Jaffna and lastly his advance towards Toppūr near the Grand Anicut, before he returned to his capital. News of the arrival of the rebels led by Jaggarāya, near Toppūr and their breach of the great dam across the Cauvery, which were conveyed to him were the immediate causes for his onward march to Toppūr. Rāmabhadrāmba describes in great detail the battle of Toppūr and Raghunātha's part therein ; and also his victorious return to Tanjore therefrom, crowned with laurels. Raghunātha is said to have planted a pillar of victory also on the field of battle, and his troops claim to have taken possession of the fort at Bhuvanagiri (in the Chidambaram taluk).

Yagnanārayana Dīkshita's account is not so full as it stops with Raghunātha's leaving his capital on a march upon his enemies; and it gives another version of the events, which differs in certain respects from

11. *Raghunāthābhyudayam*, Canto VIII, Slokas 1 to 7.
12. *Raghunāthābhyudayam*, Canto VIII, Slokas 7, 14 and 23.

the account of Rāmabhadrāmba. According to him, a war council was held by Achyutappa Nayaka and it was attended both by Gōvinda Dikshita and Raghunātha, besides others. This summoning of the war cabinet was the direct outcome of the Nēpāḷa king's complaint; he had already arrived at Tanjore, having been driven away from his kingdom by the Portuguese.[13] Gōvinda Dīkshita is said to have informed his master of the atrocities of Sōḻaga, the rise of the Pāṇdya and the Tundīra rulers and lastly the war of succession following the death of Venkatapati.[14] According to the author, these news were conveyed to the minister by a spy who was sent out to gather information.[15] The author refers to the murder of Venkatapati's successor by Jaggarāya and his arrival at Srirangam. Reference is also made to Yāchama Nayaka's desire to come to the south,[16] along with the rescued prince Rāma, who was the only survivor of the massacre and who was the second son of the murdered king of Vijayanagar; in order to receive help from Tanjore, as against the rebel Jaggarāya and his partisans. Jaggarāya is reported, in the meanwhile, to have reached Srirangam, where he was preparing for battle along with the Pāṇdyan King. Yagnanārayana Dīkshita then only describes the abdication of Achyutappa and the acession of Raghunātha. Again, another spy is introduced, who is said to have informed the new Nayak (Raghunātha) for a second time about the murder of Chikkadēvarāya by Jaggarāya and the latter's arrival at Srirangam, where he was joined by the Dramida, Chēra and the Pāṇdya kings. Yāchama Nayaka is mentioned again for the second time, but this time it is said, that he was then actually coming to the south accompanied by the Aravidu prince Rāma.[17] Immediately after, Raghunātha was informed of Yāchama Nayaka's arrival and of the damage done to the Cauvery embankment by the enemies.[18] Raghunātha, who was enraged at this news, is said to have resolved that he should first restore and instal the young prince Rāma, as the emperor of Karnātaka, by his marching towards Kumbakōnam; and then to crush Sōḻaga and other enemies.[19] Yagnanārayana Dīkshita stops at this place in his account but he gives a full description of the Tanjore army and its equipment. Thus Yagnanārayana Dīkshita's narration of events

13. *Sāhityaratnākara*, Canto VI, Slokas 66-72.
14. *Sāhityaratnākara*, Canto X, Slokas [illegible]-60.
15. *Sāhityaratnākara*, Canto X, Slokas 33, 36 and 55.
16. *Sāhityaratnākara*, Canto X, Sloka 56.

परिग्रह्य तदात्मज सयाचप्रभुरन्यैश्च समायियाराती‌ह ।

17. *Sāhityaratnākara*, Sloka 76. .....आयातिसयाचभूपतिः
18. *Sāhityaratnākara*, Sloka 78. .....त्वामभ्यागमदेष सयाच महिनः
19. *Sāhityaratnākara*, Sloka 80 and 81.

differs in important respects from that of Rāmabhadrāmba. The latter says that the king guaranteed his help to the loyal Karnātaka nobles and marched upon Sōḻaga and the Nēpāḻa enemies. This is just possible and the expedition against these might have been undertaken by him. But it will be seen from the account of Yagnanārāyana Dīkshita, that Raghunātha first installed prince Rāma, as the legitimate emperor at Kumbakōnam, then marched against Sōḻaga, leaving at the sametime the powerful combination of the enemy forces under Jaggarāya, on the west of his dominion thus risking their attack on his own kingdom. When Rāmabhadrāmba says that Raghunātha passed through Kumbakōnam on his march against Sōḻaga, Yagnanārāyana would make us understand that he went there to effect a junction with Rāma and to proclaim him as the King of Karnāta. Both of them refer to the damages caused to the Cauvery dam by the rebels led by Jaggarāya. Raghunātha's hastening to Toppūr from Jaffna was the result of his hearing this news according to Rāmabhadrāmba; and so, the victory over the Sōḻaga and the Portuguese must have happened before the Toppūr battle. But according to the Dīkshita, the same news was the cause of Raghunātha's leaving the capital for Kumbakōnam.

These two accounts are not, however, really so very contradictory as they appear to be at first sight, but are merely complementary to each other. And the historical sequence of these incidents can best be understood, if these narratives are studied in the light of internal evidence as well as of the facts contained in the letters of Barradas and the Portuguese missionaries. We have already referred to Yagnanārāyana Dikshita's confusion regarding the regular coronation of Raghunātha as ruler with his *Yauvarājyābhishēkam* and his omission of his participation in the Penukonda campaign. And this confusion may be said to continue throughout his narrative, which appears to have been compiled in a slipshod manner without due regard for historical sequence or the regular order of events. His account resembles more that of a mere chronicler of events, while Rāmabhadrāmba's version seems to be the more historically accurate and sequentially probable. However, the former's account gives greater detail and hence only a rearrangement in the sequence of facts alone is needed. The absence of unity and agreement in sequence in these two accounts, are largely due to the fact, that the compilers had in view different objects and motive . Of course, both are agreed in their attempt to praise their patron-king, but the methods employed by them differ.[20]

20. Their object was not essentially to write a history of the period. Rāmabhadrāmba wrote her account mainly to exhibit her love and regard for Raghu-

The murder of Chikkadēvaraya, the rescue of his second son Rāma who was smuggled out of the prison in a bundle of washerman's clothes by the loyal Yāchama Nayaka, and the rise of Jaggarāya are all mentioned by both Rāmabhadrāmba[21] and Yagnanārāyana and their accounts are confirmed by the narrative of Barradas. The latter says that both the armies of Yāchama Nayaka and Jaggarāya were assembled in the spacious plains surrounding Trichinopoly on December 12th, A.D. 1616.[22] The *Raghunāthābhyudayam* of Vijayarāghava Nayaka says that Raghunātha was then camping at Paḻamānēri, a village near Tanjore, in the month of August A.D. 1616 before he began his march upon Toppūr.[23] It is stated that Rāma, the prince, also accompanied him to the battle field. The Portuguese chroniclers of Ceylon refer to the success of the Tanjore forces in Jaffna, in the beginning of A.D. 1616. As both Rāmabhadrāmba and Yagnanārāyana place the invasion against Sōḻaga as the first part of the campaign it is evident that the latter's defeat must have been effected before A.D. 1616. Barradas speaks of the loyalist party led by Yāchama and the rebel combination led by Jaggarāya and to their fight before they reached Trichinopoly.[24]

nātha; while Yagnanārayana Dīkshita wrote his work with a different object altogether. He says that his attempt was to write a work on Sāhitya with particular reference to Alaṇkāras, so that it may serve as a guide for others to follow (Canto I). The author also complains that poets with no knowledge of literature and its conventions had attempted works of this kind before and had received large presents from the king. Secondly, as a pupil of Raghunātha (Canto I, Sl. 62), he thought of showing his gratitude and indebtedness by writing this work; and above all he wanted to exhibit his own scholarship and literary attainments. Hence we find more than two chapters being devoted to the description of the seasons. Dr. T. R. Chintamani says that the treatment of this *kāvya* is largely modelled on the Tamil Kāvyas (*Sāhityaratnākara*, Introduction). A reading of the work would show that the author, who complains of others' faults, is himself guilty of a '*dōsha*' known as Puṇarukti.

21. Rāmabhadrāmba does not mention the name of Yachama Nayaka. Yagnanārāyana calls him Yācha bhūpa and Yāchamahīpa.

22. *A Forgotten Empire*; pp. 222-230.

23. *Sources of Vijayanagar History*, p. 259.

24. *A Forgotten Empire*, p. 229. Yāchama Nayaka is said to have won a decisive victory over Jaggarāya and Barradas says that 'after this victory many of the nobles joined themselves to Yāchama Nayaka.

[*Further Note by the Editor.*]

Barradas explicitly states that "all came to him (Srīranga) to offer their allegiance except three," and these latter persons joined together and "swore never to do homage to the new king, but on the contrary to raise in his place the putative

Rāmabhadrāmba's account of Raghunātha's advance towards Toppūr must refer to this period (in 1616) when Yāchama had already arrived in the Cauvery Valley. Yagnanārāyana Dīkshita's mentioning Yāchama Nayaka's arrival at last, must also refer to the same time, since he speaks of the breach of the Cauvery dam effected by the enemies merely to prevent Yāchama from effecting a junction with his ally. The *Bahuḷāsvacharitam* of Dāmarla Veṇgaḷabhūpāla, gives an account of the route of Yāchama's march towards Toppūr,[25] but even from that it is

son of the deceased king." Srīranga or Ranga II had, before his enthronement been in Tanjore where he made the acquaintance, according to Queyroz, of several Balalas of Jaffnapatam. He raised these latter to various posts in his administration, shortly after his accession. Gobbūri Jaggarāya, the maternal uncle of the putative heir, Tima Nayaka and Makaraja were the chiefs who were opposed to Śrīranga. They were joined by the Dalavoy, and a minister who were alienated from Ranga and also by one Narparaju, also by Ravilla Venka and three others named Chenchu, Virappa and Yāchama. Then followed the coup by which the Dalavoy and Jaggarāya seized possession of Ranga and his family. This took place after Ranga had ruled for some time—a few months at the most. The coronation of the putative nephew was celebrated by Jaggarāya, who first treated Ranga with consideration; but put him into rigorous confinement when he tried to rise against the usurper. Barradas says that Ranga was now deserted by "all save one captain whose name was Echama Naique" and who was attempted to be cajoled and won over by Jaggarāya. Yāchama Nayak was unable to obtain any access to the imprisoned Ranga, but contrived to have one of his sons concealed in a bundle of soiled linen taken out to wash and thus brought over to his side, probably hoping to encourage his troops with the presence of the boy prince and also "perhaps in order to save the royal offspring in the case of a prospective regicide". After two futile attempts at escape, poor Ranga and all his other children were slaughtered though there is a discrepancy as to the method by which this holocaust was brought about. The Viceroy of Goa heard in December 1614 that Ranga had been killed in a short time before, perhaps in November. According to Barradas, Yāchama Nayak was infuriated by this atrocious crime and openly challenged Jaggarāya, offering battle to him. In the fight that followed, Yāchama attacked the enemy with such valour that Jaggarāya had to retreat, abandoning all the royal insignia. Yāchama Nayak proclaimed the surviving son of Ranga the rightful heir and king and soon he got the support of many of the nobles; while Jaggarāya fled to the jungles with 15,000 men only. The Nayak of Madura joined the army of Jaggarāya after this defeat. According to Barradas this first victory of Yāchama resulted in many of the captains joining Yāchama Nayak, so that in a short time his army had augmented to 50,000 fighting men; while Jaggarāya's forces had diminished to 15,000 (see Heras: The Great Civil War of Vijayanagara in the Journal of Indian History, Vol. V, pp. 164-88). Here Father Heras says that Sri Ranga himself had vainly renounced his rights on Venkata's death-bed as he was not willing to become the cause of bloodshed and the Portuguese Viceroy foresaw the coming civil war some years before.

25. *Sources: Bahulāsvacharitam*; p. 305.

not known whether Yāchama ever came to Kumbakonam at all. If reliance is based upon the *Sāhityaratnākara* then, it would mean that Yāchama Nayaka reached Toppūr from South Arcot, marching through the western portions of the Chola country; and the breach of the Cauvery dam which was effected by the rebels, in order to prevent his entry into the Tanjore country, easily explains this.[26] If this is correct, Raghunātha's going to Kumbakonam to instal Rāma as emperor, must be taken to mean his march from Tanjore eastwards to the same place on his way to the campaign against Sōḻaga. Otherwise how could Raghunātha start on an expedition against his eastern enemies when there were enemies on the west prepared for battle? Diplomacy and prudent statesmanship would not justify such a course of action. Yagnanārāyana's references to Yāchama Nayaka's 'desire to come' (समायियासति) to 'his coming' (आयाति), and lastly to 'his arrival' in the Tanjore country (अभ्यागमत्) exactly fits in with the account of Barradas. Yāchama Nayaka's arrival at Trichinopoly is dated towards the end of A.D. 1616, that is, two years after the declaration of hostilities between Jaggarāya and Yāchama Nayaka in the Karnātaka country. And Barradas says 'that the war continued these two years, fortune favouring now one side now the other.' Raghunātha's joining the army led by Yāchama Nayaka and Rāma, must be placed sometime before August A.D. 1616 when he was encamping near the village of Paḻamānēri.

Raghunātha Nayaka's first expedition began only after A.D. 1614, since the contemporary works say that he was informed of the news of the Karnātaka war of succession before he actually left his capital.[27]

26. *Sources*: *Sāhityaratnākara*; p. 274.

27.

[*Note by the Editor.*]

The loyalist chiefs sent envoys to request the Nayak of Tanjore; and these demanded of Raghunātha "to rescue the empire *once more* from destruction, as he had done before in his youth, and to destroy the party of Jaggarāya" (Sarga VIII of the *Raghunāthābhyudayam* of Rāmabhadrāmba, tells us that Raghunātha then told his ministers that the three tasks of destroying Śoḷaga in the island, driving out the enemies of the Nepala (Jaffnese) king and celebrating the coronation of the new Karnaṭa emperor would constitute his *digvijaya*) Yāchama Nayak himself had wished to go to Tanjore for the same purpose. The *Sāhityaratnākara* (Sarga X) says that "after the Karnaṭa emperor had thus been murdered in his capital, his only surviving son, a child, had been rescued by the nobleman, Yācha, who, with other chiefs, was proceeding to Achyuta for help. Achyuta had to effect a junction with Yācha and the young emperor before the Pāṇḍya (the Nayak of Madura) and his allies met the troops of Jaggarāya at Srirangam as arranged

His victories over Sōḻaga and the people of Jaffna were accomplished before the middle of A.D. 1616. In the meanwhile, the loyalist party led by Yāchama Nayaka and the rebel group led by Jaggarāya were both fighting, and Barradas tells us of the success won by Yāchama Nayaka and to his crowning of Rama as emperor before he came to the south. Jaggarāya's coming to the south, was the result of his earlier defeat sustained at the hands of Yāchama Nayaka. Raghunātha Nayaka's attention was first directed against the rebellious chief Sōḻaga who is said to have been the ruler of an island (*Aṇtarīpagataha*)[28] and *Aṇtarīpavāsam*.[29] Ṣōḻaga was causing much

between them. Then followed the abdication of Acyuta on the advice of Gōvinda Dīkṣita and the coronation of Raghunatha, performed by the latter and the retirement of Achyuta to sacred Srirangam (*sarga* XII). Raghunātha heard from his spies of the news descriptive of the troops of the Pāṇdya and his confederates and was told that "the noble Yācha....requests to be assisted by you in the cause of your common master, the Karnāṭa emperor...... Hearing that Yācha and his army are proceeding towards you with the emperor's (Ranga's) son, (Rama) and that they may not effect a junction with your troops, the Pāṇdya King (Nayak of Madura) at the instance of Jaggarāya has cut the great anicut across the Kaveri ...... On hearing this news, King Raghunātha decided to proceed to Kumbakonam to effect a junction with the emperor's son, Rama Raya, and celebrate his coronation at the place. The king then vowed that he would proceed against Śōḷaga in his island and destroy him along with his relations. He would then proceed against the Pāṇdya and his allies........would also destroy in battle Jaggarāya and his other allies, and with their skulls, reconstruct the anicut (*śētu*) across the Kaveri and put up there an inscription in memory of his great triumph there. Speaking thus, Raghunātha entrusted the whole management of the kingdom to his minister, Gōvinda Dikshita and in great anger ordered his army to get ready for the march. (*Sahityaratnākara*: Sources: pp. 273-4).

Barradas implies that, in the course of the civil war the partisans of prince Rama were gaining strength; also a Jesuit letter of Malabar of 1617 would show an advance of the loyalists into the Madura kingdom, as its Nayak ravaged the whole country before retiring; and Father Heras adds:—"It was then most likely that at the instance of Jaggarāya, the Nayak of Madura cut the great anicut across the Kaveri in order to prevent their enemies to advance further south, as related in the *Śāhityaratnākara*." At the end of 1616, when Barradas finished his account, though some time previously the Nayak of Madura had mustered more soldiers and his enemies had to retreat northwards owing to scarcity of water, "the Naique of Tanjore though not so great, was, with the aid of the young king, getting the upper hand....... Indeed they are now assembled in the field in the large open plains of Trichinepali which may contain not only a hundred thousand soldiers as each of the parties has, but several millions of people."

28. *Raghunāthābhyudayam;* Canto VI, Sloka 24.

29. *Sāhityaratnākara,* Canto X, Sloka 18.

trouble to the wayfarers and women and disobeyed the king's[30] orders. It is said that he forced thirsty people to drink heated lead and that he used to throw his prisoners to be devoured by well-trained crocodiles in his moat and to pass sharp needles into their bodies. He is compared to Rāvana of the great epic for his misdeeds, the only difference being that Sōḻaga had only one head instead of ten. Rāmabhadrāmba adds that he was a worshipper of the god Bhairava and even Viṭhala himself could not conquer him.[31] Gōvinda Dīkshita told Raghunātha that he was backed up by the Portuguese as well (Parangis).[32] Sōḻaga was a feudatory of Krishnappa Nayaka of Gingee and he is identified with Sālavaccha[33] by Father Heras. He was one of the two principal feudatories of Gingee, according to Father Pimenta, who also refers to Sōḻaga's son visiting Krishnappa Nayaka and to the former's friendship with the Jesuits, on the evidence contained in a letter of Father Du Jarric. Sōḻaga was the ruler of the south eastern portions also of the kingdom of Gingee and his capital was Dēvikōttah (Tīvukōttah, also called Jalkōta by the Muhammadan historians meaning, surrounded by water) an island fort at the mouth of the river Coleroon. According to Father Du Jarric, he must have been an old man aged about eighty years and 'was a man of great authority among his subjects feared by everybody.' Father Pimenta who visited the Coromandel Coast about A.D. 1597, speaks of his trained crocodiles which were 'put in his river for his security' and this description agrees admirably with the account of Rāmabhadrāmba.[34] Father

30. The name of the king whose orders he defied is not mentioned. As Sōḻaga was a feudatory of the Gingee Nayak, Raghunātha Nayaka could not claim any supremacy over him. Perhaps it refers to the Nayak's order not to trouble the people often.

31. Dr. S. K. Ayyangar suggests that Viṭhala must refer to Rāmarāja Viṭhala the foremost general of Sadāsivarāya who came to the south in 1546. *Sources of Vijayanagar History*; p. 286. Also *Raghunāthābhyudayam;* Canto VIII, and *Sāhityaratnākara*; Canto X.

32. *Sāhityaratnākara* refers to the Portuguese as Pārasikas by mistake while *Raghunāthābhyudayam* has Parangis.

33. *The Aravidu Dynasty of Vijayanagara*; p. 407.

34.
[*Note by the Editor.*].
According to Yagnanārāyana Dikshita, Śōlaga was giving great trouble to the people of the neighbourhood and used to inflict inhuman punishments on the innocent people of the land; he would bind them up in empty sacks and after having them well beaten with pestles, would throw the sacks containing the men into the waters of his rivers to be devoured by the crocodiles. He would also subject the Kaḷamāḷ (perhaps Kallamārs) of Achyuta's territory to unheard of atrocities by passing sharp needles into the roots of their hairs. "These do not cover even a

Pimenta also speaks of his son[35] as a great supporter and friend of the Jesuit missionaries. The *Sāhityaratnākara* also refers to Raghunātha Nayak's march from his capital against Sōḻaga with a huge and well equipped army composed of infantry (Batās), cavalry and elephantry leaving the administration of the kingdom in the hands of Gōvinda Dīkshita.[36] The elephants were all well caparisoned and were also equipped with iron howdahs,[37] while the horses were mounted upon by soldiers who wore long turbans and carried with them bows and arrows. Camels are also mentioned as a component part of his army (उष्ट्रपङ्क्तयः). There were besides, a large number of Muhammadan soldiers in his train and also *Yavanas* who were perhaps Sinhalese troopers. The Tanjore army carried with them bows, arrows, swords and a weapon called *Nālikāyudham* having an *analavarti* (fire wick).[38] The king was in armour and rode on a white elephant. Rāmabhadrāmba and Yagnanārāyana Dīkshita give a picturesque account of the Tanjore army and they also speak of a number of palanquins that accompanied the king. The former speaks of the materials used in erecting tents, besides provisions for the army and also vessels that were carried to the field of battle.[39] Boxes containing precious jewels were also removed from the capital and were taken along with the king, for safety. Yagnanārāyana speaks of the camp followers, who carried along with them besides their

small portion of the cruelties practised by Sōḻaga. If Achyuta were to subdue him and put an end to his atrocities, then the Portuguese (Pārasīkas) could be easily subdued and the Nēpāla king once more raised to his throne." For these reasons Achyuta was told that since the Nayak of Madura had concluded alliances with Śōḻaga and the king of Tundira (Nayak of Gingee) it would not be advisable on his part to fight with them at once.

Father Pimenta thus describes the Śōḻaga:—"He is old and severe and hath caused crocodiles to be put in his river for his security charging them not to hurt his own people. They nevertheless killed a man; whereupon I know not by what arts he took two of them which were the malefactors and put chains round their necks and cast them into a miry place, there to be stoned by the people and to die of famine." His son, a boy of 14, became greatly attached to the Jesuits during Father Pimenta's stay at Gingee; and he took them from that place to the castle of his father who received them very kindly.

35. Yagnanārāyana Dikshita refers to the sons and relatives of Sōḻaga (Canto XIII, Sl. 81).

36. *Sāhityaratnākara*; XIII, Sl. 84.

37. *Sāhityaratnākara;* XIII, Sl. 86.

38. *Sāhityaratnākara ;* Canto XV, Sl. 20.

39. *Raghunāthābhyudayam;* Canto VIII, Sl. 68-70.

weapons, medicinal herbs which had a good healing property of the wounds.[40] The army left the capital in full battle array and soon reached the town of Kumbakōnam[41] and Raghunātha crossing the river Cauvery[42] advanced towards the territory of Sōlaga. This rebellious chief was helped by the Portuguese and also by Krishnappa Nayaka of Gingee.[43] Raghunātha crossing the river Coleroon, is said to have offered a severe fight and laid siege to his fort. The smoke emanating from the firing of the guns (*Agniyantrās*)[44] is said to have enveloped the whole island. Sōlaga, finding that he could not withstand the attack, quickly yielded. And Raghunātha Nayaka, after a short but sharp fight, took Sōlaga and his family as captives and threw him into prison. The Gin-

40. *Sahityaratnākara*; Canto XVI, Sl. 23.

41. Yagnanārāyana Dikshita also refers to his march upon Kumbakonam but mentions it in connection with (XIII, Sl. 80) Raghunātha's assurance given to the Karnāta nobles. This was undertaken according to the author to instal Rāma as the emperor of Karnātaka. We have seen earlier that this must refer to his expedition against Śōlaga.

42. *Raghunāthābhyudayam;* Canto VIII, Sl. 76 and 77.

43. *Raghunāthābhyudayam;* Canto VIII, Sl. 78 and 79 mention *Krishna Bhūpa,* as the *king of Tundira.* Dr. S. K. Ayyangar identifies Krishna Bhūpa with Krishnappa Nayaka of Gingee.

[*Further Note by the Editor.*]

This Krishnappa was perhaps related to the chiefs, Sūrappa and Pōta Bhūpāla who were the Nayaks of Gingee before him. Anquetil du Perron states that he was a contemporary of Venkatapati and succeeded his father whose name, however, he does not mention. He escaped from prison, having been confined by his uncle and in the sequel, imprisoned the latter after putting out his eyes. In 1586 he rebelled against Venkata, who captured him and had him put in prison. Raghunatha, after his Pēnukonda campaign, interceded with Venkata on his behalf and secured his release. Krishnappa sealed his gratitude to Raghunatha by giving his daughter in marriage to him. During his imprisonment, Gingee was ruled by one Venkata, who was sent against him by Venkatapati Raya. Krishnappa was a wise and able ruler and his court and capital were well described by Father Pimenta who visited Gingee in A.D. 1597. He built Krishnapatam near Porto Novo. His feudatories were Sōlaga, the chief of Tiruvati and Lingama Nayak of Vellore. Krishnappa rebelled for a second time against the Raya in 1600 and war broke out between them in 1607. He had close relations with the Portuguese and the Dutch on the coast. He was also a staunch Vaishnava. For an account of his rule see *Histoire du Gingi* by C. S. Srinivasachari—traduit de l'anglais et annote par Edmond Gaudart, Governeur en retraite (Pondicherry and Paris, 1940)—pp. 43-63.

44. *Raghunāthābhyudayam;* Canto VIII, Sl. 80.

gee Nayak, Krishnappa, is said to have fled from the scene of battle having become disheartened and terrified on Raghunātha's approach. The expedition against Sōḻaga was a complete success for the Tanjore army which occupied his fort. This was the first victory for Raghunātha Nayaka; and Dr. S. K. Ayyangar says that this may be dated in A.D. 1615.[45]

From Dēvikōttah, Raghunātha marched south along the sea-coast, towards Jaffna, whose king is mentioned by both the authors as having accompanied the Nayaka from the very beginning of his expedition. Passing through the modern Kāvēripattanam, where the Cauvery joins the sea[46] and crossing the sea (the gulf of Manaar) by means of a chain of boats (तरी), the Nayaka landed on the Jaffnese coast. Rāmabhadrāmba says that the army also crossed the channel with the aid of wooden floats. Raghunātha offered battle to the Portuguese, who, finding themselves exhausted in spite of the furious charge of their guns, fled for their lives; while a large number of them escaped by the sea in small ships. Raghunātha inflicted another crushing defeat upon the Portuguese and reinstated the Jaffnese ruler on his throne. This victory over the Portuguese of Jaffna must have happened before the battle of Toppūr and immediately after the capture of the fort of Dēvikōttah and hence the date of this campaign may be fixed approximately towards the close of A.D. 1615 or in the beginning of the year A.D. 1616.

Nothing more is known about this expedition and the internal evidence does not throw any light as to who was the Jaffnese King that sought the help of Raghunāṭha in his endeavour to regain his lost throne. Rāmabhadrāmba says[47] that a Nēpāla[48] king along with his relatives and assistants came to Raghunātha's court and represented to him his misfortune in being driven away from his capital. The Nēpāla ruler also seems to have narrated how Raghunātha Nayaka's ancestors were great supporters of his kingdom. We saw how some Balalas of Jaffna had been in Tanjore even before this time. 'The Parangis (Portuguese) had on several occasions been defeated by his ancestors and they had been waiting to wreak their vengeance upon the king of Nēpalā.' Rowing the

45. *Sources of Vijayanagar History*, p. 286, footnote.

46. *Raghunāthābhyudayam*; Canto IX, Sl. 7.

47. *Raghunāthābhyudayam*; Canto VIII, Sl. 13 to 22.

48. Nēpāla is identified with Jaffna as it is said that the country was surrounded by ocean and other particulars of the description of this country satisfy this identification.

seas in their ships, they now attacked his capital while he was away and captured the city called Vārdhikēya. And Raghunātha promised him help. The *Sāhityaratnākara* gives some additional information.[49] It refers to the arrival of the wives of the Jaffnese ruler at Tanjore, besides the latter; and here the enemies of the fugitive are called the Pārasikas by which term the Portuguese are meant. In another place, the same author calls the Jaffnese ruler as the Yavana king.[50] His name is mentioned as Pararājabhayaṇkara and his kingdom is said to have been surrounded on all sides by the ocean. That the Tanjore army was composed of Yavana soldiers will mean that it was composed of men from Jaffna.[51] Raghunātha Nayaka's defeat of the Portuguese and his reinstallation of the Jaffna ruler on his throne are established beyond a shadow of doubt; but the question, as to who was the king that was re-anointed by him is not clear. The references to the city, called Vārdhikēya and the king Pararājabhayaṇkara do not take us far as they are not definite.

The literary evidence refers to the help given to the rulers of Jaffna during the time of Achyutappa Nayaka, and so, Raghunātha's intervention must refer to the help rendered a second time. To understand the Tanjore relations with Jaffna aright, it is necessary to have a grasp of the trend of the Jaffna politics of this period. A fair account of these political troubles is given in the Portuguese chronicles and also in the *Yālpāṇa Vaibava Mālai* of Mayilvāhana Puḷavar, composed in the beginning of the 17th century. They refer to the help given by the Nayak of Tanjore to the rulers of Jaffna even from the middle of the 16th century.[52] In all

49. *Sāhityaratnākara*; Canto VI, Sl. 65-72.

50. *Sāhityaratnākara*; XV, Sl. 50 and 52. Yavana Bhūpati.

51. *Sāhityaratnākara*; XV, Sl. 35.

The above work says that the Jaffnese ruler stayed at Tanjore for sometime and he is said to have accompanied Raghunātha in his war upon Sōḷaga. Sloka 50 has the word *Upaiti* which means "follows.'

52. *Ancient Jaffna* in Tamil, by Mr. C. Rasanayagam, p. 96.

[*Further Note by the Editor.*]

Mr. Rasanayagam thinks that the Jaffnese king who went for help to Achyutappa of Tanjore must have been Saṇkili Kumara, who had murdered Arasakēsari, the regent uncle of the minor king and usurped the regency. The Portuguese drove him out and he returned with an army of Tanjore and established himself on the throne. The Portuguese then recognised him as king, but ultimately dethroned him and occupied Jaffna. Again, under Raghunātha Nayaka there was another personal appeal from the Jaffnese King for help.

these wars the powers on the Coromandel Coast do not seem to have fared well at all. In 1547, Śankili, Śegarājasēkharan, who is said to have joined the Sinhalese ruler Māyādunnē, the ruler of Sitawāka and the younger brother of Bhuvanēka Bāhu VII, and fought against the Portuguese; appears to have secured help from the Tanjore Nayaka. This must have happened during the reign of Śevappa Nayaka and the Portuguese seems to have won a victory on that occasion. Tanjore again interfered between A.D. 1570 and A.D. 1582, when Peria Pillai, Śēgarājasēkharan was the king of Jaffna. He came to the throne with the help of the Portuguese general, De Castro, in A.D. 1570, but soon exhibited his innate hatred and hostility towards his allies by attacking their colony at Maṇṇār with the help of the Tanjore forces. The Tanjore army sustained a defeat for a second time. Peria Pillai's successor was one Puvirāja Paṇḍāram who, on his accession assumed the title of Pararajasēkharan. He was also opposed to the Portuguese and is said to have persecuted the Christians; and his attempts to capture Manaar from

Raghunātha crossed the sea by a bridge of boats, placed his own garrison in the island of Jaffna and celebrated the coronation of his ally. It is not certain whether Saṇkili went over to Tanjore for help for a second time and had himself crowned before Oliveira's forces came up and captured him, or "whether the story is a confused account of the help given to the prince of Ramēsvaram on whose behalf the people of Jaffna revolted against the Portuguese." (*Ancient Jaffna*, pp. 386-87).

THE KINGS OF JAFFNA

According to the Rev. S. Gnānaprakāsar, O.M.I., of Jaffna (*Kings of Jaffna in the Portuguese Period*, 1920) the following kings reigned at Nallūr in Jaffna:—

(1) Kanagasūriya, Segarājasēkaran 1467 A.D.
(2) Pararājasēkaran—1478 A.D.
(3) Saṇkili, Segarājasēkaran, 1519 A.D.
(4) Puvi Rāja Pandāram, Pararājasēkaran, 1561 A.D.
(5) Kachi Nayinar—Pararājasēkaran (usurper) C. 1565 A.D.
(6) Periya Pillai, Segarājasēkaran, C. 1570 A.D.
(7) Puvi Raja Pandāram, Pararājasēkaran, C. 1582 A.D.
(8) Hendarmana Singa, (Edirmaṇṇa Singha), Pararājasēkaran, 1591
(9) A minor son under the regency of
    (1) Arasakēsari—1615 A.D.
    *(2) Sankili Kumāra—1617 A.D.
(10) Oliveira, the Portuguese Governor—1620 A.D.

* There was some confusion between the two Saṇkilis in the *Yalpāṇa Vaiṗhava Mālai.*

them, on two occasions also ended in failure. The second attempt which took place in A.D. 1591 resulted in serious consequences. For then, he was attacked by the Portuguese general, Andre Furtado de Mendoza, who invaded Jaffna in October 1591, and quickly brought it under his control. Puvirāja Paṇḍāram was killed in the battle and the Portuguese installed the son of Peria Pillai, as the new ruler of Jaffna. This prince was known as Edirmaṇṇa Śinga with the title of Pararājasēkharan. He is said to have ruled from A.D. 1591 to 1615,[53] as a feudatory of the Portuguese and to have paid them an annual tribute. He was 'as might be expected, was extremely punctilious in showing his gratitude to the Portuguese, conferring many favours on them and treating them with much familiarity. Quite naturally, the latter were having it all their own way in the land.' This state of things did not satisfy the Mudaliars and chiefs of the kingdom and they soon formed a plot for placing on the throne a prince who was then at Ramancor (Rāmēswaram) and who was backed up by a select army of Moors, Badagas and Maravas under the protection of the Naique of Tanjore and the renegade Dom Joas Wimalaḍharma, King of Kandy.[54] The Portuguese on the other hand wanted to depose Wimalaḍharma, who, on ascending the throne of Kandy is said to have renounced his former religion of Christianity, oppressed his allies and persecuted the Christians.[55] The king of Jaffna Pararājasēkharan, on hearing of this intended attack and insurrection by the prince of Rāmēswaram, soon communicated it to the Portuguese captain of Manaar and the latter at once sent Manoel de Athaide with a body of men in seven ships to meet the Tanjore army. On the 26th of October A.D. 1592 Athaide charged the Tanjore forces and in the end was able to defeat them near Talaimannār.[56]

From A.D. 1592 to A.D. 1615 there was peace in the land and Pararājasēkharan was allowed to rule without further trouble. The Portuguese had their own suspicion about his attitude towards them. Edir-

53. *The History of Jaffna under the Portuguese Period*, by Rev. S. Gñānaprakāsar O.M.I. He says that his death took place in A.D. 1615 while Mr. C. Rasanayagam would place it in the following year. *History of Jaffna in Tamil*, p. 120 and 116.

54. *Ibid.*, Rev. S. Gnanaprakāsar, pp 49 and 50, and *History of Jaffna in Tamil*, pp. 118 and 119.

55. *The Portuguese in India* by F. C. Danvers, Vol. II, p. 98.

56. Rev. Gnānāprakāsar says that 'in all 400 Badagas were slain and 200 taken prisoners.'

maṇṇaśinga Ārya *alias* Pararājasēkhara—for that was his full name—shortly before his death, made his three-year-old son as his successor and appointed his own brother Arasakēsari Paṇḍāra as regent, until the time, the boy should come of age. This arrangement was communicated to the Portuguese Viceroy of Goa for ratification; but he died all on a sudden before the confirmatory order could reach Jaffna. The death of this ruler is dated A.D. 1615.[57] It is said that immediately after his death, one Saṇkili Kumāra of the royal family who was longing to usurp the throne, captured the government by putting an end to the lives of Arasakēsari Paṇḍāra the Regent, and Peria Pillai Arāchi a powerful chief. Saṇkili then became the Regent. The people of Jaffna became dismayed at the unexpected success of Saṇkili Kumāra, grew restless and rose in revolt. Chiṇṇa Migāpillai Arāchi, the son of Peria Pillai who was murdered by Saṇkili, went over to the mainland to seek the aid of the Portuguese against the usurper, who however managed to stay on. When Joao de Cruz Girao of Manaar came to Jaffna to give effect to the will executed by the late king Ediramaṇṇa Śinga, Saṇkili is said to have denied the truth of the will and to have proved it to be a fraud. Saṇkili was thus left undisturbed ruler, on his promise to pay the Portuguese the due tribute and to rule according to their wishes. Saṇkili kept up his word for some time; but soon internal troubles arose which enabled him to set at nought the Portuguese claim to overlordship by allowing the Badagas (people from the mainland) to pass through his kingdom on their way to Kandy. Again, he also became unpopular by his atrocities and cruel exactions. The news of his proposal to appoint his son-in-law as his successor, was received by the Jaffnese with indignation and they consequently rose in revolt. Even the intervention of the Portuguese captain of Manaar to bring about a truce between Saṇkili Kumāra and his subjects was of no use; and Saṇkili, being very much opposed by his own men, had to take refuge at Ūrṭṭurai, a port on the Jaffnese Coast. It is said that his womenfolk had, in the interval, made their escape to the court of Tanjore to seek the Nayak's help in putting down the revolt of the Jaffnese people and the Portuguese, who had then joined them. At last Saṇkili seems to have regained his kingdom with the aid of the Tanjore Nayak's forces sent under one Khēm Nayak and of five thousand *lascarins.* (Sinhalese warriors) led by one Varunakulat-

57. *The Portuguese in India*; by F. C. Danvers. The author places his death in 1617, Vol. II, p. 194. Mr. Rasanayagam (*History of Jaffna*) says that the confirmatory order from the Viceroy was issued on 13th May 1616, but it actually reached Jaffna towards the end of August of the same year.

tān.[58] Yagnanārāyana Dīkshita's reference to the presence of the ladies of the Jaffnese king at the court of Raghunātha, perhaps indicates this appeal made by Saṇkili's women and Raghunātha Nayaka's claim to have re-established a king of Jaffna on the eve of the Toppūr battle must also refer to this victory won by his forces on behalf of Saṇkili, though the Portuguese chronicles do not refer to the part said to have been played by the Nayaka himself in person, but record the victory of the Tanjore forces.

Since Raghunātha Nayaka is said to have been in camp at Paḻamānēri in the cyclic year *Naḷa* and in the month of *Ādi* (Ashāda) corresponding to August A.D. 1616 on his way to Toppūr, the invasion of Jaffna must have taken place sometime before that date. The Rev. Gnānaprakāsar's date (1615) for the death of Edirmaṇṇa Śinga Parārājasēkharan the predecessor of Saṇkili, confirms A.D. 1616 as the date of the Jaffnese expedition.[59] The only point of conflict between the Tanjore and the Portuguese chronicles is that, while the former speaks of Raghunātha's presence in Jaffna in person, the latter mentions only his despatch of troops under one Khēm Nayak. Hence it is known for certain that it was Saṇkili Kumāra, who came to Tanjore for the Nayak's help and got subsequently back his lost kingdom through the latter's intervention. The reference made to the Jaffnese King as Pararājabhayaṇkara (dread of enemy king) by Yagnanārāyana Dikshita, refers to Saṇkili himself. Pararājabhayankara could not be taken as referring to Pararājasēkhara on the ground that the Jaffnese rulers called themselves

58. *History of Jaffna*; p. 124. Also *Ancient Jaffna;* by Mr. C. Rasanayagam; *Danvers*, Vol. II, p. 206. The account given above is mainly drawn from the *History of Jaffna under the Portuguese*, *The Portuguese in India*, *History of Ceylon*, by H. W. Codrington, *Ceylon and the Portuguese Era*, by Dr. P. E. Pieris.

59. The dates of 1616 and 1617, given by Mr. Rasanayagam and Mr. Danvers will have to be abandoned in the light of Tanjore evidence. Raghunātha Nayaka's installation of Saṇkili as King, however, did not prove to have settled the matters finally. The Portuguese chronicles of Quieroz, Menezes and Faria Y Sousa refer to the sporadic attempts made by the Tanjore Nayak to regain Jaffna from the Portuguese, in whose hands the land has fallen about A.D. 1620. Dr. S. K. Ayyangar (*Sources*, p. 287, Footnote) fixes the date of Pararājasēkharan's death in A.D. 1617 following Mr. Danvers. Mr. C. Rasanayagam refers to the Tanjore help, on two occasions and he places Saṇkili Kumāra's reappointment during the reign of Achyutappa Nayaka. As regards the second which happened during the time of Raghunātha Nayaka according to him, the author himself is not sure whether it was made on behalf of Saṇkili for a second time, or in favour of a prince of Ramanacor, on whose behalf the Jaffnese revolted against the Portuguese. (*History of Jaffna* by C. Rasanayagam).

Pararājasēkharans and Śegarājasekharans in the order of their accession. In that case we cannot adequately explain the title of Pararājasēkharan for Saṅkili, since his predecessor Edirmaṇṇasinga was called a Pararājasēkhara[60] but there was one predecessor, Arasakēsari, in the regency.

Raghunātha Nayaka is said to have marched to Toppūr[61] from Jaffna as he was informed, at the latter place, of the troubles caused by the enemy chiefs led by Jaggarāya and the damage done to the Cauvery dam.[62] The causes that led to this momentous war are mentioned both in the Tanjore literature and in the letter of Barradas.[63] Venkatapati Raya's death in A.D. 1614 saw the beginning of a crisis which soon assumed greater magnitude and began as a regular war of succession to the Karnatāka throne. Venkatapati Raya having no male heir to succeed him, appointed his nephew Sriranga *alias* Chikkadēvarāya as his successor at the time of his death, setting aside the claims of a child who was fraudulently palmed off on him as his son by one of his queens. It is said that Venkatapati could not do anything to proclaim the real origin of this putative son as he was very fond of his queen, who was the sister of Gobbūri Jaggarāya, the then governor of Kolar and its neighbouring parts under Venkatapati. Jaggarāya, who had already entertained an ambition to acquire the throne for himself, naturally took up the cause of this young child, whom he declared to be the rightful son of the deceased emperor, and proclaimed him king by putting an end to the life of Chikkadēvarāya and his family. Only the second son of Chikkadēvarāya called Rāma, was saved from this wholesale disaster by the skilful exertion, of a washerman who had the boy smuggled out from the prison along with his bundle of dirty linen, with the connivance of Vēlugōti Yāchama Nayaka, a loyal feudatory of the

60. The Jaffnese rulers had these titles added to their names on their accession. A Pararājasēkharan was usually succeeded by a Segarājasēkharan like the Pāṇḍyas of the Second Empire who called themselves Jatāvarmans and Marāvarmans on their accession and the Cholas, Parakēsaris and Rājakēsaris.—See Dynastic List of the Jaffnese Kings in the Portuguese Era given above.—(*Ed.*)

61. *Sources:*—Dr. S. K. Ayyangar identifies this place with the modern Tōvūr or Tōhūr which is about two miles from the Grand Anicut on the southern bank of the Cauvery.

62. *Raghunāthābhyudayam;* Canto IX, Sl. 24 and 25.

63. *Raghunāthābhyudayam;* Canto XIII. *Sāhityaratnākara;* Canto XI and XIII. Barradas; *A Forgotten Empire*, pp. 222-230.

late king and the founder of the present Venkatagiri royal house. Yāchama Nayaka as the sponsor of the claims of Rāma, the legal claimant to the throne, soon gained strength and opposed Jaggarāya. According to the account given by Barradas it appears that both the parties had come into collision in a series of engagements with varying success.[64] Jaggarāya's going over to the south was the result of a defeat which he sustained about the beginning of A.D. 1616; and he perhaps had the object of securing the co-operation of the southern governors to make a final bid for victory.[65] In this he was joined by the Nayaks of Gingee and Madura besides the Chēra king, who was a tributory of the Madura Nayaka. Tanjore alone remained loyal; her Nayak took up the cause of the legitimate successor, Ramarāya, along with Yāchama Nayaka. The Tanjore literature has no reference to this first success of Yāchama Nayaka referred to by Barradas. However his advance towards Tanjore was made probably with the object of destroying the coalition of rebel chiefs under Jaggarāya.

The Madura ruler who joined Jaggarāya was Muttuvīrappa Nayaka (A.D. 1609 to A.D. 1623) and he, far from being loyal to the Empire, aimed at independence even very early; but he was not allowed to have a free hand in his attempt at independence as Venkatapati was a fairly strong ruler and was effectively helped by his loyal ally, the Tanjore Nayaka in maintaining the Imperial overlordship. By A.D. 1616 Muttuvīrappa had grown powerful enough to rise in opposition and as a first mark of his hostile attitude, he changed his capital from Madura to Trichinopoly.[66] Father Leon Besse says that 'the Nayak of Madura removed his court and army to Trichinopoly in A.D. 1616 with the object of making war with the King of Tanjore' and Dr. S. K. Ayyangar says[67] that his change of capital seems to have been 'the direct result of the combination that culminated in the battle of Toppūr; and by A.D. 1616 the hostility between Madura and Tanjore had settled into a habitual kind of relation between the two Nayakships.' And it was this perpetual enmity with Tanjore that made Muttuvīrappa join the rebels.[68]

64. *A Forgotten Empire*, p. 229.
65. *A Forgotten Empire*, p. 230.
66. *La Mission du Madura*, p. 3 and
The Nayaks of Madura; p. 103; Foot-note.
67. *The Nayaks of Madura*, p. 103, Footnote.
68. Tanjore's loyalty to the empire and her co-operation with Venkatapati in the battle of Vallam against Madura, were sufficient causes for Madura's distrust and hatred.

Gōvinda Dikshita is said to have told his master that the Pāṇḍyan ruler (Nayak of Madura) and others were bearing ill-will and hatred towards Tanjore out of ignorance;[69] and Dr. S. K. Ayyangar again says that this combination of the Madura and Gingee Nayaks with Gobbūri Jaggarāya against the loyalists, was effected mainly with the object of overthrowing the Imperial control at this favourable juncture and this could be done only if the loyalists were crushed.[70] They seem to have done all they could to prevent the junction of Yāchama Nayaka, who was then coming towards Tanjore with Prince Rama to join Raghunātha Nayaka and the reference to the breaking off the Cauvery dam was perhaps their first act of destruction towards this aim. Rāmabhadrāmba says that the damage to the dam was caused by the rulers of the west, while *Sāhityaratnākara* says that some one did it at the instigation of Jaggarāya.[71] And Raghunātha is said to have remarked that he would reconstruct the dam with the skull pieces of his enemies.

An account of the battle of Toppūr is found in the *Raghunāthābhyudayum*, the *Raghunāthābhyudaya Nātakam* by Vijayarāghava, the narrative by Barradas and the *Bahuḷāsvacharitam*.[72] Barradas says that "Yachama Nayaka had with him fifty thousand men in his camp, while Jaggarāya with only fifteen thousand followers, fled into the jungles where he was joined by more people, so that the war has continued these two years, fortune favouring now one side, now the other. But the party of the young prince has always been gaining strength; the more so because, although the great Nayak of Madura—a page of betel to the King of Bisnagar—who pays a revenue every year of some say 600,000 pagodas and has under him many kings and nobles as vassals, such as he was of Travancore—took the side of Jaggarāya and sustained him against the Naique of Tanjaor. Yet, the latter though not so powerful is, with the aid of the young king, gradually getting the upper hand." Both Rāmabhadrāmbha and Yagnanārāyana Dīkshita speak of the union of the Madura and Gingee rulers and the Pāṇḍyan chief of Teṇkāsi with Jaggarāya, while the latter mentions also the Chēra

69. *Sāhityaratnākara*, Canto X, Sl. 26.

70. *The Nayaks of Madura;* p. 104, Footnote.

71. *Raghunāthābhyudayam;* Canto IX, Sl. 26. *Pāśchātyabhūmipatayaha* and *Sāhityaratnākaram;* Canto XIII, Sl. 78 and 83. Father Heras considers it likely that the Nayak of Madura did it at the instance of Jaggarāya—see Note by (Ed.).

72. *Sources of Vijayanagar History;* p. 305.

King[73] as among the rebel allies. The reference to the Dramida and the Maghadha kings is nothing but mere poetical rhetoric. Mysore seems to have held aloof from this war of succession.[74] The *Raghunāthābhyudayam* and the *Sāhityaratnākara* give a detailed account of the preparations made by Raghunātha Nayaka.[75] The Tanjore army was composed of elephantry, cavalry and infantry besides a corps of troopers. The elephants were all equipped with iron howdahs[76], each containing soldiers and the well caparisoned horses were all mounted by high-turbened riders who carried with them bows and arrows. The soldiers also had with them broad swords and matchlocks (Agniyaṇtrās).[77] The infantry troops which were composed of Pāraśikas and Yavanas besides the natives, were armed with bows, arrows, spears and a deadly weapon called *Nālikāyudha*.[78] Yagnanārāyana Dikshita also refers to a small batch of young soldiers, who were recruited from the class of nobles of the land.[79]

The reference to the Pāraśikas and Yavanas is rather inconclusive. Yagnanārāyana Dikshita uses the word Pāraśika to mean the Portuguese and the word Yavana must refer to the Jaffnese or Sinhalese since he speaks of the Jaffnese ruler as Yavanabhūpati.[80] Dr. S. K. Ayyangar[81] and Mr. K. Sitaramayya following him say that the Pāraśikas must be taken to mean the Dutch and not the Portuguese, since Raghunātha had already shown his hostility towards them by driving them away from their coastal settlement in his kingdom. The

73. *Raghunāthābhyudayam;* IX, Sl. 25 and 26. *Sāhityaratnākara;* X, Sl. 57 and XIII, Sl. 78. Dr. S. K. Ayyangar says 'the Nayak of Madura, the Nayak of Gingee, the Pāṇḍyas of Tinnevelly, the Portuguese and perhaps even distant Travancore stood ranged on the side of the traitor.'

74. *The Nayaks of Madura;* Introduction, pp. 19 and 105, Note.

75. *Raghunāthābhyudayam;* IX and X; *Sāhityaratnākara;* XIII and IV.

76. *Sāhityaratnākara*; XIII, Sl. 86 and 88.

77. *Sāhityaratnākara*; Sl. 8-10.

78. *Sāhityaratnākara;* XI, Sl. 20 and 21. The whole of Canto XIII is devoted to a description of the Tanjore army and the preparations made on the eve of the war. Unfortunately this description is taken to mean the enemies by Dr. S. K. Ayyangar. *Sources*, p. 273. However, a close reading of the Canto would show that it was the spy, who had arrived at Tanjore, saw these things before he met Raghunātha.

79. *Sāhityaratnākara;* XIII, Sl. 37.

80. *Sāhityaratnākara;* XV, Sl. 35 to 52.

81. *The Nayaks of Madura;* p. 124, Note.

employment of Dutch soldiers by the Tanjore Nayaka seems improbable in the light of the evidence furnished by the Dutch records. The Dutch at Pulicat to whom Venkatapati had issued a charter on the 24th April, A.D. 1610 permitting them to build a factory, were friendly with the Karnātaka Emperor. A second charter of the same Raya dated the 9th of June, A.D. 1612 was issued from Vellore to the Dutch in ratification of the first; and its last clause refers to a *cowle* granted by Jaggarāya, who was then the chief minister of Venkatapati and as well as the governor of Kōlar. Bāyammā or Vayyāmbika, Jaggarāya's sister and the chief consort of Venkatapati, is said to have given the Dutch, facilities for building the fort called Geldria at Pulicat. Moreover, the Dutch were not on unfriendly terms with the ruler of Gingee as they had established themselves at Tegnapatam by this time; but their hostility towards the Portuguese remained unabated. Above all, Hans de Haze, who came to Masulipatam on the 12th of November, A.D. 1616 to improve the Dutch prospects on the Coromandel Coast, is said to have followed a policy of strict non-intervention in the native affairs and in the war of succession that followed the death of Venkatapati. It is said that 'Haze thought it wise to remain neutral.' The English Factory Records tell us of the unsuccessful attempts made by the Dutch to found a factory in the kingdom of the Tanjore Nayak and these show the obvious improbability of the Dutch joining Tanjore against Jaggarāya.[82]

The *Raghunāthabhyudayam* of Vijayarāghava says that Raghunātha was encamping at Paḷamānēri near Tanjore before he started for Toppur, the scene of the historic battle. It also gives a detailed account of the king's march towards Toppūr accompanied by bodieṣ of officers and numerous followers. Raghunātha is said to have been mounted on an elephant under a white canopy, accompanied by his son, Rāmabhadrā Nayaka. Purushōttamayya and Narasappa (the two town Madālasis) rode on the second elephant while Aṣtappa (or Hastiappa) and Aḷagappa, the two other officers rode on the third elephant. They rode respectively before and behind Raghunātha. Rāmarāya the legitimate ruler is said to have also accompanied Raghunātha to the battle field. Vijayarāghava gives a long list of thirty-two officials and chiefs who went out to fight in company with Raghunātha. Among them Ōbala Rāju the uncle of the king,

82. *Sardesai Commemoration Volume*. The last days of Vijayanagar; by Prof. K. A. Nilakanta Sastri. Also *The Dutch Beginnings in India* by T. I. Poonen, Madras University.

the chiefs of Kaluva, Cuddapah, Palēla, Panta, Balamuri, Māṇdva and the Reddis of Kambam figure prominently.[83]

83. Barradas refers to the Karnātaka nobles, who joined Yāchama Nayaka and supported the cause of Rāmarāya.

[*Further Note by the Editor.*]

The chiefs mentioned in the list given in the *Raghunāthābhyudayam* of Vijayaraghava Nayaka, are interesting as showing the distribution of feudal power in the country at the time.

(1) Kōnēti Kondarāju.
(2) Kaṭṭa Rangapa Rāju.
(3) Kastūri Rāju.
(4) Sampeta Nāga Rāju of Mittāpālem.
(5) Rāma Rāju.
(6) Raghunātha Rāju of Owk.
(7) Māma, Obala Rāju.
(8) Manuboli Rāju.
(9) Srīrangapati Rāju.
(10) Srīgiri Rāju.
(11) Vīrarāghava Rāju.
(12) Viṭhala Rāju.
(13) Chiṭrāju of Nandela.
(14) Nārapa Rāju.
(15) Kanḍanavol Rāju.
(16) Gaḍi Timma Rāja.
(17) The Chiefs of Kālurva.
(18) The Chiefs of Cuddapah.
(19) The Pālela Chiefs.
(20) The Panta Chiefs.
(21) Srīpati Rāju and his mercenaries.
(22) The Jūpalli people.
(23) Dēsūr Reddi clans.
(24) Mūrteppa.
(25) Kumāra Rangayya.
(26) Pāmināyanivāru.
(27) The Balumūri chiefs.
(28) The chiefs of Manduva.
(29) The Reddis of Kambam, Koṇḍavīdu and Koṇḍapalli.
(30) Mallappa.
(31) Mādana.
(32) Perumāl Mudaliar.

These were the chiefs, who had joined the rightful prince after seeing his cause supported by the Nayak of Tanjore.

Chapter VI.

RAGHUNĀTHA NAYAKA (*Continued*).

Rāmabhadrāmba speaks of the matchless and gallant fight put up by the Tanjore forces. It is even said that Raghunātha himself took the field in person, when it was brought to his notice that his troops were not faring well at all.[1] In the battle, Jaggarāya fell dead, and his allies Mākarāju,[2] Rāvilla Venka and his general (Rāya Dalavāy) Chencha took to their heels.[3] The Nayak of Gingee and the disheartened Madura Nayaka are also said to have fled from the field, in order to save their lives. Rāmabhadrāmba again says that the losses on the enemy's side were great and Raghunātha generously pardoned the Madura ruler,[4] when he and his allies surrendered to him. Raghunātha after winning the battle, is said to have proclaimed prince Rāma as the Emperor of Karnāta[5]; and it is further said that he planted a pillar of victory on the site of the battle-field in memorial thereof.[6] From the subsequent account of Rāmabhadrāmba it is known for certain that the Toppūr battle did not bring to a close the hostilities between the loyalists and the rebels, as she says, that soon after this decisive engagement intelligence was received by the Tanjore Nayak, of the intended counter-combination of Krishnappa Nayaka of Gingee and Yatirāja, the brother of Jaggarāya. Krishnappa is said to have collected together and reorganised his forces immediately after his flight from Toppūr, and once more advanced to fight the loyalists. Raghunātha now despatched his commander with a large army, to fight the Gingee Nayaka; and he himself was encamped at Tiruvaiyār awaiting the issue of this new advance. Soon Raghunātha was informed of the success of his army, which captured the fort of Bhuvanagiri on the N. Vellar river near Chidambaram and forced Krishnappa and his ally, Yatirāja, to retire from their positions. The Tanjore Nayak, thus

1. *Raghunāthābhyudayam;* X, Sl. 25.
2. Mākarāju is identified with the chief of Kārvetinagar by Mr. H. Krishna Sastri. *Report of the Archaeological Survey of India* (1911-12).
3. *Raghunāthābhyudayam;* X.
4. *Raghunāthābhyudayam;* X, Sl. 60 to 64.
5. *Raghunātha Vilāsa Nātakam*; 4th Anka.
6. *Raghunāthābhyudayam,* X, Sl. 62. The *Rāmarājiyamu* (*Sources,* pp. 243-44) also refers to this war and the success won by Yāchama Nayaka and Raghunātha Nayaka. The war is compared to the great Mahabharata War and Raghunātha is likened to Lord Krishna.

crowned with success and immortal glory, now returned to his capital where he was received with all honours by his loyal subjects.

From the references contained in the literary sources, the date of this important battle may be fixed within reasonable limits. Vijayarāghava, in his *Raghunāthābhyudayam,* says that Raghunātha was encamped at Paḻamānēri in the month of *Āshāda* (Ādi) of the Cyclic year *Nala,* corresponding to August A.D. 1616, before he started for Tōppūr.[7] Barradas writing on December 12, A.D. 1616, says that both the armies of Jaggarāya and Yāchama Nayaka 'are now assembled in the field in the large open plains of Trichinopoly not only the hundred thousand men that each party has, but as many as a million soldiers.' It is evident from these two records that the Toppūr battle must have been fought sometime earlier in A.D. 1617[8]; and the interval between August and December 1616 was probably spent in reconnaissances before the final struggle.

The important and far reaching consequences of this historic battle can hardly be over-estimated. His victory at Toppūr made Raghunātha supreme among his fellow Nayaks and the most powerful ruler of the southern kingdoms, and the crushing defeat sustained by the rulers of Madura and Gingee was so signal that it took years for them to recover their normal strength. The death of Jaggarāya shattered their fond hopes of achieving independence; and Muttu Vīrappa Nayaka of Madura never again entertained, either an openly hostile or even an impliedly aggressive attitude towards Tanjore till his death in A.D. 1627.[9] Even Tirumala Nayaka, the brother and successor of Muttu Vīrappa, who ruled from A.D. 1623 to A.D. 1659 and who was the arch fomenter of disloyalty towards his suzerain, found himself helpless so long as there

7. Anchita Nalavatsarāshāda Suḍḍha panchami Pushyārka Parigayōga muna Swamivaru Paḻavā(mā)nēri Nagara Nāmatīrtamu, Purānasravanāmbu Rāma vigraha Pūja Rāmajapambu Sri Mūrti dānādhya sēshadāna muluga vinchi Vijayambugalu Kanakshatāha Sri Vaishnavulo sanga sīra muna dālchi Āditya hridaya japānantara muna, etc., *Raghunāthābhyudayam Nātakam.* Raghunātha is said to have left Paḻamānēri and offered battle the next day.

8. Dr. S. K. Ayyangar also places this battle early in 1617 A.D. and the accession of Rāmarāya took place in the latter part of that year. Rāmarāya of Vijayanagar by Dr. S. K. Ayyangar. *Sardesai Commemoration Volume*, p. 203. *The Aravidu Dynasty of Vijayanagara*, p. 481. Father Rubino, the master of the College at San Thomé, in a letter dated 29th November, 1617 says that the war had not come to an end by that time. Perhaps he had in mind the subsequent operations against Krishnappa and Yatirāja.

9. *The Nayaks of Madura* p. 112.

was Raghunātha ruling at Tanjore.[10] The Toppūr battle was the last great war of Raghunātha; and the immediate result of it was the re-establishment of the diminished power of the Hindu Empire under Rāmarāya, with the consequent check it gave to further Muhammadan advance for the time being. Tanjore's victory once more asserted the supremacy of the Raya and helped to keep the disruptive and disintegrating forces of insubordination and disloyalty in complete check for a time.

The successful termination of these wars, however, did not prove, in fact to be the end of all troubles for Raghunātha, since the Portuguese accounts of Queiroz, Faria Y. Sousa and Sa. Y. Menezes refer to the subsequent invasions made by the Tanjore Nayak upon the Portuguese of Jaffna.[11] Śaṇkili Kumāra, who had been placed on the throne of Jaffna by Raghunātha Nayaka in the beginning of A.D. 1616, was not allowed to rule in peace for long. There were internal risings among the Jaffnese themselves, as they were not satisfied with his administration. They could not also reconcile themselves to Śaṇkili's coming to power with the help of the foreign Nayak of Tanjore. In addition to this, Śaṇkili, perhaps relying too much upon the Tanjore Nayak's support, began to defy the Portuguese supremacy by withholding the tribute due from him.[12] The accounts of the Portuguese say that he even went to the extent of helping the Kaṇdyan king in the latter's efforts to drive away them from his land. The Kaṇdyan king, who received this help must have been Māyādunnē who, it is said, was for sometimes a refugee at the court of Tanjore before he returned to Kaṇdy towards the end of A.D. 1617[13] and successfully overcame his rival, king Sēnāret. The Portuguese after defeating Māyādunnē and capturing his capital Meddegāma, turned upon Jaffna to punish Śaṇkili. De Sa Noronha was then the Portuguese Viceroy at Goa; and in A.D. 1619 he despatched his captain, Major Philippe de Oliveira, to deal effectively with the insubordi-

10. Tirumala's policy of conquest and insubordination began only after A.D. 1634, since in that year his subordination to Venkata II, is recorded in the Kūniyūr plates. Prof. Sathianatha Iyer says that his allegiance to Venkata 'could have only been nominal.' *Ibid.*, p. 126.

11. There is no reference to these wars of Tanjore in the internal literary evidence. Perhaps the defeats sustained by Tanjore are the reasons for this omission.

12. *History of Jaffna*, p. 124. Mr. Rasanayagam referring to the year of 1619 says that 'Śaṇkili had not paid it (tribute) these three years.'

13. *The Dutch power in Ceylon*; Dr. P. E. Pieris, p. 52. *History of Ceylon*; by H. W. Codrington, p. 111. Also The Portuguese in India; F. C. Danvers, Vol. II, p. 203.

nation of Jaffna with an army of 130 Portuguese and 3000 *lascarins* (Sinhalese soldiers). Śaṇkili suffered a complete defeat at Oliveira's hands; and when he tried to escape, he was taken prisoner and sent to Goa where he was subsequently put to death. Jaffna was immediately taken possession of by the Portuguese and Oliveira was appointed the first governor of the place, with the titles of Captain General and Major in A.D. 1619-20. However, a few attempts to recover the kingdom from the Portuguese were made in the following two years by the chief of the *Kareas* (Karaiyar—a class of fishermen on the Coromandel Coast to the south of the Gulf of Manaar) with the help of the Tanjore troops. Portuguese accounts refer to six such attempts made in the years 1620 and 1621; and we learn that in every one of these, the Tamil army sent by Tanjore seems to have sustained defeats.[14]

At first, the chief of the Karaiyars rose in revolt and offered resistance to the Portuguese, with the help of a large body of men from Tanjore. Oliveira is said to have defeated him near Nallūr and the Portuguese chronicles say, that the defeated Tamils 'fell like mosquitoes.' The second attempt was made by Dom Luis (*alias* Chiṇṇa Migapillai Arāchi), who tried to enthrone a prince of Ramanaçōr in Jaffna. He obtained the help of a thousand men, who went out in twelve *dhonies* from the Tanjore coast and landing at Talaimannār, offered battle to the Portuguese in its neighbourhood. On this occasion the Tanjore Nayak claims to have sent his captain, Khēm Nayak 'who had not long before assisted Śaṇkili'.[15] He is mentioned by the name of Vāruṇakulattān by Queiroz. Varuṇakulattān has been identified by the Rev. S. Gnānaprakāsar with Khēm Nayak and he says that it was perhaps his caste name. According to the *Tolkāppiyam,* the fisherfolk of the coast country worshipped the God of the Sea; and Varuṇakulattān (he of the tribe of Varuṇa's descendants) means evidently a chief of a clan of fishermen and sailors. Oliveira sent Antonio de Mota Galvao, with a body of two hundred men and secured another victory over the Tamils. In the meanwhile, the Captain General of Colombo viewed these developments with a great deal of concern and in all haste, he sent Luis Teixeira de Mecado 'of the Seven Corlas' with four companies and five hundred *lascarins,* to Oliveira's help. Teixeira's

14. This and the following account of Jaffna are largely based upon the *History of Jaffna*; by Mr. Rasanayagam, pp. 124-130; History of *Jaffna under the Portuguese period*; by Rev. S. Gnānaprakāsar, pp. 64-75; *The Portuguese in India;* by F. C. Danvers, pp. 204-207 and *A Short History of Ceylon;* by H. W. Codrington.

15. Faria Y. Sousa, c. IV, p. 151; and *History of Jaffna under the Portuguese;* by Rev. S. Gnānaprakāsar, p. 66.

advance, which 'was more like a race than a march,' was marked by many barbarous deeds and atrocities. It is said that 'he clove men with axes like trees, opened the wombs of women and put in their children snatched from their arms.' Chiṇṇa Migappillai Arāchi and the prince of Ramanaçōr were defeated and the latter is said to have surrendered to the visitors. The attempt made by a Mudaliar, nicknamed Das Mamin-has (the heavy breasted) in this connection, was also a failure. Dom Luis, *alias* Chiṇṇa Migappillai Arāchi, escaped to India and persuaded the Nayak of Tanjore to make himself King of Jaffna. The Nayak again seems to have taken advantage of this opportunity of acquiring Jaffna, and so he sent a force consisting of two thousand Badagas across the waters. Hostilities were resumed in November 1620 with the determination 'to conquer the kingdom for the Nayak of Tanjore.' Oliveira, meeting the Tanjore army, was able to defeat it for a third time. 'The Tamils were driven back after a severe fight in which, Oliveira himself was wounded.' The Nayak of Tanjore, unmindful of these reverses, made a fresh attempt to take Jaffna 'by raising more Badagas still hoping to make himself master of Jaffnapatam'; and here again, the Tamil army 'met with a disastrous defeat from Oliveira's troops.' On the 2nd February A.D. 1621, Oliveira was at Nallūr. Soon intelligence was received that the Nayak of Tanjore 'was sending out a powerful army—this time not only to conquer Jaffna, which he claimed as his tributary fief, but also to colonise it with Indians.' Galvao, waited for the arrival of the Tanjore army at Point Pedro (Paruttiṭurai). The Tamil army was once again defeated by the Portuguese, who fell on the enemy and massacred them 'until they were weary of it.' This proved the last and the final attempt made by Raghunātha Nayaka to conquer the kingdom of Jaffna; and the Jaffnese, finding themselves helpless finally submitted to Portuguese domination.

Thus, it will be seen from the Portuguese accounts that Raghunātha Nayaka had to pursue a vigorous, but very unsuccessful foreign policy, in his attempts to recover the kingdom of Jaffna from the Portuguese hold for his protege, the prince of Ramanaçōr. The series of defeats sustained by his army at the hands of the Portuguese, must have compelled him to abandon all idea of overrunning Jaffna, after the failure of the last attempt that he made in A.D. 1621.

Nothing more is known regarding his foreign policy, as there occurred no more wars with the neighbouring kingdoms till the end of his reign. Raghunātha continued his old attitude of loyalty and co-operation towards his new suzerain Rama, as he pursued in the reign of Venkatapati Raya. He was the most powerful upholder of the unity of the Hindu Empire. The evidence of the Jesuit letters, on which Father

Heras bases his conclusion that 'Raghunātha's relation with Venkata are a little suspicious', is not easily sustainable, as it goes against the basic ideas of the Nayak's policy.[16] The Jesuit letter in point says that Raghunātha was not only disloyal, but was actively engaged in opposing the Emperor, since it is recorded that about A.D. 1610 when Venkata was besieging the city of San Thomé, Raghunātha helped the Portuguese inhabitants of that place; and Raghunātha is also said to have received a letter in appreciation of his services to the Portuguese at San Thomé, from Dom Philip III, King of Spain and Portugal. The letter which is dated 20th February A.D. 1614, is said to have been sent to the Portuguese Viceroy, Azeveda, directing him to forward it to the Nayak. Father Heras continues :—'Unfortunately neither this letter nor a copy of it has hitherto reached our (Jesuits') hands. We know only that it was sent to the Bishop of Mylapore by whom it had to be despatched to Tanjore. "The letter of your Majesty to the Nayak of Tangaor (Tanjore)" says the Viceroy in his reply to the king, "is being sent to the Bishop (of Mylapore), who will hand it over to him." This letter of the Viceroy in reply to King Philip's letter, is dated 21st January A.D. 1613 and Father Heras asserts that the king's letter was sent to Mylapore. Evidently there must be a mistake in the transcription of the dates of these two letters; otherwise how could the Viceroy write a reply to the King some twelve months before, in anticipation of a letter from the latter, and which letter he is said to have actually received only after 20th February A.D. 1614. Moreover, the contention of Father Heras will not hold good in the light of internal criticism for, if Raghunātha Nayaka should have been hostile in his attitude towards Venkatapati in A.D. 1610, then how could he have taken part in the Toppūr battle which had for its avowed object, the restoration of the Vijayanagara throne to that line of heirs, which was nominated for succession by Venkatapati? But there is evidence to show that the Nayak of Gingee was not on friendly terms with Venkatapati and since the siege is said to have taken place at San Thomē, it is possible that the Gingee Nayak might have assisted the Portuguese. Besides, the Viceroy's despatch of the King's letter from Goa to the Bishop of Mylapore, instead of sending it to Negapatam (then a Portuguese settlement) to be delivered to the Nayak of Tanjore, might also lend support to the fact that the reference contained in the Jesuit letters, was largely due to the misconception and confusion of the political affairs prevailing in the Gingee country with those of the Nayaks of Tanjore. Above all, the subsequent wars of Raghunātha with the Portuguese in the years A.D. 1614 to A.D. 1621, clearly show that he could not have been so friendly at all towards them as to offer

16. *The Aravidu Dynasty of Vijayanagara*, pp. 402 and 448.

free assistance. On either side, the evidence shows that Raghunātha's supposed insubordination and opposition to his overlord is only a figment of the misconceptions in the minds of the Jesuit fathers.

There is no doubt that his wars would have cost him a great deal of money and men; and the English Factory Records very naturally speak of his greed for wealth. What became of those conquered territories such as the dominion of Śōḻaga, whether they were annexed to the Tanjore kingdom or not is not definitely known. Dēvikōttah was most probably annexed to the Tanjore kingdom, since a letter dated 1664 refers to the Tanjore Nayak's refusal to allow the English to establish a factory at Dēvikōttah.[17] The Chronicles which refer to the imprisonment of Śōḻaga and the Pāṇdyan king, say that the latter alone was released. What became of Śōḻaga is not mentioned in them.[18] In Negapatam the Portuguese continued to carry on their trade and it is surprising to note why they were not dislodged from the place on account of Raghunātha's obvious hostility towards them. Perhaps some sort of truce might have been effected between them, by which, security must have been assured to the Portuguese by the Nayaka ; and this suggestion will remain tentative in character till we detect further evidence in this respect.

Raghunātha Nayaka's reign also witnessed the arrival of other European merchants like the Dutch, the Danes and the English on the coast. The Dutch, who had already made their appearance in the Eastern Seas and made a bid for a share in the trade of the Indian Ocean towards the close of the 16th century, were soon followed by other nations such as the Danes and the English. The Portuguese had already established themselves at San Thomé and Negapatam, while the Dutch had acquired Tegnapatam about A.D. 1610. There was keen rivalry between the Portuguese and the Dutch, who 'worked havoc to the Portuguese ships in the sea but on land the latter endeavoured by clandestine efforts to prevent the Dutch from getting a foothold.' However, the native powers sought the Dutch help to drive away the Portuguese; and the Dutch chronicles record that 'similar supplication for help from the Dutch of

17. *The English Factory Records*, 1661-64, p. 365.

18. An Inscription coming from Nodiyūr (Tanjore District: 200 of 1932) registers an annual grant of 30 *pon* made to one Vēdaṇdichōḻan of Śengilinādu as remuneration for the latter's services in having captured and killed a certain Pērichchi Sōḻagan. Since the record contains only the Cyclic year Śobakrit, the exact date is not easy to calculate. If Pērichchi Sōḻagan can be identified with Śōḻaga of Dēvikōttah, whom Raghunātha defeated and imprisoned, then the epigraph would have us understand, that he escaped from prison and fled for life. Vēdaṇdi Chōḻan might have captured this culprit while he was roaming about, and put an end to his life.

South Coromandel Coast against the Portuguese were made by the rulers of Jaffnapatam, Cochin and the Nayak of Tanjore.' The Dutch finding themselves much opposed by the Portuguese, made attempts to get a footing in the South. Bourgonji, the Dutch factor at Tegnapatam says in a letter dated 26th July A.D. 1610 that negotiations were carried on with the Nayak of Tanjore for securing a place called Triminipatam (Tirumalarāyanpattinam) and even though a *cowle* was expected from Tanjore to that effect 'no reply was received up to 7th April A.D. 1609.'[19] He also says that 'much was expected of the cloth trade at Triminipatam situated in the Tanjore Nayak's country between Tegnapatam and Negapatam. It appears from this, that the earliest attempt of the Dutch to found a factory in the kingdom of Tanjore, proved unsuccessful. The English Factory Records also show that the Nayak of Tanjore was not for according permission to erect forts in favour of the Dutch 'who were earnest suitors to the Naick to his country'. The Nayak refused to have them 'live in his country' and had demolished 'what they had begun, saying he had heard how they encroached upon other princes' dominions and countries and therefore should not live in his.'[20]

The annual return of the Portuguese and Dutch ships laden with large quantities of gold and commodities got as profits in the Eastern trade, stirred up the other enterprising nations of Europe to take to oceanic enterprise. The Danes and the French were the most important of them. The Danes appear to have visited the court of the Tanjore Nayak a few years earlier than the English. The first Danish settlement of Dansborg (Tranquebar) on the Coromandel Coast and in the kingdom of Raghunātha Nayaka, was founded on the 19th of November A.D. 1620 by Ove Geede, who was sent out to India as the commander of the first Danish fleet of four ships by King Christian IV of Denmark. But the first arrival of the Danes had already taken place sometime earlier when Roelant Crape, a Dutchman, in the Danish service 'was received with thirteen of his men graciously by Ragnādo (Raghunātha Nayaka) of Tanjore.'[21] The foundation of the Danish settlement

19. *The Dutch Beginnings in India*, T. I. Poonen, Chapter VII.

Triminipatam is the modern Tirumalairājanpatnam situated in the Nannilam Taluk of the Tanjore District. It is located between Tranquebar and Negapatam in Linschoten's map. See also the map of India by Sanson d'Abbeville (1652).

20. *The English Factory Records, Vol. II,* (1622-23) p. 337.

21. J.R.A.S., 1898, p. 625. The Danish settlement of Tranquebar—Donald Ferqusson. The author disproves the date of 1612 assigned for the foundation of the Danish settlement of Tranquebar and mentioned in the *Imperial Gazetteer* as it is too early for it.

of Tranquebar took place by mere accident as it were. The Danish East India Company was started in Copenhagen (Denmark) under the patronage of King Christian IV, as early as A.D. 1616 but it took two years for the Company to fit out an eastern expedition. In their early voyages the Danish Company, for want of their own men with sufficient knowledge of the trade routes in the Indian Ocean, had to employ the services of the Dutchmen, who were available; and the sending out of two of their ships in the course of A.D. 1618 was largely due to the exertions of a Dutchman, Marcellus de Boschowver, who went on a political mission to Holland.[22] Boschowver finding that he could get no help from the Dutch, as the Batavian government was preoccupied with their schemes regarding the acquisition of Moluccas, turned to Denmark in November 1617 which was now determined to set out an expedition in order to trade with the East, consequent of the successful end of their war with Sweden in A.D. 1603.[23] Boschowver on behalf of the Kaṇḍyan king negotiated a treaty with the king of Denmark with forged credentials. As a result of this treaty the '*Oeresund*' started first with Roelant Crape on August A.D. 1618 and this was followed after three months by Ove Geede, who set out with four vessels, the '*David*' and the '*Elephant*' provided by the King and the '*Christian*' and the '*Copenhagen*' belonging to the Company. Roelant Crape reached the coast of Ceylon and informed the Kaṇḍyan King of the news of the forthcoming arrival of Ove Geede. Roelant Crape being persuaded by King Sēnāret of Kaṇḍy to enter into hostilities with the Portuguese, captured a number of small Portuguese junks laden with rice and arecanuts. The news of Crape's success soon reached the ears of Andre Boetelho de Costa, who was the Portuguese Governor of Jaffnapatam; and becoming enraged at this, he at once despatched six galleys 'to chastise the interlopers'. Crape, who was then anchoring near Karikal was suddenly attacked by the Portuguese fleet, and in his attempt to escape he was stranded near the coast. Crape taking along with him the remaining thirteen of his crew, swam across to the shore and made his way to

22. Boschowver, the Dutchman who was in Ceylon promised help to King Sēnāret of Kaṇḍy in the latter's attempt of driving the Portuguese out of his kingdom. He sailed to Tegnapatam A.D. 1613 to get help from the Dutch Factors there, but finding no help forthcoming, he sailed to Holland. Even there he could not get help from the Government and so to fulfil his promise given to Sēnāret, he negotiated with the King of Denmark using forged credentials since Sēnāret never gave him power to negotiate with the Danes. Boschowver, who sailed along with Ove Geede to the East, died on his way and the dead body was interned in Ceylon.

23. *J.R.A.S.*, Vol. 30, p. 169. *The Danes in Ceylon;* Dr. P. E. Pieris.

Tanjore, where they were given protection by the Nayak. Ove Geede, landed in Ceylon in May A.D. 1620 and found to his great disappointment that the king of Kaṇḍy was then in friendly relations with the Portuguese and besides, Boschowver's credentials were also discovered to be unauthorised fabrications made, on his visit to king Sēnāret. However, Geede made use of the king's desire to win the Danes to his side, and made a treaty by which Trincomali was formally ceded to the Danish Crown. Geede then sailed towards the Coromandel Coast to know more about Crape of whose previous misfortune, he had heard already in Ceylon. Geede visited the court of Raghunātha Nayaka and concluded a treaty in November 1620 as between the Danish Company and the Nayak by which, Raghunātha permitted the Danes, without any objection on his part to supply materials, to build a fort at Tranquebar and to trade freely with his subjects. Geede appointing Henrick Hess to be the commandant of the fort and Crape to an equally important post, then sailed away.[24] The fort at Tranquebar constructed by Geede 'is a quaint old structure in the Gothic style and quite baronial in appearance in spite of modern restoration.'[25]

The foregoing account clearly shows, that the arrival of the Danes in Tanjore and their founding a settlement in the Nayak's country happened without any previous plan; and the Nayak's help to Crape at the hour of distress when his life was in danger, his offering them help and permission to build a fort, are not without significance and importance in the history of the Eastern Commerce in general and in the Nayak's relation with the Portuguese in particular. Within a short time the Danes were able to gain ground and compete effectively with other European nations in the eastern market; and an English letter dated A.D. 1621[26] refers to their prosperity in trade. The letter records that 'this coast is not yet freed of all the Danes' and the building of a small fort at Tranquebar is also mentioned. By August 27, A.D. 1622 the fort at Tranquebar had been strengthened and fortified and President Fursland writing to the Directors of the English East India Company says 'that the Danes trade under the name of the English and are marvellously well used. He

24. Fenger: *The Tranquebar Mission*. This little book gives detailed information about the founders of Tranquebar which was known in an inscription of a Paṇḍya, as Sadangapadi and subsequently as Tarangampadi (wave-village) —[*Editor*].

25. *The Annual Report of the Archaeological Department*, Southern Circle, 1912-13, p. 09.

26. Letter from Methwold to the Company. *The English Factory Records*, Vol. I, Introduction and p. 266.

(Nayak of Tanjore) has given them a town and a place to build a castle which is finished and hath thirty-six pieces of ordnance mounted therein.'[27]

A similar attempt to establish a factory in the Nayak's territory was made by the English in the year A.D. 1624. But their negotiations ended in failure consequent upon the Nayak's demanding a large sum and a heavy rent as well, for their proposed factory at Karikal. About A.D. 1622 The English had their factories at Masulipatam and Pulicat on the Coromandel Coast; but the unprofitable trade carried on at the latter place led the Presidential Council at Bantam to order the dissolution of the Pulicat factory, on July 11, A.D. 1623.[28] Another reason that contributed for the immediate abandoning of Pulicat was the fact 'that Coromandel cloth will not be required in future as long as they discontinue their trade with Moluccas'. Another letter refers to the wrongs done by the Dutch to the English at Pulicat, as they were also in possession of that place under the patronage of the local governor Yatirāja, the brother of the rebel Jaggarāya, the victim of the Toppûr battle. The Dutch and the English at Pulicat made joint efforts to procure Indian cloth in sufficient quantities for purposes of export, but the Dutch appear to have insisted 'on the strict dividing of the cloths received in accordance with the respective proportions of the two Companies' investments, but making the English pay their full share of the expenses.' In A.D. 1622 information was sent to the Superior Council at Bantam that the Nayak of Tanjore was very desirous of opening trade with the English and this news was communicated to the Directors in England by Brockedon, the President of the English settlements in the East and also of the Council at Bantam, towards the close of A.D. 1623.

Brokcedon in his letter[29] says that "the prince of Tanjore of those parts has often invited us to live in his country promising great privileges and favours and now by the *Ruby* (which reached the coast on November 23, from Batavia) there is come an Englishman Johnson, who came out master of one of the first Danish ships, who has lien about 18 months at the Nayak's court as a pawne for the pepper first sent home by the Danes, who reports the Naick having heard the English to be a peaceable nation that seek not to encroach on other men's territories was earnest with him to move into us the favourable opinion he had for our nation and great desire that we should trade in his dominions

27. *The English Factory Records*, edited by Sir Foster, Vol. II, p. 117.
28. *The English Factory Records*, Vol. II, Introduction, pp. 37 and 38.
29. Letter from President Brockedon from Batavia to the East India Company dated, December 14, A.D. 1623 *The English Factory Records*, Vol. II, p. 337.

wherefore understanding that better cloth of all sorts is made there than at Pulicat and Masulipatam and pepper likewise to be gotten in reasonable quantities; we have resolved to send a ship thither within these three months to make trial what good may be done in those parts. The Portugals have lived long in his country but without fortification, he taking their protection upon him and offers the like to us or to fortify as the Danes have done. The Dutch have been earnest suitors to the Nayak to fortify in his country and had begun a fort at Tegnapatam,[30] but the Nayak refuses to have them live in his country and has demolished what they had begun saying he had heard how they encroached upon other princes' dominions and countries and therefore should not live in his." The decision to send a ship to the coast of Tanjore was arrived at on the strength of a letter written by an Englishman, John Johnson of whom we have again an account preserved in a letter dated 4th March A.D. 1622,[31] and written by Johnson himself. John Johnson came out to India in A.D. 1620 as a sailor in the *Christian* of the Danish fleet and found his way to the court of the Tanjore Nayak along with the Danes, when the latter negotiated with Raghunātha for obtaining Tranquebar. Soon, Johnson and another Englishman Richard Hatfield by name, found themselves stranded alone with no money or provisions to find their way home or to reach the nearest English factory. Johnson himself says in a despatch to the President that he was staying at Tanjore quite against his own will. In the same letter he wrote for money, giving information regarding the possibility of founding an English settlement in the Tanjore Nayak's country. He says 'the great Naick demands of men what the reason is that the English do not desire to trade in his land as well as the Portugal, saying that they shall have pepper and anything the land doth afford and likewise buy those commodities that they do bring with them as tin, lead, iron and red cloth is well sold. Little does our nation know how they are expected all this land, therefore the Danes do trade under the name of the English and are marvellous well used...... " In the following year, Johnson seems to have made his way from Tanjore to Masulipatam and thence reached to Batavia.[32] He moved the President at Bantam to send a ship to Tanjore where the English, he said, would soon have a prosperous trade in pepper and large quantities of excellent calico. He also mentioned the Dutch attempts to establish a factory in Tanjore Nayak's territories and the refusal of the Nayak to allow them that freedom. These representations and the Nayak's anxiety to receive

30. Tegnapatam, the modern Fort St. David, belonged to the Nayak of Gingee and not to Tanjore.

31. *The English Factory Records*, Vol. II, p. 51.

32. *The English Factory Records*, Vol. III, Introduction, p. 39.

them and grant them favourable terms tempted the English Council at Batavia to send a ship, the *Hart,* to the Nayak's port of Karikal under the captaincy of Thomas Bickley with Joseph Cockram, a member of the Council as 'chief factor' and four assistants.[33] The stock was fixed at 52,000 rials, 4/5 of which was to be invested in pepper and the rest in calicoes. A letter was also sent to the Nayak requesting his gracious treatment of the factors and the concession of necessary privileges. John Johnson went as pilot.[34]

President Brockedon wrote on January 17, 1624 to the Company, of his intention to send the *Hart* to the place which the Danes have fortified on the Coast of Coromandel, saying that good clothes and paintings and store of pepper may be had in abundance. He had also referred to the invitation of the prince of that country and to the fact that the Danes in a week's time had laden 3 or 4 hundred tons of pepper, and that the Portuguese bought almost all their clothes in their country (Tanjore). Regarding the ruler of that country, he says 'he is accounted the most warlike prince in all those parts, an observer of justice and will protect all those that trade in his country.'[35] The *Hart* left Batavia on March 27, 1624 accompanied by the *Unity,* which was to go to Masulipatam. The President wrote also a personal letter to the ruler of Tanjore, which runs as follows:—"They trust that His Highness's letter to their agent at Masulipatam (lost by the latter's negligence) will excuse this abrupt coming to him before they could commend his gracious favours into their own sovereign and since they have learned by Mr. Johnson's relations his good inclination towards their nation, they have despatched the bearer Mr. Joseph Cockram with the aforesaid Johnson to offer their service in the accommodation of the commerce, that it may for ever remain inviolable a band of amity between the houses of Tanjore and Great Britain. Their intent is only to transport such commodities of his kingdom as can conveniently be spared to furnish, in return for such English and other goods as one wanted and one in their power to supply. They

33. They were George Brewen, John Cartwright, Richard Robinson and Edward Powell. George Brewen was to be left behind as principal of the proposed English factory on the Tanjore Coast.

34. *Ibid.,* Vol. III, p. 39. Also *Consultations held at Batavia,* March 2, A.D. 1624.

35. *Consultations at Batavia,* Vol. III. The letter written by Raghunātha Nayaka inviting the English was conveyed to Thomas Mills at Masulipatam by Johnson. That the letter was not sent to Batavia is seen from the reprimands made by the President to Mills for keeping that letter.

do not doubt his Majesty's gracious favour for the grant of necessary privileges on which point the bearer is empowered to negotiate."[36]

On the same day, the President also issued instructions to Joseph Cockram and others for setting up a factory at Tanjore. The letter containing those instructions is as follows:—" On arrival at Śerical (Karikal) a *caul* (cowle for safe conduct) is to be procured from the governor before landing. Mr. Johnson or some other should next be sent to the Nayak to procure a farman 'that you may come safely unto him,' which being granted, you shall present him with our letters and such presents as we have sent and demand the grant of suitable privileges. The *Unity* is to be sent on to Masulipatam within 5 or 6 days of their arrival with advice of cloth likely to be procured at the new settlement. No attempt should be made to build a factory house until they should be satisfied that the trade is worth pursuing. 'The chief thing we aim at is the procuring of large quantities of pepper wherefore if pepper be extra ordinary dear or but little to be gotten, we hold it unfitting to remain there unless the place afford extraordinary good cloth and good cheap and that there be hopes to vend quantities of our English commodities which you are especially to inquire after.' 'To be cautious in landing goods until well assured of the Nayak's affection; also in giving credit to the Natives. We are informed there is a great *commitie* (kōmati) in the Naick's country named Malaya[37] which we make account will be your merchant and will undertake great matters. He showed himself very honest in his dealings with Mr. Mills at Pulicat, yet by dealing with inferior komatis, You shall better understand the market and know how to bargain with Malaya with more certainty.' To be especially careful in choosing good colours as there is much deceipt in the red (the most usual colour); also in seeing that the goods correspond with the sample. Packing should not

36. *The English Factory Records*, Vol. III. A copy of this letter is found in the *Factory Records* at Java.

37. Mallai or Mallaya *alias* Chinniah or Chenana Chetti, was an influential merchant through whom the Dutch had been conducting their transactions with Indian traders, weavers, etc. The Dutch assisted Mallai, who had been made to supersede Damarla Venkatappa Nayak. some years later, *i.e.*, after the founding of Madras; and he became after 1644 the effective master of the coast country round Madras. Mallai played the decayed Raya against the Dutch and *vice versa*. Mallai had a large body of soldiers under him and took part freely, frequently changing sides, in the struggles of the Raya, the advancing Muhammadans and the Europeans of the coast. One of his dependents was Seshadri Chetty of Porto Novo who subsequently rose to be the chief Indian merchant at Madras. Mallai had even a small fort at Tegnapatam. He was a prominent figure in the politics and trade of the coast for nearly half a century. [*Editor*].

be carried on in moist weather while the clothes are still damp.[38] They must look vigilantly to the delivery of the goods at the time appointed, and must have packing materials prepared in time. Should the Nayak be very earnest for a piece of ordnance, they may spare him one of the ship's guns 'with all his furniture'. Keep good correspondence with the Danes and the Portugals, but trust them not and have as little conversation with the Portuguese as may be for, they are exceeding treacherous and will poison you if you eat with them. As our people by oweful (woeful) experience in Siam have made trail (trial) with the loss of their lives. Mr. Johnson may be left at the new factory or not as may be found expedient; but he is not to be trusted with the Company's cash. Two Portugal women and men sent in this ship are to be landed at Negapatam or San Thomé and an endeavour to be made to procure the release of Mrs. Forbisher. Should it be decided to leave a factory Mr. Brewen is to be chief, John Cartwright second and Richard Robinson third with four or five Englishmen. If sufficient pepper be not obtained the *Hart* should be despatched to the West Coast of Sumatra for a supply and so to Batavia. While in port the sailors are to be allowed 'four fresh meals the week either fish or flesh and if butter be dear let them have salt fish to eat with their rice.' You may entreat the Nayak's favour to bring from thence 15 bricklayers that have skill to lay 'plaster of Paris' (chunam) and fifteen coolies to labour which you shall buy though they cost 20 rials per piece or upward. And lade as much plaster of Paris (pallist) and tiles aboard the *Hart* as she can conveniently take in for, we shall have great occasion to use them. Private trade is to be rigorously suppressed." The same day John Bicklay also received instructions for the voyage from the President which says, that the ship must stop at the Sunda Islands to cut wood for the intended factory at Serical (Karikal). "Mr. Johnson would guide them to the latter port. Authority to help the mariners and to help the merchants. Not to meddle with the Portuguese while in the ports of the Nayak but in going or coming he is to endeavour to capture any Portuguese vessels he may meet. A piece of ordnance to be given to the Nayak if necessary. The ship to go to Sumatra if lading of pepper cannot be obtained at Karikal. Thirty (blackmen) to be procured at the latter place. Not to remain beyond the end of September except in an emergency. To stand always on his guard. The sailors etc. are not to buy any goods at Karikal until the merchants have agreed with the kōmatis as to price." The President sent also presents, which were to be made over to the Nayak and they included two *Demiculverins.*

38. This clause was necessitated by the fact that the Factors at Jambai complained about the bad condition of the goods got from the coast. Vol. III, p. 12.

On May 21, A.D. 1624, the ships sighted Tegnapatam and the *Unity* shortly after, set sail to Masulipatam. The *Hart* coasting along the south, passed the Danish fort of Tranquebar and anchored at Karikal on May 23 1624. On the next day the Captain went ashore and was received by the governor of Karikal, who at once despatched to Tanjore the news of the arrival of the English ship. While the English were awaiting a reply, the Danes made two attempts to frighten them away, alleging that they held an exclusive concession from the Nayak for all the ports between Negapatam and Pulicat. Joseph Cockram and Bickley with courage returned defiant answers and the Danes themselves, immediately afterwards, sailed away quietly when the English captain hoisted the British flag. On June 8, in response to an invitation from the Nayak the English departed for Tanjore, where they were all given a warm reception both by the Nayak and his nobles and were 'by the Nayak by his own mouth promised free trade and that they should have the port of Karikal at an easy rate. But the Portuguese and the Danes were greatly against it and most cruel enemies.' The latter it is alleged gave the Nayak great bribes and when Cockram was confronted with a demand for a yearly payment of 7000 rials of eight, for permission to use the port of Karikal, he could not accept the outrageous demand and broke off the negotiations and returned to the *Hart* on July 9. The English were the less disposed to satisfy the Nayak's greed for money as they found the pepper of the country to be limited in quantity and of 'a very sort and that always much wet with fresh water in portage from the upland mountains.'

The *Hart* visiting Tranquebar and calling at Tegnapatam, anchored off Pondicherry on July 19. The Governor of the District came on board and invited Cockram to settle a factory in that port. Cockram is said to have told him, that the English would visit Pondicherry next year with the necessary permission to found a factory. The *Hart* sailed again on August 3 and four days later reached Masulipatam where the *Unity* lay, being condemned and not fit for further voyaging. Remaining there till October, the *Hart* reached Batavia on November 20, 1624. Johnson was blamed for deluding the English in the business of Tanjore and he was mulcted of his wages. But Johnson on his going to England and on making an appeal to the Board of Directors, got back his wages by justifying his action.[39]

39. The foregoing account is drawn from the *English Factory Records* Vol. III, 1623-29. The English decided to send a ship to Pondicherry on January 12, 1625 but the troubles that ensued prevented further attention. A letter received by the Company in 1626 states that the Danes had intercepted for paintings (painted cloths). A Dutch letter from Pulicat written towards the close of 1625 mentions that the

From this account, it becomes evident that the first attempt of the English to get a foothold in the Tanjore Nayak's country for purposes of trade proved a lamentable failure. The causes that led to the despatch of the *Hart* to Tanjore, were to procure large quantities of pepper which was reported to be in abundance and to purchase cloth only if it is of 'good quantity and sort and also cheap.'[40] According to the report of Johnson 'sufficient quantity of pepper to lade the *Hart* may be had in three months at 18 rials per *bahar* (Bāram ?) of about 330 lbs.' And the reasons for the abandoning of the settlement at Karikal are recorded in John Goring's Diary, which refers to the country's yielding 'but little pepper of a very small sort and that always much wet with the fresh water in portage from the upland mountains.' The Nayak also, was found to be 'very coveteous expecting very great presents yearly', besides the payment of 7000 rials as rent for the port of Karikal, which 'he would appoint for us.'[41]

Berckley's account of the same voyage contains valuable and interesting information. He says that the failure of the English was largely due to the intrigues of the Danes, who bribing the Nayak, poisoned his mind against them. Berckley adds that the Nayak's demanding 7,000 rials as rent was due to 'the Danes being the cause thereof.' 'As for the king, he cares not who it be that has his ports to rent so he may have them what he will demand for he is for all what you will give him and so are all his great men.' The rivalry of the Danes, who were enjoying a considerable amount of influence with the Tanjore Nayak, was the main cause for the failure of the English and the records show that the Danes had even gone to the extent of influencing the governor of Pondicherry, under the Nayak of Gingee, as to prevent the English from founding a factory there. The Factory Records of this period show that the trade of the Coromandel Coast was carried on in a large measure by one Malaya Chetti, a rich kōmati, who had his house and godown at Tegnapatam.

Raghunātha Nāyaka's later years of rule were a period of comparative peace and tranquillity, marked by the absence of bloody wars and internal troubles. The kingdom did not seem to have suffered any dimi-

Danes had endeavoured to procure calicoes at *Pouls Cera* (Pondicherry) and Porto Novo and a subsequent letter says that the Danish merchants left at both places, had been imprisoned by the Nayak.

40. *The English Factory Records,* Vol. III, p. 12.

41. The English agreed to pay 3,000 rials of eight as rent for the port of Karikal.

nution in its extent and the presence of Raghunātha's epigraphs beyond the limits of the Tanjore district, show his rule and supremacy over the neighbouring territories. His powerful hand seems to have extended as far as Tirukkōshtiyūr in the Ramnad District,[42] Lālgudi in the Trichinopoly District,[43] Gōvindavādi in the Chingleput District[44], Nedungunram and Nārattampūndi in the North Arcot District.[45] His records at Nedungunram where his ancestors and now his agent Śonādriayyan are said to have made gifts to the local temple show again the close association of the Tanjore Nayaks with that place. The presence of the Tanjore Nayaks' epigraphs and especially those of Raghunātha at Nedungunram has led the Government Epigraphist to suppose that Raghunātha 'was a governor under Venkata in some portions of the North and South Arcot Districts.' There is also another inscription[46] found at Nedungunram and it is dated in the cyclic year Tārana. The record which registers a gift of land to the temple of Dharmaputtirar at Nedungunram by the inhabitants of the village and by one Tiruvambala Pillai, who is termed as the deputy of Timma Nayak and the agent of the king, is issued in the name of Vijaya Raghunātha Nayaka. If Vijayaraghunātha Nayaka can be identified with Raghunātha Nayaka, then the cyclic year would correspond to A.D. 1584. In that case this record will be the earliest of Raghunātha's epigraphs. The Government Epigraphist has assigned this record to A.D. 1644 and in that case, it will refer to Vijayarāghava Nayaka. Since it is not known whether Vijayarāghava was also called Vijaya Raghunātha, the supposition of the Government Epigraphist, that Raghunātha was viceroy under Venkata would require further confirmation before it can be safely accepted. However, epigraphs of both Achyutappa and Raghunātha show that they had agents at Nedungunram.[47] Tiruvannāmalai, where we have Śevappa and Achyutappa's records has none of Raghunātha Nayaka.

The inscriptions of Raghunātha Nayaka refer to a number of agents, who were, in all probability, in charge of small administrative divisions. His great minister Gōvinda Dikshita, figures largely in his epigraphs and in one of them he is called Pradhāni and in another he is termed as the agent of the king.[48] Ellappa Nayaka, son of Mādaiya Nayaka is mention-

42. 308 of 1923 dated Saka 1529. Tirukkōshtiyur.
43. 151 of 1928 from Nattamāngudi (Lalgudi Taluk)
44. 40 of 1923. Gōvindavādi.
45. 705 of 1904 from Nedungunram and 379 of 1925 from Nārattampūndi.
46. 112 of 1924. Also A.R.E. 1924 and 1925.
47. 705, 706 and 709 of 1904.
48. 331 of 1923 and 290 of 1927.

15

ed as one of his agents, in an inscription found at Achyutamaṇgalam.[49] Achyutamaṇgalam is perhaps the same village called Achyutasamudra *alias* Arivīḻimaṇgalam which was given away as gift to Vijayīndra Tirtha by Achyutappa Nayaka. One Naraśingarāja, who made an assignment of thirty *pon* to the Nodiyur temple from the amount payable to the palace by the villagers for worship of god, was another agent.[50] Koḻundappar was a third agent of Raghunātha and he is said to have made provisions for feeding Brahmans and celebrating some festivals in the Tirukkōshtiyūr temple in A.D. 1607.[51] Mādayya Nayaka, son of Mallappa Nayaka, was also his agent at Srīvāṇjiyam. He is said to have made a gift of certain taxes in favour of the dancing girls (dēvaradiyār) attached to the temple in lieu of services.[52] Tattapillai was another agent[53] besides one Narasinga Dikshita, who is mentioned in aṇ epigraph coming from Nārattampūndi and dated in A.D. 1614.[54] A record from Nāchchiārkoil[55] dated Saka 1540 is interesting as it refers to an official of the king called *Aṭṭavaṇai* (accountant). *Aṭṭavaṇai* Raṇgappayyan built a mantapa to the goddess, for the merit of Raghunātha Nayaka. Apart from these gifts made by the King's agents, the numerous benefactions made by the Nayaka himself are also known. An Inscription from Nārattampūndi (North Arcot District) dated A.D. 1604 and issued in the name of Venkatapati Raya, refers to a *sarvamāṇya* gift (free of all taxes) of an entire village called Kailāsapuram to god by Raghunātha, for his own merit.[56] Another record coming from Kōttūr (Mannargudi Taluk) registers a gift of ten *velis* of land by the same Nayaka and the purpose for which this grant was made, is not to be traced since it is damaged.[57] The epigraphs also stand testimony to his impartial patronage of Śiva and Vishnu temples and other religious faiths. Raghunātha is said to have honoured the great Madhwa teacher Sudhīndra, the successor of Vijayīndra, with Kanakābishēkam (bathing in gold).[58] The patronage extended to Christian Frang merchants and their being allowed to settle at Negapatam and Tranquebar, show his broadmindedness and tolerance.

49. 412 of 1925.
50. 194 of 1932.
51. 308 of 1923.
52. 77 and 78 of 1911.
53. 57 of 1923.
54. 371 of 1925.
55. 286 of 1927.
56. 379 of 1925.
57. 465 of 1912.
58. *Sources: Rāghavēndra Vijayam*; Canto II, Sl. 53.

The *Raghunāthābhyudayam* and the *Sāhityaratnākara* refer in glowing terms to the numerous gifts made by him. Rāmabhadrāmba says that the water poured as libations in giving away the numerous gifts by the king (*dānōdhaka*) flowed down like a river, and she adds that the water thus poured out collected in the moat round the Tanjore fort. Yagnanārāyana Dīkshita gives a detailed account of the many and costly gifts made by the Nayaka on the day of his coronation.[59] He says that he performed the *Tulāpurushadāna* (weighing against gold) twice and distributed them among the Brahmans. Gifts of precious stones and jewels were distributed even among those who were disabled. In addition he performed the great gifts called *Hiraṇyagarbha* and *Mahābhūtagata*: Cows made of gold were also given away as gifts and all paraphernalia that go to make kingship were also gifted away. Apart from this he also founded numerous *agraharas*, where he settled learned Brahmans well-versed in all the Vedas. The author says that his gifts even surpassed the presents mentioned in Hēmādri's *Dhānakāṇda* (a work enumerating the gifts to be made). Rāmabhadrāmba says that on every day he gave large and rich presents as soon as his morning prayer and worship were finished. Gōvinda Dikshita in his introduction to the *Sangīta Sudhā* says that Raghunātha often performed the *Tulāpurushadāna* and with his gifts the Brahmans felt happy. He also speaks of the agraharas founded by him and each was composed of a thousand families. Raghunātha is said to have fed countless Brahmans daily.[60] The temples also were carefully looked after. The *Sangīta Sudhā* and the *Tanjāvūri Andhra Rājula Charitamu* give credit to Raghunātha for building the Rāmaswamy temple at Kumbakonam.[61] And the former adds that he also built temples for Rāma at Rāmēswaram and Srirangam. The gopura of Lord Kumbhakōṇēswara (Kumbhēswara) at Kumbakonam and a maṇtapa also are said to have been built by him. Raghunātha is praised for his interest in the celebration of Rathōtsavams (car festivals) to the gods Jalpēsa at Tiruvaiyar and Dhēṇunātha at Paśupatikōil.[62] It is also claimed that he added buildings to the temples of Srinivāsa sthala (identified with Uppiliyappan koil in the Kumbakonam Taluk) and Champēsa (Mannargudi).[63] He continued all the charities established by his predecessors and instituted many new ones.

59. *Sāhityaratnākara*; Canto XII, Sl. 62 to 93.

60. *Sangīta Sudhā*; Sl. 57 to 60.

61. Dr. S. K. Ayyangar says that the temple was built in commemoration of his victory and of the anointment of Rāmarāya as the rightful emperor.

62. *Sangīta Sudhā*; Sl. 54 to 56.

63. *Sources*; 268.

The literary works give a fine picture of Raghunātha Nayaka's towering personality,[64] his military exploits and literary attainments. Raghunātha was an expert in the art of sword play,[65] a fine marksman and a skilled master in the art of horse riding[66] The remarkable skill with which he handled the various weapons of war is also spoken of very highly. His victories over his enemies stand as testimony to his military accomplishments. He was also a great scholar in letters (*sāhitya*) and music (*sangīta*) and a renowned poet in Sanskrit as well as in Telugu. He had also a profound and deep knowledge of Daṇḍanīti[67] (political science). The *Sāhityaratnākara* refers[68] to his early education when Raghunātha is said to have learnt the alphabets, by writing them on a board strewn with precious stones. Yagnanārāyana Dīkshita says that Achyutappa Nayaka's putting Raghunātha to study at a very tender age was not very much liked by his queen Mūrtimāmba.[69] Raghunātha exhibited wonderful scholarship and learning and became famous as an author as well very early, and it is said that he was able to compose a Kāvya called *Pārijāthāpaharaṇam,* within two *yamas.* He is said to have written a good number of Kāvyas, Prabhandas and Yakshagānams in Sanskrit and Telugu. Rāmabhadrāmba says that he was unequalled in the art of verse-making and poetic composition and his knowledge of the various vrittas (meters) and prasthavanas was well-founded.[70] The most important of his works in Telugu are *Pārijāthāpaharaṇam, Vālmīkicharitam, Rukmaṇīpariṇaya Yakshagānam,* and *Rāmāyanam* while his Sanskrit works include *Sangīta Sudhā* and *Bhārata Sudhā.*[71] He was also a great authority on the science of Music and is deemed to be the founder of Karnatic Music. The *Sāhityaratnākara* refers to his skill in playing different tunes on the Veena and which he learnt while a youth.[72] The *Sangīta Sudhā* says that he was the author of new *rāgas* like Jayantasēna and new *tāḷas* like Rāmānaṇda, and he also taught music to others. The authorship of the *Sangīta Sudhā,* an important work on Music, has not been definitely settled. Raghunātha is held to be the author of this work to which Gōvinda Dikshita wrote an introduction. Verses 71 to 76 of the introduction to the *Sangīta Sudhā* refer

64. *Sāhityaratnākara;* Canto VI, Sl. 43 to 60.
65. *Raghunāthābhyudayam;* Canto III, Sl. 27.
66. *Sāhityaratnākara;* Canto V.
67. *Raghunāthābhyudayam,* Canto VIII, Sl. 35 to 46.
68. *Sāhityaratnākara,* Canto V, Sl. 1 to 40.
69. *Sāhityaratnākara:* Canto IV, Sl. 66.
70. *Raghunāthābhyudayam;* Canto III, Sl. 13 to 16.
71. *Sangīta Sudha;* Sl. 62 and 63. Also *Tanjavūri Añdhra Rājula Charitamu;* Introduction by Mr. V. Prabhakara Sastri.
72. *Sāhityaratnākara;* Canto V and VI, 10 to 28.

to Gōvinda Dīkshita's request made to Raghunātha to write this treatise in *dvipada* metre and publish it so that, all might enjoy it. Veṇkatamakhi's reference in his *Chaturdaṇḍiprakāsika,* that *Sangīta Sudhā* was written by his father, Gōvinda Dīkshita, at the request of Raghunātha, has led some to think that the whole was the work of the Dikshita himself,[73] but was given out in the name of the Nayaka. Neither of these views is impossible since both Raghunātha and Gōvinda Dikshita were reputed musicians and taking the two versions together it may be said without much fear of contradiction that the work was written by Raghunātha in collaboration with his minister, Gōvinda Dikshita. The work can claim the joint-authorship of the Nayak and his minister.

As Raghunātha himself was a renowned scholar, it is but natural that he should extend his patronage to other scholars and poets. The *Raghunāthābhyudayam* and the *Sāhityaratnākara* speak in laudable terms of his patronage shown to men of letters. Numerous poets and poetesses flourished in his court. Raghunātha is called an ocean of learning where, the learning of pundits who were equally renowned; is said to have formed the rivers that flow into that ocean. Rāmabhadrāmba says that Tanjore became the seat of Vāṇi (goddess of learning) and even the small children of the royal harem were noted for their versatility and keen intellects. Yagnanārāyana Dikshita refers to the king's gifts and costly presents to the poets and musicians (*Kavi budha gāyakābhimata Kalpataru*) and the Nayak is likened to the Kalpa tree noted for its large bounty. His benefactions to learning and patronage of pundits must have made his name so familiar in the land, as to attract other learned men to his court. Among them the visit of Koṇda Kōnaṇgi Kavi Chowdappa, the court *vidwan* of Mātla Anantarāja, to the court of Raghunātha is important[74] and the poet is said to have expressed his surprise and admiration of the remarkable talents of the literary men who fitted his court. Among the galaxy of his famous poets, the names of Gōvinda Dīkshita, his two sons, Yagnanārāyana Dikshita and Veṇkatamakhi, *alias* Veṇkatādhwari, Rāja Chūdāmaṇi Dīkshita, Bhāskara Dikshita and Kumāra Tātāchārya,[75]

73. *Chaturdaṇdiprakāsika.*

74. *Tañjāvūri Andhra Rājula Charitamu,* Vavilla Edition, Introduction, p. 28.

75. His active life extended from about A.D. 1575 to A.D. 1630, as gleaned from lithic records. He was the grandson of Tōlappācharya. He was the Rajaguru of the Imperial family and perhaps crowned Venkata II in 1630 (Saka 1552). He had also to his credit the gilding of the Ānandanilaya Vimana of Sri Venkatēsvara at Tirumalai and also the Kalyānakōti and Puṇyakōti Vimānas at Conjeevaram (*see* The Tirupati Davastanam Epigraphical Report by S. Subrahmanya Sastri (1930)—pp. 312-13). [Editor].

Rāmabhadrāmba and Madhurāvāṇi are important and they figure more prominently. Each has written a number of works. Yagnanārāyana Dīkshita says that his master was the Nayaka himself and the *Sāhityaratnākara* was written to record his gratitude and regard for his master from whom he learned the Sāhityaśāra.[76] He was well versed in Vēdānta, Tarka and Mīmāmsa.[77] Rāmabhadrāmba the poetess, was also an equally gifted and talented scholar and writer, who was much favoured by the king. She bore the distinguishing titles of Śatalēkhini (one who could write a hundred venes) Samaśamayalēkhini and Aṣtabhāshā lēkhini (one who knows evident who could write in eight languages) and one who had ascended possible of literary domain (*Chaturvida Kavitānu pranita Sāhitya Sāmrājya bhadra pitārūdaha*).[78] She was the pupil of one, Kālayya.[79]

This revival of literary activities must have reached its zenith in the latter part of Raghunātha's reign, when the country returned to peaceful conditions after a series of wars. Most of the works must have been written only after A.D. 1617. At any rate that the *Sāhityaratnākara*, the *Sangita Sudhā* and the *Raghunāthābhyudayam* were written only during this period is evident from their contents. Rāmabhadrāmba referring to Raghunātha's return to Tanjore after the battle of Toppūr speaks of his durbar that was held and was attended by numerous poets who were proficient in eight languages.[80] Mention is also made of the fact that the king sent regular despatches and news-letters from the field of battle to the capital, regarding the progress of his operations[81] The poets and poetesses are mentioned as writing the history of his wars in all possible languages.[82] Since these works record his victories over the Pāṇḍya and other enemies, it is certain that they were composed only after 1617. Even though the *Sāhityaratnākara* is not available in its complete form, yet evidence is not wanting to prove that portions of the complete work were lost. Chēmakūru Veṇkata Kavi,

76. *Sāhityaratnākara;* Canto I, Sl. 62.

77. *Sāhityaratnākara;* Canto I, Sl. 52. The author calls himself as one well versed in the Vēdas and Sāstras and belonging to the school of literature nurtured by the grace of Raghunātha Nayaka. (*Prauda Sri Raghunāthabhūpati Kripāspārita bavōtsāhita sāmrājya nigamāgamārta nipunaha Sri Yagnanārāyanaha.* (Colophon).

78. *Raghunāthābhyudayam*; Colophon.

79. Kalayya refers to his pupil in his *Rājagōpālavilāsa*.
Also *Raghunāthābhyudayam*; Introduction, by Dr. T. R. Chintamani.

80. *Raghunāthābhyudayam;* Canto XI, Sl. 24 to 28.

81. *Raghunāthābhyudayam;* Canto XI, Sl. 54.

82. *Raghunāthābhyudayam;* Canto XI, Sl. 55 to 79.

the author of *Vijaya Vilāsam* dedicated to Raghunātha Nayaka, tells us that the great Nayaka took interest in theatricals and there was also a theatre in the royal palace in which plays were enacted in the Nayak's presence. The *Raghunāthābhyudayam* of Vijayarāghava Nayaka tells us that such plays were enacted in the palace theatre before the king, who was in the habit of holding very frequently pandita parishads, at which learned men as well as women, competed with one another in exhibiting their attainments. It is said that on those occasions, the king asked the poets to set śmasyas (the art of verse making with given words) to the young ladies assembled in the court. Rāmabhadrāmba seems to have come out successful on one occasion.[83] It was during his glorious reign that the southern school of Telugu literature noted for its special contribution of the Yakshagāna type of drama had its origin. A great impetus was given to learning in all languages and in particular to Telugu and Sanskrit.

Raghunātha Nayaka was a great ruler, a profound scholar and a liberal patron. By his learning and patronage, wars and victories, he earned an immortal name and lasting glory. The *Vijayavilāsam* and the *Sāhityaratnākara* give him numerous titles and distinguishing birudas such as *Abhinava Bhōja, Sōḷaga māna banjana, Nēpāla Nripāla sthāpana samara nisṣanka, Karnātaka prabhu sukha pradaha, Saurya dairyaha* and *Sāhitya Bhōja.*[84] If indigenous works give him so much praise for his learning and patronage of arts, contemporary foreign evidence gives him an equally high place among the powerful rulers of the land and praise his even handed administration of justice and protection of foreigners. If a foreigner should speak of Raghunātha 'as the most warlike prince in all those parts, an observer of justice and (one who) will protect all those that trade in his country,' no further testimony woud be needed to show his greatness.[85] The same high praise is given to him by a later writer on Tanjore, who calls Raghunātha Nayaka as the 'Solomon of his age in wisdom and the Absalom of his time in personal beauty.'[86] An image bearing a torch in the Chakrapāniswāmi temple at Kumbakonam is taken to represent Raghunātha Nayaka, but this identification will have to remain provisional since authorities are not agreed. Some hold it that it represents

83. *Raghunāthābhyudayam*, Introduction
84. *Vijayavilāsam*. Also *Sāhityaratnākara*; Canto II, Sl. 71.
85. *The English Factory Records*; Vol. III. Consultation at Batavia. Letter from President Brockedon to the East India Company, dated January 17, A.D. 1624.
86. *The Maratha Principality of Tanjore; the Eden of the South* by W. Hickey.

Achyutappa Nayaka, while still others conclude on a closer examination, that it must represent a Vaishnava devotee and nothing more.[87] The end of his reign will be considered in connection with the accession of Vijayarāghava Nayaka, his successor.

87. *The Tanjore Gazetteer*, p. 218 says that it resembles Achyutappa. See also V. Rangacharya; *Inscriptions of the Madras Presidency*, Vol. II, 1235.

CHAPTER VII.

GŌVINDA DĪKSHITA

Neither the rule of the Tanjore Nayaks in general, nor the reign of Raghunātha Nayaka in particular, would be complete and full without a reference being made to Gōvinda Dīkshita, the illustrious Brahman minister of the kingdom. Gōvinda Dīkshita was minister to both Achyutappa Nayaka and his son Raghunātha, and it was to him that these two Nayaks owed a large measure of their successful and glorious rule. The Dīkshita played a very prominent part in the good administration of the country, and it may be said that his fame even eclipsed that of the Nayaks. If Raghunātha Nayaka could be compared to the great Krishnadēva Raya of Vijayanagar, Gōvinda Dīkshita may well be ranked with the latter's minister, Sāluva Timma. Gōvinda Dīkshita's name is still green in the memory of the people of the Chōḻadēśa and the generation that is fast disappearing, speaks of his greatness and fame as an administrator, as an erudite scholar and as an able minister besides, his high sense of justice and fairness which were all brought to bear upon his high office of minister His meritorious services with which he enriched the people and the land as well, are held in much esteem even at the present day.

The existence of numerous villages and streets besides other memorials, named after him, stand testimony to his greatness and to the regard which the people and the rulers had for him and his personality. The villages of Gōvindapuram, Gōvindakudi, Ayyampēt and the streets known as Ayyaṉkadai street in Tanjore, Yāgasālai street in Kumbakonam and tanks such as Ayyaṉkuḷam, all these are monuments that go to commemorate his name. In spite of all these remembrances, it is really an irony of fate that very little should be known authentically of such a great person, who lived and played a considerable part in maintaining the prestige of the Nayak rule. In the temple of the village called Pattīswaram in the Kumbakonam Taluk, there stands 'in oriental majesty and grandeur, a statue of this great minister dressed in the state garb with the long robe and with the curious head-dress of the day.' Besides him stands in like manner the magnificient statue of his wife. And Liṅgās called Dīkshitaliṅgas, are still worshipped in the temples of Kumbēswara at Kumbakonam and Panchanadīswara at Tiruvādi (Tiruvaiyar). Whether these Liṅgās are consecrated by the Dīkshita himself or established in his name, are questions that remain

16

to be settled. But all the same, nothing definite is known about him and his early life, beyond the traditional accounts which though interesting, are so varied as not to admit of easy verification. Pattīswaram and Tirunāgēswaram in the Kumbakonam Taluk and Tiruppaḷāttu-rai in the Pāpanasam Taluk, are held by the people as places, where he lived and spent his life. The statement that he lived at Pattīswaram and went to Tanjore daily in his palanquin to discharge his duties as minister, looks not only improbable but incredible considering the distance of the place and the importance of his high office.[1] However, the historical remains of a statue and the ruined site shown as the place where his house once stood, as well as epigraphs and the present custom of a section of the community called *Paṭṭunūlkārar* going to Pattīswaram to settle their minor differences before the shrine of Gōvinda Dīkshita even now,—all these support the statement that in all probability he might have lived and spent his last days at Pattīswaram or it might have been a favourite place of residence of his.

The literary evidence of this period contains only casual references and from them a good account cannot be made of him. Even Yagñanārāyana Dikshita, the son of this famous minister and the biographer of Raghunātha Nayaka, does not give a full account of his father, though he shows in many places that his father was associated with the government of the Nayaks, during the reigns of Achyutappa and Raghunātha. But as regards the minister's early life, it is not possible to derive any knowledge from his son's references. Tradition has it that Gōvinda Dīkshita was a Kannada Brahman belonging to the Vasishṭa gōtra and Āśvalāyanasūtra and that he migrated to the Chōḷa Country about the middle of the 16th century. Even of this, there are two versions. One version says that Gōvinda Dīkshita, a Kannada Brahman, was noted even as a young man, for his remarkable knowledge of Hindu Sāstras and Astrology. He is said to have been born of very poor parents; and so to find employment he made his way to Vijayanagara at the early age of seventeen. There, he soon became a favourite of Achyutarāya, (A.D. 1529 to A.D. 1542). Gōvinda Dīkshita's first meeting with the Rāya is said to have taken place about A.D. 1532, when he went to the royal palace along with several astrologers who had been summoned by the Rāya, to cast the horoscope of a child that had just then born to him. Achyutarāya was very much impressed by the Dīkshita's deep

1. An account of Gōvinda Dīkshita embodying all the traditions and stories is given in an article entitled *Gōvinda Dīkshita* by Mr. N. K. Venkatesam Pantulu, in the *Journal of the Andhra Historical Research Society*, Vol. II, pp. 220-241.

knowledge of astrology, showered on him his favours and employed him in his service. When Achyutarāya gave Śevappa Nayaka, the principality of Tanjore and appointed him to be its governor, the latter is said to have taken along with him, his former master and friend, Gōvinda Dīkshita.[2] It is even claimed that the Nayaka requested Gōvinda Dīkshita to accept the governorship of the province, but the latter excused himself by saying that he, being a Brahman, should not encroach upon the right or *dharma* of a Kshatriya, whose duty it was to wield the sceptre. And so he helped Śevappa to become the ruler and himself became his minister. It is said that he continued to be minister of the state for more than the duration of the rule of Śevappa and Achyutappa and even unto the reign of Raghunātha.[3] Another version, says that he was a Kannada Brahman and was born of poor parents in Mysore, and he migrated to Vellore, where he took service under his uncle, who was the rāyasam (secretary) of the Ārni Nayaka. Later he was transferred to the Tanjore Samasthānam, when a daughter of this poligar was married to a prince of the Tanjore line. Here, in Tanjore, he rose to prominence and became the minister of state. Neither of these accounts is supported by the literary evidence nor by the epigraphic testimony, but the fact that he was a Kannada Brahman and a great scholar is beyond doubt.[4] The rest of the tradition of his rise to power cannot withstand internal criticism; for one thing, the epigraphs prove the impossibility of Śevappa being a servant of Gōvinda Dīkshita and the former's rise to prominence through him.[5] Apart from this it is also

2. An account of this traditional story is given in Chapter II. Also *Sāhitya-ratnākara*, Introduction by Dr. T. R. Chintamani.

3. An apt parallelism may be traced between the long ministerial career of the Dīkshita at Tanjore leading to the consolidation of the State and to an increase in its prestige and the remarkable services of Ariyanātha Mudaliar, the co-adjutor and Daḷavāy of Visvanatha Nayak, the founder of the Madura Nayak kingdom. He was for over 50 years the "second in power" in the State. Ariyanātha was especially responsible for the organisation of the Pālaiyam system in the Southern Tamil country, and the poligars were specially attached to Ariyanātha and his memory. In one grant his name is associated along with that of the Nayak himself (of 1560 A.D.). Ariyanātha was the Daḷavay and Pradhāni of the State; and his equestrian statue in the Pudumantapam at Madura and the thousand-pillared hall in its great temple are "substantial relics of his importance". Both Ariyanātha and Gōvinda Dīkshita were roughly contemporaries and engaged in work of the same character and both were responsible for the consolidation of the two great Nayak States of the south.—[Ed.].

4. The Kaṇṇada origin of Gōvinda Dīkshita is established by the fact that His Holiness Srī Saṅkarāchārya of Kāmakōti Pīṭha in his *pūrvāśrama* belonged to this family and he is of Kaṇṇada origin.

5. See Chapter II.

obvious from a study of the records that Gōvinda Dīkshita could not have been minister to Śevappa, the first Nayaka. Gōvinda Dīkshita is mentioned only once in the records of Achyutappa and Raghunātha and the earliest inscription mentioning him by name, is dated A.D. 1588.[6] This record registers a gift made by the Nayaka for the merit of Gōvinda Dīkshita. The literary evidences of *Raghunāthābhyudayam* and the *Sāhityaratnākara* also speak of Gōvinda Dīkshita only during the reign of Achyutappa and Raghunātha and not before. If Gōvinda Dīkshita had any association with Śevappa, at least his son Yagñanārāyana would have made mention of it. Moreover, Gōvinda Dīkshita's migration from Vellore is not also supported by internal evidence, since there is nothing to prove the marital alliance of the Tanjore Nayaks with the house of Ārni. Hence these traditional accounts are of no material help to the historian.

Mr. N. K. Venkatesam Pantulu[7] says that Gōvinda Dīkshita began his career as minister under the first Nayak Śevappa and continued in office through the reign of Achyutappa; and he also was of help to Raghunātha in the early years of his reign. He does not support the statement contained in the *Tanjore District Manual* which says that Gōvinda Dīkshita also lived during the time of Vijayarāghava Nayaka, the last ruler; on the ground that this supposition was consequent on the writer of the *Manual* identifying Achyutappa Nayaka, the second ruler, with the last king, called Vijayarāghava and Achyuta Vijayarāghava in the records. He further adds that this view is incredible when between Śevappa and Vijayarāghava, there was an interval of a century and there was no possibility of his having lived for such a long time. The literary evidence also proves the impossibility of Gōvinda Dīkshita having continued as minister under Vijayarāghava. The *Chaturdaṇḍi prakāśika* distinctly says that Vēṇkatēswara Dīkshita, one of the sons of Gōvinda Dīkshita, was Vijayarāghava's minister and so the father was evidently dead by that time. Therefore the question of Gōvinda Dīkshita's early association with Śevappa alone remains to be settled. Mr. Venkatesam Pantulu says that his early association with Śevappa is established and quotes two inscriptions in support of his statement.[8] He takes the word 'Śevappa Nāyakkarayyan' occuring in

6. 119 of 1930.

7. *The Journal of the Andhra Historical Research Society*, Vol. II, 1928, p. 223.

8. *Ibid.*, p. 224.

one of them[9] to mean both Śevappa Nayaka and his minister Gōvinda Dīkshita on the ground, that the latter was called Ayyan out of respect. Ayyan, he further adds, is derived from the Sanskrit word Ārya which means 'worshipful.' This argument is not only inconclusive, but also untenable. Unfortunately, one of the epigraphs produced by him for our consideration, does not contain either the name of Śevappa or his minister; while the second inscription which was issued by Achyutappa records that he was the son of Śevappa; (*Śevappa Nāyakkarayyan Achyutappa Nāyakkarayyan Tanjāvūr taṭṭārukku kodutta dharma sāśanam*) and that he made a gift to the goldsmiths of Tanjore. The reference to Śevappa Nāyakkarayyan must be taken to refer to Śevappa Nayaka alone and not to mean himself and his minister. Gōvinda Dīkshita is also called in his epigraphs as Dīkshitarayyan and the Tanjore records give the rulers the appellation of Ayyan added to their names. Mr. Venkatesam Pantulu, who reads the word Śevappa Nayakkarayyan as referring to two distinct individuals, *viz.*, the Nayak and the Ayyan, in order to prove the association of Gōvinda Dīkshita with Śevappa, is not inclined to read and interpret in the same manner the epigraphs of Vijayarāghava Nayaka, which contain references as Vijayarāghava Nāyakkarayyan.[10] In that case, it must be said that Gōvinda Dīkshita also lived during the reign of the last Nayaka Vijayarāghava; but Mr. Pantulu says that he could not have been minister to Vijayarāghava; and hence his view of Gōvinda Dīkshita's association with Śevappa from the epigraphs, remains to be proved. The argument that Gōvinda Dīkshita was not associated with Vijayarāghava, on the ground that the former could not have lived for more than a century, applies equally to the statement that he was associated with Śevappa very early. Because, Gōvinda Dīkshita's latest epigraph is dated A.D. 1634 and if he should have come to Vijayanagar in his 17th year corresponding to A.D. 1532, before the rule of the Nayaks began at Tanjore, then it would give him a very long life of more than a century; and this is also extremely impossible.[11] There is also no literary evidence to establish Gōvinda Dīkshita's early association with the administration of Śevappa. The *Sangīta Sudhā* alone contains a reference to prove that

9. The epigraphs referred to are, Achyutadēva Raya's inscription recording a gift of land by Taṭṭappa Nayaka, son of Mallappa Nayaka to Toppāram Kētta Pillaiyar and 22 of 1897 dated Saka 1499 and issued by Achyutappa Nayaka in favour of goldsmiths. Mr. Venkatesam Pantulu basing his conclusion on the traditional evidence, works out the epigraphs to suit his conclusion.

10. 513 of 1918 and 709 of 1904.

11. According to tradition he came to Vijayanagar in his 17th year and his first meeting with Achyutarāya took place about A.D. 1532 when a son was born to him. Gōvinda Dīkshita had then Śevappa as his servant.

Gōvinda Dīkshita was in the court of Śevappa and here, this fact is given out by Gōvinda Dīkshita himself, when he praised Raghunātha and brought to his notice that even his grandfather had predicted in open court that he (Raghunātha) would become a great ruler. This appreciative reference is said to have been made by Śevappa, when Raghunātha was a tender child interested in play.[12] This statement would only prove that the Dīkshita was present in Śevappa's court only from the latter part of his reign, since Raghunātha, his grandson is mentioned as having been a child then.[13] Even Yagñanārāyana Dīkshita speaks of his father's association only with Achyutappa Nayaka and his son, and not with his predecessor. From the *Sāhityaratnākara* it is known for certain that Gōvinda Dīkshita was minister to Achyutappa; and the latter took his advice on all matters relating to the internal and foreign policies of the state. Gōvinda Dīkshita attended the war council held by Achyutappa on the eve of the great Karnataka civil war of succession, and it was he, who helped in the coronation of Raghunātha Nayaka and the abdication of Achyutappa. Gōvinda Dīkshita is said to have also crowned Raghunātha and performed his *Pattābhishēka* ceremony. He taught Raghunātha the science of politics and other śāstras and claimed him as his pupil. Raghunātha Nayaka's march upon Sōḻaga and other enemies was the result of Gōvinda Dīkshita's wise counsel. When Raghunātha started on his expedition, he is said to have left the administration in the hands of Gōvinda Dīkshita Raghunātha Nayaka's confidence in his minister and the great regard which he had for his learning and experience in administration, are fully borne out by Yagñanārāyana Dīkshita in his references in the *Sāhityaratnākara* as well as in several places in the *Raghunātha Vilāsa Nātakam.* According to the evidence contained in the latter work, it appears that when a drama was enacted in the palace theatre both Raghunātha Nayaka and Gōvinda Dīkshita were seated together on the same seat. Yagñanārāyana Dīkshita also speaks in glowing terms of the victories won by the Nayak and of the high reputation enjoyed by his father, Gōvinda Dīkshita. These references go to show that Gōvinda Dīkshita continued to live during the reign of Raghunātha; and the same internal evidence proves that he did not survive in

12. *Sangita Sudhā*, Sl. 48.

पूर्वं समेतां वयमत्रयुष्मत्पितामहं चेव्वमहीमहेन्द्रम् ।
आशीभिरानन्दयितुं तदग्रे त्वय्यादधानेखुरलीषु केलिम् ॥
तदाभवन्तं सविलोक्यहर्षादस्मान्मुदावाचमिमामवोचत् ।
अस्माकमेतेन भवेत् प्रतिष्टा धर्तुंसमर्थश्च स एष राज्यम् ॥

13. *Sangita Sudhā*, Sl. 49.

the time of Vijayarāghava Nayaka. Venkaṭamakhī, another son of Gōvinda Dīkshita and the author of the *Chaturdaṇḍi prakāsika,* says that he wrote the work at the instance of Vijayarāghava, when he was minister to him for some time. If Gōvinda Dīkshita continued to live then, Venkaṭamakhi would have mentioned him. Since the latest epigraph[14] of Gōvinda Dīkshita is dated in A.D. 1634, it is certain that he lived till then. His earliest record is dated in A.D. 1588[15] and so, his association with the government of the Nayaks will have to be mainly based on the evidence of the epigraphs, between A.D. 1588 and A.D. 1634. This period does not include the years which he spent in the court of Śevappa, whose death had taken place about A.D. 1580. Since Śevappa is said to have seen his grandson, Raghunātha, playing as a boy, Raghunātha's birth may be placed in or about A.D. 1575. As Gōvinda Dīkshita bears witness to Śevappa's blessing the child Raghunātha, it is probable that Gōvinda Dīkshita had then already settled at Tanjore. Since he says that he was one of those, who were assembled at the durbar hall when Śevappa expressed his high expectations of Raghunātha, it is possible to surmise that he had not then become the minister of state, but was probably employed in the palace as the royal *purōhita.*[16] Hence under the present circumstances, Gōvinda Dīkshita's association with the administration of Tanjore may be broadly held to have lasted from A.D. 1575 to A.D. 1634, and in this period of nearly six decades, he was serving the Nayaks in a double capacity both as their 'Kulakūṭastha purōhita' (family priest) and 'Kula manṭri.'

From the foregoing account it is evident that Gōvinda Dīkshita, a Kannada Brahman hailing from the Mysore country made his way to the court of the Tanjore Nayak during the last years of Śevappa, the first ruler; and he was well received and respectfully treated on account of his profound scholarship and deep learning. Soon the Dīkshita made his mark there and rose to be the royal purōhita, then to that of a tutor to the prince and lastly to the high office of minister solely by dint of merit.[17] Achyutappa Nayaka's great regard for this minister is best seen in his records referring to the gifts made by him for the merit of Gōvinda Dikshita. Raghunātha Nayaka's veneration for and gratitude to his minister were something extraordinary, since Gōvinda Dīkshita was also

14. 257 of 1927.
15. 119 of 1930.
16. The *Sāhityaratnākara* refers to Achyutappa's request made to Gōvinda Dīkshita to fix an auspicious day for the celebration of Raghunātha's coronation. *Sāhityaratnākara,* Canto X, Sl. 103. Also Canto XII, Sl. 46. Here Gōvinda Dīkshita is called Guru.
17. *Sāhityaratnākara:* Colophon.

his teacher. And in the later years of Raghunātha's reign which witnessed the revival of literary activities, Gōvinda Dīkshita must have also played a prominent part; but of this we have no direct evidence.

Gōvinda Dīkshita was an orthodox Brahman and he is said to have performed numerous sacrifices. Tradition says that he never neglected to perform Agnihōtra (daily fire worship) and was never wanting in the strict performance of *dharma* as enjoined in the Vēdas and Śāstras. Yagñanārāyana Dīkshita speaks of his performing the *Sāgnicitya*, the *Vājapēya* and the *Sarvatōmukha* sacrifices and in the performance of the *Vājapēya* sacrifice he was assisted by the Nayaka, Raghunatha, who it is said, held the umbrella over his head. The Yāgasāla street and the Yāgamantapa at Kumbakonam are even now pointed out as marking the places, where Gōvinda Dīkshita performed these sacrifices. It is also said that he made large gifts and benefactions on the occasion of the completion of these sacrifices; and his great gifts numbering sixteen (*Ṣōdaśa mahādānas*) and his gift of a village in the name of each tithi (15 days of a *paksha*) are also well known. The modern village called Ēchchangudi *alias* Ekādasī Agrahāram and the village called Mahādhānapuram, Mulliakkudi *alias* Dīkshita Samudra and important streets called Mahadhāna streets, in the towns of Mayavaram, Tiruvidaimarudur and Tiruvaiyar besides others, are all pointed out as great gifts made to the Brahmans on such occasions. Gōvinda Dīkshita's name is even now associated with the repair and construction of the sixteen mantapas on the bunds of the Mahāmakham tank at Kumbakonam.[18] It is said that the Nayak, who was pleased with the Dīkshita for his charitable endowments, gifted to him a quantity of gold equal to his own weight for further repairs. Gōvinda Dikshita is also spoken of as the builder of several Pushyamantapas at different places such as Tiruvaiyar, Kumbakonam, Tiruvidaimarudur, Tiruvaḷanjuḷi and Vriddhāchalam. As Achyutappa Nayaka also is mentioned by the Dīkshita as the builder of these maṇtapas at these places,[19] it is possible that these works were carried out at the instance of Gōvinda Dīkshita. The Rāmaswāmi temples at Kumbakonam, Vijayarāghavapuram and Srirangam were erected during his time.[20] The temple at Pattīswaram is said to have received large gifts as well as additions made to its precincts. He is mentioned as the builder of the Āchāravāśal, and the Anaṇtakalyāna maṇtapa of the Sāraṇgaswāmi matha at Kumbakonam in A.D. 1631[21] and also the Turaikkāttuvār

18. A.R.E., 1926-27, p. 117.
19. *Sangīta Sudhā*.
20. A.R.E. 1926-27.
21. 270 of 1927.

mantapa in the Viḷanagar temple situated in the Mayavaram Taluk.[22] Apart from these magnificent charities and public works, tradition has it that he also devoted much attention to the cause of education. The Rājā Pātasala at Kumbakonam traces its origin to the bounty of Gōvinda Dīkshita; and several institutions for the teaching and propagation of the Hindu Śāstras and Vēdas were also maintained by him. Even though Sanskrit learning enjoyed special favour, yet the growth of and fostering of the Tamil literature and culture do not seem to have suffered at all for want of patronage either royal or otherwise. Gōvinda Dīkshita himself was responsible for the translation of the *Tiruvaiyār Mahātmyaṃ* into Tamil about A.D. 1605.[23]

In addition to being a good administrator, Gōvinda Dīkshita was also a renowned author. He is said to have written commentaries on the *Jaimini Sūtras* and *Kaumārila Daṛsana* besides the *Sangīta Sudhā*. He is called *Advaita Vidyācharya*; and Yagñanārāyana Dīkshita says that he was not only proficient in the Advaita Philosophy, but had a thorough knowledge of the six systems of philosophy (Shad darsanas). Vēṇkatēswara Dīkshita (or Vēnkaṭamakhi), another son of this great minister says that his father reestablished the Advaita school of Philosophy of Śri Sankara and he was the elder contemporary of the great Advaita scholar, Appayya Dīkshita. Both of them are said to have made efforts to propagate advaitism.[24] While Gōvinda Dīkshita completed his *Kaumārila Daṛsana* (a commentary on Kumārila Bhatta's *daṛsana*), Appayya Dīkshita wrote in comment, his *Parimala* at the former's instance. Appayya Dīkshita's reference to an *Advaita Vidyāchārya* in his *Siḍḍhāntalēsa Saṇgraha,* is taken to mean Gōvinda Dīkshita himself, for whom the author had a high regard.[25] Gōvinda Dīkshita was also very proficient in the science of music and may well be called the founder of Karnātic music. Vēnkaṭamakhi says that the *Sangīta Sudha* was in reality written by his

22. 164 of 1925.

23. There is a passage in the *Tiruvaiyār Purāṇam* which reads:

மலிபுணல் சூழ்சோணாடு தஞ்சையிற் காத்திருமாசர்
மதியமைச்சர் ஒலிமறைதேர் கோவிந்த தீட்சதராயன்
திருவாக்குடைமையாலே, கலியுகத்துச் சகராண்டு
மூவைஞ் ஞூற்றிருபதின்மேல் காணுமேழாய்பொலி
வருடத்தை யோற்றுப் புராணவடமொழி தமிழாய் புகலுற்றேன்

24. *Gōvinda Dīkshita* by Mr. N. K. Venkatesam Pantulu, *Ibid*.

25. Gōvinda Dīkshita is wrongly called the author of *Harivaṃsa Charitam* composed of twenty-three cantos on the ground, that the author of this work is also called Gōvindamaṇtrin. But this is not possible since the latter is said to have belonged to Sāṇdilya gōtra whereas Gōvinda Dikshita belonged to Vasishta gōtra. (See The Tanjore Sarfoji Maharaja's Saraswathi Mahal Library Catalogue edited by Prof. P. P. S. Sastri.)

father.[26] Both Yagñanarayana Dīkshita and his brother Vēnkaṭēswara Dīkshita were all good musicians and the latter is given credit for his standard work on music the *Chaturdaṇḍiprakāsika*,[27] wherein he had "reduced the old twenty-two *svaras* to twelve and designed the present *Vīna* adapted to the twelve *svaras*." "It appears also that Vēnkaṭamakhi was the author of the *Mēḷakarta* that is in vogue at present in Southern India." Gōvinda Dīkshita was also the author of a work on Astrology, since reference is made to his work in the *Tāṇdava Mālai*.[28] The contemporary works say that Gōvinda Dīkshita had numerous titles such as *Pada vākya pramāṇa pārāvāraha* and *Advaitāchārya*. He was also known by other names as Gōvinda Ādhvari, Gōvinda Yajva and Gōvinda Makhindu.

From the colophon to the *Chaturdaṇḍiprakāsika*, it is known that Gōvinda Dīkshita's wife was called Nāgamāmba, the daughter of one Nārāyana Dīkshita.[29] Gōvinda Dīkshita is said to have been the father of eight sons, of whom only two are well known. Yagñanārāyana Dīkshita has won immortal fame by his works, the *Sāhityāratnākara*, the *Raghunātha Vilāsa Nātaka* and the *Alankāra Ratnākara*; and he also performed the *Sāgnicityā* and the *Sarvatōmukhā* sacrifices.[30] He studied both under his father Gōvinda Dīkshita and his patron Raghunātha, who taught him all the Sāstras including *Vyākarana, Tarka, Mīmāmsa* and *Vēdānta*. His brother Vēnkaṭēswara[31] was also an all round genius and wrote a number of works. The *Vārtikābharaṇam*, a commentary on the *Tuptika* of Kumārilaswāmi is classified along with other important works on *Mīmāmsa*. He also wrote the *Karmānta Vārtika*, a commentary on a portion of *Bōdhāyana Srauta Sūtras, Sulba Mīmāmsa*, a treatise on

26. ततोनु रघुनाथेन्द्र मेलविनानिरूप्यते तल्लक्षणं नु सङ्गीत सुधानिधिरिति श्रुते । चेव्वमाच्युत भूपालरघुनाथ नृपाङ्किते अस्मचातकृते ग्रन्थे प्रोक्ता श्लोकांलिखामितान् ॥

Chaturdaṇdiprakāśika.

27. The work is not available in its entirety.

28. Report on the Sanskrit and Tamil Mss. for 1896–97, Madras. The introduction of the *Tāṇdava Mālai* says (pp. 261 and 262):

இன்னூலென்னூலின் வழித்தெனின் 'மாவிந்தை சோதான் மலரடி வணங்குங் கோவிந்த தீட்சிதீயத்தின் வழித்து' எனவும், கோவிந்த தீட்சிதர் தங் கொள்கையினுற் கூறுகின்ற மாவிந்த நூலின் வழக்கறிந்து தேவிந்திசர் போற்றும் பிண்டியஞ் செல்வன் சீர்கூறி வருவணப்பா வையன் வந்து.

Also the *Journal of the Andhra Historical Research Society*, Vol. II, p. 237.

29. 'Sri Gōvindadīkshita Nāgamāmba vara tritīya nandanasya.'—*Chaturdaṇdiprakāśika*.

30. Colophon to the *Sāhityaratnākara*.

31. He calls himself as the third son of Gōvinda Dīkshita in his *Chaturdaṇḍiprakāsika*, Colophon.

Vēdic Trignometry and also *Sangīta Sāmrājya.* But he is well known by his great work on Music, the *Chaturdaṇdiprakāsika.* He was also the teacher of Rājachūdāmani Dīkshita, the author of *Rukmaṇī pariṇayam*[32] and of Nīlakaṇta Dīkshita, a grand nephew of Appayya Dīkshita. One Liṇgādhvari, the author of *Sivasahasranāmabhāshya* and *Vēdartha ṭatva nirnaya* is said to have been a third son of Gōvinda Dīkshita.[33] Rājachūdāmani Dīkshita in his *Taṇtraśikhāmaṇi,* a work on the *Jaimini Sūtras,* says that Vēnkatamakhi also performed several *yagñas.* Nīlakaṇta Dīkshita, the author of *Siva Līlārṇava* and *Gangāvatarana Kāvya,* speaks of Vēnkatamakhi, his master, as belonging to Vasishta gotra and as the son of Gōvinda Dīkshita.

Gōvinda Dīkshita also appears to have been an authority in *Dharma Sāstras* and also a permanent court of arbitration. His administration of even-handed justice is recorded in an inscription coming from Pattīswaram. The epigraph is dated in the cyclic year Bhava, corresponding to A.D. 1634; and Gōvinda Dīkshita is called by the venerable name of Gōvinda Dīkshitaswāmi. The record registers a settlement made by him when the *paṭṭunūlkārars* (Saurashtrian weavers) presented him with a petition (Vaḷakkumuṛai) as a result of some differences arising in social matters. It appears that there was some difficulty in the order of precedence in the distribution of betel and nuts among the weavers and the merchants (Chettis). Gōvinda Dīkshita hearing both sides. seems to have arbitrated and settled the question amicably;, but the exact terms of the settlement are not known. The agreement reached among them by making a person liable to offer a new cloth worth five fanams and 30 arecanuts and 100 betel leaves to the goddess of the local temple, if he should transgress the rules, shows clearly that the settlement was made satisfactorily to both the contending parties, who are said to have made up their minds to observe this rule by making a vow in the name of the king.[34] This record is also the latest so far known of him and this would show that he was living till A.D. 1634. Since Vēnkatamakhi says that he was for some time the minister of Vijayarāghava (accession 1633) it is probable that Gōvinda Dīkshita died shortly after his accession. This is further supported by the fact that no more reference is made to Gōvinda Dīkshita in the contemporary literature. Even Yagñanārāyana's name is not mentioned in the reign of Vijayarāghava Nayaka. The absence of any mention of these two

32. Vēnkatamakhi is also said to be the author of *Jātaka Chandrika*—a treatise on Astrology. This has been translated into English by Mr. B. Suryanarayana Rao.

33. *Sāhityaratnākara,* Introduction by Dr. T. R. Chintamani.

34. 257 of 1927.

names or their whereabouts in the works of Vēnkatamakhi and in the Telugu works of Vijayarāghava, has led some writers to think that both of them must have died about the same period[35] and how far this view is correct, will have to be determined by future research.

Gōvinda Dīkshita's association with the administration of the Nayaks, is also taken as the cause for the latter's patronage of Saivism. Since the Nayaks were all Vaishnavas by their religious persuasion, it is said that their patronage of Saivism was made possible only by the powerful influence of Gōvinda Dīkshita, the great Advaita scholar of the times. Even though his influence over them cannot be undervalued, yet the statement that he was responsible for their catholicity and religious toleration remains to be well established; since the Nayaks in general do not seem to have ill-disposed towards or persecuted any of the rival faiths. Gōvinda Dīkshita, though not a native of Tanjore, soon became one; and a review of his life which starting from humble and poor circumstances soon attained to the zenith of power and honour; shows the high regard and esteem which the Nayaks had for learning and scholarship. His rise to power was made easy by the royal patronage and favour and the high sense of duty, honesty, loyalty and charity which Gōvinda Dīkshita had in abundance, were responsible for his ultimate success as a great administrator. These qualities made him a hero of the day and when he died, the people deified him. It is popularly believed that he spent his last days in the Maṇgalāmbika shrine at Kumbakonam, performing severe penance.

35. Mr. K. Sitaramayya: *The Tanjore Andhra Nayaka Charitam*, p. 252.

CHAPTER VIII.

VIJAYARĀGHAVA NAYAKA.
(A.D. 1633 to A.D. 1673).

I

Achyuta Vijayarāghava Nayaka[1] better known as Mannārudāsa[2] and as Vijayarāghava, was the son of Raghunātha Nayaka and succeeded his father on the throne. For his reign and for the subsequent period, there is available only the evidence of the native chronicles and of the Jesuit letters. With regard to the date of his accession, his epigraphs which are few and far between, remain silent, while the chronicles mention no date at all. Raghunātha Nayaka's inscriptions show, that his rule must have extended down to the year A.D. 1634 since a record of his, dated in the cyclic year Bhava corresponding to A.D. 1634 refers to a vow made by two communities at the feet of Nayakkarayyan, who was no other than Raghunātha himself.[3] The same epigraph mentions Gōvinda Dikshita also and since it is known for certain, that Gōvinda Dīkshita did not continue as the minister to Vijayarāghava also, the reference to Nāyakkarayyan must be taken to mean Raghunātha, and hence the latter ruled as king for about twenty years from A.D 1614 to A.D. 1634, but his association as co-ruler with his father, dates back atleast from A.D. 1600. Considering the duration of all the individual reigns of the Tanjore Nayaks, it becomes evident that Raghunātha, the most illustrious ruler of this family had but a relatively short reign and his death will have to be placed about A.D. 1634.

It is not known for certain whether he nominated his successor in his own life time and performed the *Yauvarājyābhishēkam*. The internal evidence contained in the *Raghunāthābhyudayam* of Vijayarāghava[4] says that he (Vijayarāghava) performed the sixteen great gifts (shōdasa mahādānas) on a day in the year of his coronation. Chengalvala

1. 461 of 1922 from Papanasam is recorded in the name of Achyuta Vijayarāghava Nayaka. Also *Mannārudāsavilāsam*, page 2.

2. Father Proenza in his letter dated 1659 says that the Nayaka called himself as the son of God Mannāru of Mannārgudi, *La Mission Du Madure*, Vol. III, p. 51.

3. 257 of 1927 from Pattiśwaram (Tanjore District). The Inscription is dated in the cyclic year Bava which corresponds to A.D. 1634.

4. *Sources of Vijayanagar History*, p. 255.

Kālakavi, the author of *Vijayarāghava Vaṃsāvali*[5] and the court poet of Vijayarāghava, has recorded that these sixteen great gifts were made in the cyclic year Srīmukha and in the month of Srāvaṇa; corresponding to August-September, A.D. 1633. These two statements taken together prove that Vijayarāghava's accession must have taken place in the year 1633 and that it was celebrated sometime before the death of Raghunātha.[6] Mr. K. Sitaramayya also agrees with this date and says that Vijayarāghava's coronation took place in A.D 1633. This date is further supported by the evidence contained in the *Tantrasikhāmaṇi* of Rājachūdāmani Dīkshita, a disciple of Vēṇkatamakhi a son of the illustrious Gōvinda Dīkshita. The author says that he wrote his work at the instance of his master, who is referred to have been then the minister in the court of Vijayarāghava. Vēnkatamakhi in the Introduction to his *Chaturdaṇḍiprakāśika,* mentions that he, in turn, wrote his work at the instance of his patron, Vijayarāghava Nayaka, the ruler and that too when the latter had already donated the sixteen great gifts. It is also stated therein that Vēnkatamakhi was the establisher (consecrator) of a Chola king and this reference to his part in helping a Chola to the throne must in all probability refer to his help rendered to Vijayarāghava Nayaka himself, as there could not have been then, any possibility for any Chola to have contested the throne. Incidentally this reference shows that the work was written sometime after the coronation of Vijayarāghava and perhaps, when the author himself was occupying the high office of minister.[7] But the date of his work, *Chaturdaṇḍiprakāśika* is not known. However, from the chronogram expressed in the *Tantrasikhāmaṇi*, it is clear that it was written in Saka 1559[8] corresponding to A.D. 1637 and it further goes to prove that Vijayarāghava had already become the ruler and that his coronation must have taken place sometime before A.D. 1637.[9] Hence, the reference made to the Nayak's gifts by Vēnkatamakhi in his own work and the date of the *Tantrasikhāmaṇi,* settle the year of Vijayarāghava's coronation finally by saying that his accession to the throne must have been an accomplish-

5. *Vijayavilāsam,* alias *Vijayarāghava Vaṃsāvali* by Kālakavi, published in Cocanada by the Andhra Sāhitya Samsodha Mandal.

6. Raghunātha must have been then fifty-nine years old. The epigraphs mention him from A.D. 1600. Śevappa, according to the *Sangīta Sudhā* lived to see his grandson, Raghunātha. Śevappa's death took place in A.D. 1580.

7. There are more than one reason to believe that Vēnkatamakhi was his minister only for a short time and that too in the early years of his reign.

8. *Tantrasikhāmani:* धीमान्मन्ये शकस्याब्दे will give 9551.

According to the rule अक्षराणां वामतो गतिः it will yield S. 1559=A.D. 1637.

9. Also the *Tanjavur Andhra Nayaka Charitam*, p. 252.

ed fact before the year A.D. 1637, which is the date of the Tantrasikhāmani. These two works, thus bear indirect evidence to the fact that Vijayarāghava's coronation took place in Srimukha (A.D. 1633) the cyclic year given in the *Vijayarāghava Vamśāvali.* In that case Raghunātha Nayaka must have anointed Vijayarāghava, as his successor, shortly before his death.

It is sometimes held that Vijayarāghava, the illegitimate heir, usurped the throne. Vijayarāghava was the son of Raghunātha by his chief consort Kalāvati, the daughter of Vēṃparāja and Lakṣhmamma. Vēṃparāja, son of Chiṇṇa Malla, was Raghunātha Nayaka's uncle.[10] The *Raghunāthābhuyudayam* of Vijayarāghava says that Vijayarāghava had a brother of the name of Rāmabhadra and that the latter is said to have accompanied Raghunātha to the Tōppūr battle field in A.D. 1617. Mr. T. S. Kuppuswami Sastri, in his *History of the Tanjore Nayaks,* says that Rājachūdāmani Dīkshita in his *Ānaṇdarāghava Nātakam* has made mention of two sons of Raghunātha, namely Achyuta and Rāmabhadra.[11] Vijayarāghava in his *Raghunāthābhyudayam* calls Rāmabhadra as *Kumāraratnam.* Of these two, Vijayarāghava would appear to be the eldest son according to the genealogy given in the *Raghunāthābhyudayam.*[12] But it is said in another place of the same work that Rāmabhadra alone accompanied his father Raghunātha to the field of Tōppūr battle and Vijayarāghava Nayaka, the elder son, is not at all mentioned among the participators of Tōppūr battle. But Mr. Hickey says that of the two sons, Vijayarāghava the younger "excelled his elder brother and consequently the kingdom was given over to him on account of his physical powers and mental acquirements. His elder brother was fain to be content with what he got *viz.* the territories of Tirukāttuppalli (near Tanjore) and Paṇdanallūr (near Kuttalam)." However, Mr. Hickey does not mention the source from where he drew this conclusion. That Raghunātha Nayaka had more than one son is also known from the

10. *Raghunāthābhyudayam;* Sources, p. 254. Also *Mannārudāsavilāsam* and *Ushāparinayam* by Raṇgājamma, the poetess. The *Ushāparinayam* says that Raghunātha had Cheṇchi Lakṣmamma and Kalāvatamma for his consorts. Raghunātha is said to have worshipped god Kastūri Krishna for the birth of a son. The God appearing before Lakṣmamma is said to have narrated to her the story of Dēvaki and Yasōdha and that he would now be born to Kalāvati this time. This means that Vijayarāghava was born to Kalāvati.

11. In the Bharatavākyam of the *Ānandarāghava Nātakam,* Rājachūdāmani Dikshita says:

सारस्यं भजतां मनस्सुमनसां सारस्वते शाश्वते शय्यामाकार्सुस्त्रशेखरे भवतुवः श्यामारुणि चेमुषि
जीयादच्युतरामभद्रजनकः श्रीचिन्नचेव्वाच्युतक्ष्मास्भृद् भू रघुनाथ भूमिपतिरप्याचन्द्रमातारकम्
quoted on p. 264 of Mr. K. Sitaramayya's work.

13. *The Maratha Principality of Tanjore,* p. 43.

evidence contained in the Jesuit letters. A Jesuit letter dated 1659[13] says that when the Kaḷḷans (thieves) plundered the land and set free the prisoners, who were imprisoned in the Vallam fort, there were among them "two brothers of the Nayaka, whom he had shut up in prison, after pulling out their eyes to remove all possibility of succeeding him." This letter shows that Vijayarāghava had two brothers instead of one and the name of the third brother is not known. And from this it is also inferred that these brothers were leading a miserable life as they were blinded and detained as prisoners at the Vallam fort. The reference to Vijayarāghava's 'putting out their eyes to remove all desire on their side of succeeding him,' proves that Vijayarāghava's right to the throne was not above challenge by rivals; and the Jesuit letter incidentally bears witness to his accession only by foul means. Moreover, the internal evidence, even though it remains silent on this quesion, does not any where mention, that Rāmabhadra was ever killed in battle or predeceased Vijayarāghava. Mr. K. Sitaramayya glibly assumes Rāmabhadra to have been an elder brother of Vijayarāghava and concludes, after a careful and critical examination of the available literary sources that Vijayarāghava got the throne through violent usurpation. He advances Vēnkatamakhi's reference in his *Chaturdaṇdiprakāśika.* that he established a Chōḷa king on the throne, as evidence to this point and to prove that Vijayarāghava got the help of Vēnkatamakhi at the time of his coronation.[14] He further adds that the statements contained in the *Raghunāthābhyudayam* are inconclusive and self-contradictory. For, Vijayarāghava says therein, that he wrote it even while Raghunātha was alive and the latter is said to have offered the succession to him in appreciation of his scholarship. But in the *Prastāvana* (Introduction) it is said that he told his master Tātāchārya, that he had been directed by God Mannāru to write this work and the royal preceptor on hearing this, seems to have blessed him, "called here as the king" and directed him to compose the work in *dvipada* metre. And the *Raghunāthābhuyudayam*[15] begins like an address made by Tātācharya to Vijayarāghava, the ruler. Besides, the same work recounts

13. Bertrand: *La Mission du Madure,* Vol. III, p. 53.
Mentioned in the *Nayaks of Madura,* on page 271-2.

14. *The Tanjore Andhra Nayaka Charitam,* p. 252. The reference to a Chōḷa ruler (Chōḷakṣmājane) must be taken to mean a ruler of Chōḷadēśa of the times and hence Vijayarāghava is referred to. Vēnkatamakhi also calls himself as *Karnātarājyapratishtāpanāchārya.*

15. *Sources,* pp. 256-7. Tātācharya says that he had already obtained the blessings of God Mannāru as well as his own. Tātācharya asked him to write the work embodying his achievements so that the whole may be offered to the deity as a garland (Tāraka Hāra).

the deeds of both Raghunātha and Vijayarāghava and Mr. Sitaramayya asks the pertinent question that if the work was written at the instance of Tātāchārya by Vijayarāghava when he had already become the ruler, how Raghunātha could have appointed him as ruler in appreciation of this work? That the work was really written long after Vijayarāghava's coronation is further established by the fact that it contains references to the help given by Vijayarāghava to the Vijayanagar Emperor, Srirangarāya III, whose accession took place in A.D. 1642. And hence the composition of this work cannot be referred strictly to the time of his accession, but only to a date approximately about a decade after the event. These observations show, that Vijayarāghava had usurped the throne with the aid of Vēnkatamakhi and Mr Sitaramayya adds further colour to the violent temper of Vijayarāghava by referring to his imprisonment of his son Mannāru, as mentioned in the *Tanjāvūri Añdhra Rājula Charitamu.*[16] And the non-co-operation and the disloyalty shown by his subjects on the eve of the Muhammadan invasions upon Tanjore and Vallam about the middle of his reign, are also taken as consequences of Vijayarāghava's violence and lack of popular support. However, Raṇgājamma says that Vijayarāghava was born to Raghunātha and his chief consort (Pattampurāni) by the grace of God. She says that when Raghunātha was praying along with his wives (*Āa sathulanugudi*), Maṇṇāru, the family deity, appeared before him in a vision and blessed him with the birth of a son.[17] This would show that Vijayarāghava was of legitimate birth. The mention of Raghunātha's numerous courtesans as praying along with him, might suggest the possibility that other sons might have been born to him, of whom Rāmabhadra was probably one. The poets of the court did not take the trouble to mention his other sons, as they were not born of his chief consort; and so Rāmabhadra could not have been on the direct line of succession. And hence, Raṇgājamma's account leaves no doubt regarding the legitimacy of Vijayarāghava's succession. And the reference in the *Ānandarāghava Nātakam* to two sons of Raghunātha, namely, Achyuta and Rāmabhadra, is not securely established; and since it is not quite known for certain, that Achyuta Vijayarāghava was also called Achyuta Rāmabhadra, it is not possible to pursue the point further. More evidence would be required to prove that Achyuta and Rāmabhadra refer to the same person Vijayarāghava. However, the general character of the Nayaks themselves and their peaceful rule as borne out by the literary evidence, do not admit the possibility of an usurpation. And

16. *Tanjavūri Añdhra Rājalu Charitamu.*
17. *Mannārudāsa Vilāsam.*

hence, on account of all these observations, Vijayarāghava's illegitimate succession cannot be admitted until further research into the still unearthed sources should be forthcoming.[18]

Vijayarāghava ruled for an appreciable length of time and it is said that he was an octogenarian at the time of his death.[19] All are agreed that he died on the battle field. The early years of his reign immediately following the death of Raghunātha, saw the continuance of peace and tranquillity, and the loyalty of Tanjore to Vijayanagar remained unquestioned. Even though his epigraphs do not bear evidence to prove his loyalty to his suzerains the Vijayanagara Emperors, Venkatapati Raya II and Sriranga Raya III, yet it appears certain, in the absence of any contradictory evidence,[20] that he conducted himself as became a loyal feudatory of the empire and did not take advantage of the weak reign of Venkatapati Raya II (1630 to 1642), who was a lover of peace and who did not interfere into the affairs of his feudatories, as he was engaged in repulsing the attacks of the Muhammadan armies of Golkonda and Bijapur converging on his capital. This non-intervention of the Raya in the affairs of the southern Nayak kingdoms was taken full advantage of by the Madura Nayaka, Tirumala, who pursued a vigorous anti-imperial policy and even refused the usual tribute. Venkatapati Raya II had no time to teach Tirumala a sense of subordination; and the Kūniyur plates (1634) of Venkatapati II issued 'in accordance with the wishes of the prosperous and eminent ruler Tirumala,' show that even from the beginning of his reign, Madura displayed only a nominal allegiance and mere outward subordination to the Empire. But Vijayarāghava appears to have remained sincere and loyal towards the Raya and upheld the cause of the empire. And it

18. From the *Raghunāthābhyudayam* of Vijayarāghava and the *Vijayarāghava Vamsāvali*, it is clear that the accession of Vijayarāghava had taken place in the year *Srimukha*, i.e., A.D. 1633, when Raghunātha Nayaka was alive. The literary evidence bears no evidence to show whether Ramabhadra Nayaka, who is said to have been a son of Raghunātha and to have accompanied his father to the Tōppūr battle, was either killed in the action or returned in safety. Even assuming that Ramabhadra did survive the war, one is not able to understand any usurpation on the part of Vijayarāghava in A.D. 1633 when there was Raghunātha Nayaka alive and whose death will have to be placed in the following year, on the authority of his epigraphs.

19. *The Tanjavūri Añdhra Rājula Charitam* and also Taylor's Mss. say that he was eighty years old at the time of his death.

20. Both the internal and foreign evidence agree on the question of Tanjore's loyalty. The *Raghunāthābhyudayam* of Vijayarāghava, contains references to his help given to the Emperor, Srirangarāya. The Jesuit letters also speak of his loyalty and co-operation with the empire.

was perhaps this loyalty of Tanjore to the empire and the emperor's countenance and support to Vijayarāghava in turn, that were responsible for the keeping of Tirumala Nayaka's ambitious and aggressive activities out of Tanjore politics in the early years of his rule and when, the latter was engaged in the fortification of the important citadels of his kingdom and bore also an indifferent attitude towards the empire.[21]

[*Note by the Editor.*]

21. It is however held by Prof. R. Sathianatha Iyer that there is no definite evidence as to the objective of Tirumala, in organising the defences of his kingdom even at the very outset of his rule, though preparedness for war was essential even without any clear objective. He thus concludes:—"The features of the policy of Tirumala Nayaka towards the Vijayanagara emperor developed only later on under the pressure of circumstances. His original idea was probably to humour the emperor with occasional presents without paying regular tribute. But he was not allowed to continue this ambiguous relationship for long." Dr. S. K. Aiyangar holds that Tirumala's attitude towards the emperor depended upon the conditions of the empire for the time being. The diversion of the attention of Bijapur and Golkonda during the Mughal wars with Ahmednagar in the early decades of the 17th century "synchronised with the active movement of Tirumala towards independence in the South." "The policy of the Nayaks of Madura generally . . . . cannot be regarded as having taken into calculation the actual political condition of the times. The empire was struggling for existence during the first forty years of the century......being driven successively from one capital on to another. Penukoṇḍa had to be vacated ...... Chandragiri had to be similarly abandoned; and early in the reign of Sriranga III, Vellore was being laid siege to. These changes did not happen in a short campaign or two, but by persistent effort of no less than three decades. The absorption of the Chennappattana viceroyalty by Mysore enabled her to make a stand against the aggressions of Bijapur.......... The whole brunt of the efforts of Golconda had to be borne by the empire practically single-handed. If Tirumala had only realised the situation and had the foresight to see the political consequences of the disintegrating movement of which he had made himself the sponsor, if not the author, he would have certainly adopted a policy of co-operation with the empire. The question of Tirumala's loyalty or disloyalty therefore depends on the question whether, in the political conditions of his time, he could have foreseen the direct results of his action. The action of his predecessors and their attitude towards the empire must necessarily have made it impossible for him to take an impartial view of the situation at the time. The interests of Mysore and the empire ran together a great way. It was the governments behind those two that were for the time saved from the attacks of the Muhammadans. It cannot but have been clear to these, chief among them Tirumala, that what befell the empire would befall them soon after. If Mysore saved herself by sustained effort, the joint efforts of the emperor and his greater feudatories should have been equally successful. That Tirumala and his friends did not adopt this course of action argues either disloyalty or want of political foresight, either of the alternatives not redounding to the credit of the great Nayak of Madura."

This long quotation shows the part that Tirumala has justly to share of the blame and responsibility for the break up of the Hindu power in the South in the 17th century.

But there is no definite evidence to help us to determine whether Tanjore paid her tribute to the empire regularly.

Vijayarāghava was not destined to enjoy a peaceful reign as his latter years were full of troubles and unsuccessful wars. He was driven by force of necessity and incompetence, to purchase peace at a very heavy price from the Muhammadans. His subsequent vacillating attitude towards Sriranga III, was largely due to his single-handed efforts to maintain his own prestige and the safety of his kingdom against great odds. He was hemmed in by the powerful Madura ruler Tirumala, on the one side and the invading Muhammadans on the other. The political circumstances of the times forced him to give up the policy of co-operation and sympathy towards the emperor. And the political conditions were such that they offered only two alternatives to Vijayarāghava, either to co-operate with the Emperor and thus work out his own ruin at the hands of the Muslims or to abandon him to save himself from immediate destruction.

The accession of Sriranga Raya III to the Vijayanagar throne in A.D. 1642[22] saw the beginning of the troubles and wars, which brought about not only the decline and ruin of the empire itself, but also the fortunes of Tanjore. Sriranga, unlike his predecessor, was a talented and courageous ruler. At the time of his accession the empire was in a state of rapid decline. On the north, the Sultans of Golkonda and Bijapure began to renew their vigorous attacks on the empire, when their own safety was guaranteed by means of settlement made by the Mughal emperor in A.D. 1636. In the South, the viceroyalty of Madura was truculent and tending to become independent. Mysore had already established herself independent under Kanthīrava Narasa and Tirumala Nayaka of Madura began to give up even the show of a nominal allegiance to the empire. The Nayak of Gingee[23] in accordance with their family traditions, joined Tirumala and co-operated with him in his attempt to overthrow the supremacy of the empire. Tanjore alone seems to have remained traditionally loyal. It was under these discouraging political conditions, that Sriranga came to the throne and soon he had to face the

22. His accession is placed on the 29th day of October, A.D. 1642; but an inscription dated A.D. 1630 of his, indicates that he had been selected as Yuvarāja in that year.

23. *The English Factory Records* mention one Tubaki Krishnappa as the Nayak of Gingee.

difficulties on either side.[24] As he had a good training and experience in the administration of government, he reversed the peaceful policy of Venkata II and declared a policy of war against his enemies amongst whom, the opposition of Madura loomed large. For, he thought that the safety of the empire and the power to repulse the Muhammadans lay entirely in the unity and co-operation of his various feudatory rulers. With this object in view, he declared war upon Madura soon after his accession, before proceeding to stabilise his other resources. Vellore was then the Raya's residence and Sriranga Rāya also wanted to regain the lost territories of the empire from the Muhammadans. Thus it becomes evident that Madura was solely responsible for the emperor's serious intervention in the affairs of the South. As subsequent history will show, Sriranga was not destined to work out successfully his ambitious policy and soon he became an emperor without an empire and a refugee in the court of one of his feudatory Nayaks of Bednore. He was the last ruler of his line and with him the history of Vijayanagar comes to an inglorious termination.

From the time when Sriranga began his military operations in the south, the Nayak of Tanjore also had to face serious consequences. According to the evidence of a Jesuit letter,[25] Tirumala Nayaka of Madura, the most resourceful of them, formed an alliance with the Nayaks of Tanjore and Gingee to oppose the onward march of the Emperor by making them believe, that in the opposition of the Emperor lay the prosperity of their respective governments.[26] The same letter speaks of the Tanjore Nayak's betrayal of his confederates' plans against the Emperor by divulging the same to Sriranga. The Emperor, being informed of the schemes of Madura and Gingee, is said to have attacked the latter. Tirumala though disappointed by the actions of the Tanjore Nayak,

24. According to Foster's extracts the Muhammadan kings of Golkonda and Bijapur began to invade the territories of the Hindu King in A.D. 1642 immediately after the death of Venkatapati II. They are even stated to have occupied the whole country on the coast. *Archaeological Survey of India*, 1911-12, p. 193. The Jesuit letters mention the Muhammadan invasion as a result of Srirangarāya's dealings with the southern Nayaks.

25. *La Mission du Madure*, Vol. III, p. 43.

26. The Jesuit letter says that Tirumala concluded a league with Tanjore and Gingee against their sovereign. Mr. Sitaramayya says that Vijayarāghava at first joined them; but when he came to know their disloyal attitude towards Sriranga, he withdrew from the league unhesitatingly. However, the hostile attitude between Tanjore and Madura from 1610 would stand against the possibility of Tanjore entering into a league with Madura.

Vijayarāghava, did not lose courage and made a successful appeal to the Sultan of Golkonda to invade the emperor's territories and to attack Vellore in order to divert Sriranga's attention from the south. His appeal had its desired effect, since Sriranga is said to have retreated to his dominions and gained a victory over the Muhammadans. These must have happened about A.D. 1643.[27]

What happened in the south, consequent upon the emperor's withdrawal from Gingee is not known for certain. However, the political relationships and animosities of the times would show that Madura and Gingee must have been opposed to Tanjore as they could not acquiesce with the latter's betrayal. Some positive offensive must have also taken place between Tanjore and the allies and even though we have no direct evidence on this point, yet Vijayarāghava's claims in his *Raghunāthābhyudayam* that he compelled the Pāṇḍya (Madura) and the Tuṇḍira (Gingee) chiefs to sue for peace, when they opposed Srirangarāya and that he helped the latter by making those chiefs to wait at his door, must have reference to this period. The above statement refers to Vijayarāghava's forcing the allies to come to terms and it may not be improbable if it is held, that he co-operated with Srirangarāya in his siege of Gingee and also continued it for sometime, even after the emperor's retirement to the North.[28]

The victory gained by Srirangarāya over the Muhammadans did not in any way prove to be final and the Sultan of Golkonda, dismayed

[*Note by the Editor.*]

27. In 1643 and perhaps in the early part of 1644, Sriranga had succeeded in putting down the opposition of Damarla Venkatappa, who had intrigued with Golconda and had also defeated and turned back the Golconda forces which had advanced as far as Pulicat. He had thus contrived to establish himself firmly in power and to push back the advance of Golconda. Sriranga's position was very strong in 1645 when he gave a charter to the English at Madras in September.

A little later, we find in the Dutch records, a reference to the defeat of Sriranga within the walls of Vellore by a Bijapur army, and forced to pay a war indemnity; though two years earlier he had secured the Bijapurian help in return for 15 lakhs of pagodas and 24 elephants. "This (change) was brought about through the intrigues of Mirjumla, who, after suffering the defeat referred to before, negotiated both with Bijapur and with Kantirava Narása Raja Udaiyar of Mysore to bring about an attack on Vellore."

After this, the rebel Nayaks of the empire seemed to have come back to their proper allegiance and support of the Raya. Foster tells us that "the three rebellious Nayaks were those of Tanjore, Madura and Sinsider (Gingee ?) who inflicted a severe defeat on the royal forces in December 1645 (*The English Factories in India* (1646-50), pp. 24-25).—[Ed.].

28. This seems fairly plausible since subsequent events do not support Vijayarāghava's help to Srirangarāya.

at the success of the Hindu army, made active preparations for another attack. Finding himself insecure, Sriranga again thought that a solution of the problem lay only in the hearty co-operation of his Nayak feudatories of the South. Mr. Sathianatha Aiyar says that 'encouraged by their new attitude, he (the emperor) worked with them to devise plans for the expulsion of the Muhammadans from their recent conquests.'[29] Proenza's letter says that Sriranga 'finding the chance of success but in an alliance with the three Nayaks, invited them to join him' and offered them favourable conditions which were accepted.[30] The same letter adds that Sriranga came to the south 'to better concert together the means of defence and attack.' But according to the same evidence even his new policy did not produce any result. Proenza says that Sriranga spent more than a year in bringing about a good understanding between the Nayaks, during which the Muhammadan armies quietly achieved the conquest of his dominions. But finally, the Nayaks whose selfish interests and jealousies were insuperable, rejected the call for co-operation with Sriranga and so the latter forsaken and abandoned, lived for sometime in the forests lying to the north of Tanjore and from where he proceeded towards the west when a Muhammadan detachment composed of cavalry from Gingee was sent further south in pursuit of the emperor.[31] Since the Jesuit letter refers to this chase and to the subsequent siege of Gingee by the Golkonda forces, it may be taken that these events happened about A.D. 1646 which is the date of the fall of Gingee fort[32] into the Muhammadan hands.

The Jesuit evidence would have us believe that Tanjore also was opposed to the emperor when it says that Sriranga invited the three Nayaks and offered them favourable terms. But from the general attitude and character of the Tanjore Nayaks, it is not possible to entertain any suspicion as regards the loyalty of Tanjore and the arrival of Srirangarāya near Tanjore on the eve of his proposed negotiations, would only confirm Vijayarāghava's more friendly attitude towards the empire. However, nothing tangible was achieved as Proenza refers to the break-

29. Sriranga III of Vijayanagar. (Third Oriental Conference Report). The reference to the new attitude of the Nayaks was perhaps due to the exertions of Vijayarāghava mentioned before.

30. Bertrand III, p. 43. Sriranga's invitation to the Nayaks and his offer of favourable conditions imply that he no more stood on his technical rights as emperor regarding his relations with his feudatories.

31. Bertrand, p. 43. Sriranga's flight from Tanjore was mainly to escape from the attack of the Muhammadans.

32. Prof. C. S. Srinivasachari, 'History of Gingee,' p. 11. Also 'The Nayaks of Madura', p. 133 and Note 60

down of the negotiations.[33] Since it is not mentioned that Vijayarāghava upheld the cause of the empire but strangely enough allowed Sriranga to go to the west, the loyalty of Tanjore calls for some explanation. Proenza's letter referring to the conquest of Vellore and other territories by the Muhammadan army of Golkonda and to the retirement of Sriranga from Tanjore, speaks of the siege of Gingee by Golkonda. Thus it becomes clear that Sriranga despaired of the prospects of a joint action on the part of his feudatory Nayaks, and disheartened, by the onward march of the Muhammadan forces which were sent in pursuit of him, had to leave Tanjore, leaving Vijayarāghava to his own fate. Perhaps the emperor thought it insecure and also futile to remain at Tanjore and to oppose his enemies with the aid of Vijayarāghava alone. Moreover, the recent success of Sivappa Nayaka of Ikkēri (Bednore) in raising the second siege of Vellore for a time and his momentary victory[34] would have tempted the emperor to join him, so that he could try his chance of winning success by attacking his enemies from the rear. Thus Vijayarāghava was left without any help from the empire, when he was attacked by a detachment of Muslim cavalry. The old animosities between him and Madura would not allow any possibility of entering into an alliance against the Muhammadans and it was this uttter helplessness and lack of self-confidence that led him to adopt the extremely unwise but the expedient policy of purchasing peace with his enemies by 'surrendering

33. What led to the failure of this proposed union is not known. Perhaps Madura's growing idea of independence and her suspicion of Tanjore were responsible, besides other factors, for the termination of the negotiations.
[*Additional note by the Editor.*]

"Tirumala Nayaka, seeking safety in his unsound policy, committed a second folly, which brought about the ruin of all these kingdoms. His ambassadors went, in his name, to treat with Idal Khan (Adil Shah) or the king of the Dakhan who sent him 17,000 horse. With this imposing cavalry and 30,000 infantry of his own, he marched to Gingi. But the Muhammadans of the two armies easily came to an understanding among themselves. The *subah* of Golkonda concluded a treaty with the general of Idal Khan and retired to the kingdom of Bisnagar to consolidate its conquest; while the 17,000 cavalry of Idal Khan, along with some regiments of infantry continued the siege of Gingi which they were called for to defend. The 30,000 Madura infantry entered into the place, and joined the troops of the king of Gingi...... Soon disagreements and diversions sprang up among these men (the besieged) so diversified in nationality and manners. A revolt broke out, in the midst of the general confusion, the gates of the citadel were thrown open to the enemy who rushed into it, and delivered the town, the richest in all these countries, to pillage." (The Jesuit letter, quoted above.)

34. *Sources: Sivataṭvaratnākara.*

himself at discretion.'[35] Proenza says that the arrival of a detachment composed of cavalry in Tanjore itself 'created a panic in the citadel.'

Tirumala Nayaka stood firm by the side of the Nayak of Gingee and when the latter was besieged by the forces of Golkonda, he was able to enlist the help of Bijapur against the besiegers. He is said to have despatched an army composed of 30,000 infantry along with 17,000 cavalry supplied by Adil Shah, the Bijapur Sultan, to raise the siege of Gingee. When these two armies arrived at Gingee, the general of Golkonda seeing that it was led by the Bijapur general, the Khan-i-Khanan, who was also a faithful follower of Islam like himself, concluded an agreement with him by which the Golkonda general retired to the North, leaving the siege of Gingee in the hands of the Bijapur general. The Madura army, again disappointed, now joined the forces of Gingee and made a protracted siege possible. But a revolt among the besieged, who were composed of heterogeneous groups, soon upset all calculations of success and the Muhammadans easily captured the city. Proenza speaks of the immense booty 'consisting of silver, gold, pearls, and precious stones of inestimable value' captured by the enemies.

Encouraged by the successful siege and capture of Gingee, the Muhammadan army marched against the Nayaks of Tanjore and Madura. According to the Jesuit account, Vijayarāghava at first displayed his cowardice by hiding himself in the inaccessible forests of his kingdom, but had to come out when his territory was overrun by the enemies, who carried plunder and devastation wherever they went. Vijayarāghava had to purchase peace again at a heavy cost by meekly submitting to the will of the conqueror.[36] Proenza finds fault with Vijayarāghava for his submission, without the least defence and also for his short-sighted policy of not attempting to advance the cause of the empire,[37] even after the re-

35. Bertrand III, p. 45. Mr. Nelson says that Vijayarāghava submitted by sending an embassy to Gingee. *Vide* the *Madura Manual*, p. 134.
[*Additional note by the Editor.*]

The Jesuit letter thus tells us about the doings of the Nayaks of Tanjore :—"The Golkonda army advanced on the territory of Gingi. The Nayak of Tanjore knew that he could not give pitched battle to an enemy whose mere number had created so much terror, but he could no longer count on his ally of Madura whom he had scandalously betrayed. Obliged to take sides, he.......delivered himself up to the king of Golkonda and concluded with him a treaty by which he surrendered at discretion." There is much that cannot be cleared up in the above passage regarding the conduct of the ruler of Tanjore, for which an elaborate explanation is offered here.

36. *La Mission du Madure*, Vol. III, p. 47. Also Taylor's *Catalogue Raisonée*, III, p. 40.

37. *Ibid.*

turn of the enemies. But a close study of the political movements of the times would only support the stand taken by Vijayarāghava, however bad and impolitic it was. Sriranga's leaving Tanjore helpless at a critical time, only exposed Vijayarāghava to the attacks of the Muhammadan and Madura forces. However strong and well disciplined the Tanjore forces might have been, yet, on account of her small size and slender resources and middle position, she could not offer an effective check against the torrential stream of the Muhammadan advance. Besides, his loyalty to the empire which led him to betray Madura and Gingee, now made him an irreconcilable foe to Madura and so no alliance with her was possible. Madura, with the idea of achieving independence, would not join Tanjore, which was for the continuance of the Empire. It was this utter helplessness that greatly handicapped him in his active co-operation with Sriranga Rāya. Under these circumstances, only two alternatives remained for immediate solution and Vijayarāghava had to choose between his own safety by submitting to the enemy and taking up the cause of the emperor at his own risk. In the latter course he could not think of joining Mysore which was then loyal to the emperor, because the distance and the immediate presence of Madura between these two would not be suitable for carrying on any united action. Hence it becomes apparent that Vijayarāghava's preferring his own safety was largely the outcome of political sagacity and statesmanship and cannot be called either want of sympathy or short-sightedness or disloyalty. However, his purchase of peace at a very heavy cost definitely proves that he was very much wanting in leadership and courage as well.

This event which happened about A.D. 1646 was a shadow of the coming evils and according to the Jesuit evidence, Khan-i-Khanan, the Bijapur general, invaded Tanjore immediately after his conquest of Madura[38] and levied a huge ransom. Proenza says that the general

38. The advance of Khan-i-Khanan upon Mysore was the result of Tirumala's invitation made to Bijapur. The causes for this second Bijapur invasion are said to have been Mysore's protection given to Sriranga and the latter's attempt to regain his territories with the aid of Mysore. Proenza says that Sriranga with an army of Mysoreans 'entered the field, reconquered a part of his provinces and repulsed the army of Golkonda which advanced to attack him.' Prof. Sathianatha Aiyar says that Madura was not all conquered but was obliged to pay subsidy for the help which Tirumala received. *Nayaks of Madura*, p. 131.

Mr. Nelson referring to the event of this period says that Raghunātha and Tambi Sētupati had annexed Pattukkōttai, Mannār Koil, Dēvākōttai, Arantangi, Tiruvarur and Tanjore. But he does not mention the source. *The Madura Manual*, p. 131.

raised large contributions and returned to Bijapur, full of plunder.[39] The second invasion of Bijapur upon Mysore and its ultimate success brought to an end the ambitious policy of Srirangarāya and Kanthirava Narasa (1638 to 1659) humbled and frustrated in his policy of Vijayanagar expansion, and finding his hospitality and generosity towards Sriranga were the sources of all his recent troubles, withdrew his co-operation and finally gave up the cause of the emperor. Since this is said to have happened in 1653, the second Bijapur invasion, must have taken place about the same year. Sriranga, thus abandoned for a second time. had to lead a miserable life in the jungles on the confines of his kingdom.[40] The disappearance of Sriranga from the political field marked the rapid decay of the empire. In the destruction of the empire, Tanjore lost a valuable protector and trusted friend, though from this time onwards, Vijayaraghava Nayaka ceased to be a depen-

39. Bertrand, p. 48.

40. Even though there are pieces of evidence to show that he appealed to Shah-Jahan for help through Aurangzeb by offering himself to become a convert to Islam and that he also made attempts in 1657 and 1658 for the recovery of his kingdom, yet nothing intelligible is known about him after A.D. 1659. "Sriranga III of Vijayanagar" by Prof. R. Sathianatha Iyer. However epigraphs and literature refer to his remaining alive as refugee under Sivappa Nayaka of Ikkēri until A.D. 1675. See *'The Nayaks of Madura,'* p. 131 Dr. S. K. Ayyangar places (p. 131 note) his death about 1675. Prof. R. S. Aiyar says that the date of his death cannot be taken later than that of Shivaji's *i.e.* A.D. 1680.

[*Additional note by the Editor*]

When Mir Jumla fell out of favour with his master of Golkonda, on account of the intercession of Shah Jahan on his behalf, Sriranga tried to recover his power. A Dutch letter from Batavia tells us that about January 1657, Sriranga had captured Tirupati and was planning the conquest of the neighbouring districts. These must have happened in 1656. But the Raya's cause was injured by the faithlessness and disaffection of his own officers, *e.g.* the defection of his general, Koneri Chetty. Early in 1658, he was defeated by Tubaki Krishnappa, who was in the service of the enemy, Mir Jumla and who was himself attacked by the Golkonda forces. In 1659 the trade of Madras was greatly injured by the continued operations of the armies of the Raya and of the Muslims in its neighbourhood.

Even in 1661 the Raya continued to enjoy some authority. But the English guns and gunners in the service of the Muslims had contributed to his defeat in many places. Dr. S. K. Aiyangar holds that 1668 A.D. definitely marks the passing of the Carnatic from the Vijayanagar rule to Muslim sway; and after this date Sriranga Raya had to shift for himself outside this region. In 1661-2, the new Madura Nayak, Chokkanatha, planned boldly to re-establish the Raya in his power, to restore Gingi to its Nayak line and to remove the evils that had resulted from the mistaken policy of Tirumala Nayaka. He contrived to defeat the Nayak of Tanjore, reduced him to submission and turned back the Bijapur generals Maula and Sagosi (Shahji) back into Gingi. Then followed an invasion of the Bijapur troops and a second invasion by the Madura forces into the Tanjore country. (See *Journal of Indian History*, Vol. XVIII, Part I, pp. 39-41.)

dent ruler. The disappearance of the empire was followed by the expansion of the Muhammadan armies of Bijapur and Golkonda farther south. Thevenot remarks that "the king of Golkonda seized those dominions of the Coast of Coromandel which lay conveniently for him and the king of Bijapur, having taken what lay next to him, pursued his conquest as far as the Cape of Negapatam," and adds that the kingdom of Bijapur is bounded on the south by the country of the Nayak of Madura, "whose territories reach to the Cape Comorin." The vassalage of Vijayarāghava Nayaka to Bijapur is proved by the observation of Thevenot:—"There are many Naiques to the south of St. Thomas who are sovereigns. The Nayaks of Madura is one. He of Tangiour (Tanjore) is at present a vassal to the king of Bijapur."[41] Robert Orme says that in 1652 the Carnatic was invaded by the armies of Viziapore (Bijapur) and Golkonda acting separately; but agreed it is supposed in the objects and division of their conquests which were accomplished in 1656.[42]

These observations of the Jesuits and other writers show that the supremacy of Vijayanagar in the south came to an end by A.D. 1646 and by A.D. 1656 the Muhammadan supremacy was established in its stead. The kingdom of Gingee was completely annexed, that of Tanjore became a vassal and Madura paid yearly tributes. From this time onwards Vijayarāghava's foreign policy was mainly concerned with Madura, as he had adopted a policy of submission towards the Muhammadans. After Khan-i-Khanan's leaving Tanjore about A.D. 1653, Vijayarāghava was allowed to rule peacefully for a short period till A.D. 1659. During this short time, Vijayarāghava was perhaps interested in the fortification of the important places of his kingdom even though the internal and foreign evidence do not prove this conclusively.[43]

By reading between the lines of the Jesuit letters one is led to think that Vijayarāghava by his short-sighted policy and ruinous re-

41. Travels, Pt. III, Pp. 91 and 105.

42. *Orme*: *Historical Fragments*, p. 62.

43. Bertrand, III p. 50. Father Proenza says that 'the king of Tanjore instead of imitating his (Muthuvirappa Nayaka) example' i.e., in fortifying the citadel and on p. 51 he says that 'the Vallam fort by its natural position and fortifications which art had added it' was considered impregnable. The *Tanjāvūri Añdhra Rājula Charitamu* says that he was responsible for the extension of the fort of Tanjore and adds that the forts of Arantāngi, Pattukōttai, Relāthalli, Tiruppattūr were all begun and completed in one day. Another tradition says that he built the forts of Tirukkāttuppalli, Vallam, Paṇdanallūr and Sākkōttai in addition to those mentioned in the *Añdhra Rājula Charitamu*. Since subsequent events were full of wars and there is also no reference to show that any of these forts was damaged, it may be said that Vijayarāghava utilised this short period in repairing and fortifying the vulnerable points of his kingdom.

ligious zeal and fervour, neglected his duty of protecting the people from foreign aggression. By his own neglect of duty and want of statesmanship and diplomacy, he made Tanjore a prey to his enemies. About the same time the contemporary Madura Nayaks were devoting their attention in the fortification of their strongholds. Tirumala does not seem to have entered into open hostilities with Tanjore as he was engaged in the settlement of the affairs of the Sētupatis of Ramnad and in his expedition against Mysore.[44] He died in A.D. 1659 and was succeeded by Muthu Vīrappa Nayaka in February of that year.[45] He differed from Tirumala in his policy towards the Muhammadans, and shortly after his accession, he added to the fortifications of Trichinopoly and placed it under the command of his general Liṅgama Nayaka, so that Trichinopoly might serve as an impregnable defence against future Muhammadan invasions. The Jesuit letter says that he even refused to pay the tribute to Bijapur. The extensive measures of defence taken by him must have had their consequence upon the neighbouring Tanjore and the Jesuit evidence records an appeal made by Vijayarāghava to Adil Shah of Bijapur in that year, instead of co-operating with the Nayak of Madura.[46] Even though there is nothing to show that Muthu Virappa was at war with Vijayarāghava, yet, the reference to the latter's appeal to Bijapur for help shows that the old family feud between these two houses continued unabated and there was also distrust and suspicion among them. What became of Vijiyarāghava's appeal to Bijapur is not known, but from the subsequent events it becomes clear, that Bijapur was indifferent towards him. However, his appeal seems to have enabled the Sultan to understand that the time was best suited for carrying on a conquest of the south. Encouraged by the absence of unity among the Southern Nayaks, the Sultan despatched a large army under 'Sagosi' and 'Mula' with the object of conquering the Nayaks' dominions. The army arriving at Trichinopoly and soon finding that the fort was well fortified and warlike preparations made for her defence, moved towards the east and made a surprise attack upon Tanjore.

The fierce advance of the enemies upon Tanjore itself made Vijayarāghava to lose courage and to take shelter in some other place, without offering them battle. The Jesuit letter says again that Vijayarāghava

44. For an account of the measures of defence taken by Tirumala, see *The Nayaks of Madura*, p. 144.

45. '*The Nayaks of Madura*,' p. 150.

46. '*The Nayaks of Madura*,' p. 152. Prof. Sathianatha Aiyar says that Muttu Virappa Nayaka 'urged the Nayak of Tanjore in vain to join him.' The Jesuit letters, Bertrand III p. 269 makes no reference to this attitude.

fled to Vallam leaving Tanjore to be defended by his 'son-in-law.' The date of this attack according to the same source was 19th of March 1659. Proenza[47] says:—"This town, situated in the midst of a fertile plain, was not inferior to the strong citadels of Europe. Defended by strong artillery and numerous troops, provisioned for several years, it could defy the besiegers, who had not a single cannon at their service. The commander of the fort, a son-in-law of the Nayak, boldly ascended the ramparts, and was struck by an arrow which inflicted a light wound on him; at once his bravery vanished, and he gave up the place shamelessly. The *rajas* also protested against his cowardice. These are warriors of a very noble caste and renowned for their courage. They use only the sword and the lance; they scorn the bow and the gun, and leave as they themselves say, these arms to cowards who dare not face danger closely. Their maxim is never to retreat before the enemy, to conquer or die is to them a sacred law. Faithful to this law, they threw themselves desparately admist the conquerors and met with a glorious death, which they preferred to a dishonourable life." 'Sagosi' and 'Mula' capturing the fort without hard fighting, proceeded towards Maṇṇārkōil (Maṇṇārgudi), which was 'situated seven leagues east of the former' and which contained a well fortified fort. This fort was also easily taken by the Muhammadans. Encouraged by their easy success they advanced towards Vallam, 'three leagues south-east of Tanjore,' where they were informed that the Nayak had taken his shelter along with his family and hoarded treasures. The fort of Vallam situated 'on a steep rock within which ramparts are erected with incredible labour and expense' and by its natural position and fortification was an impregnable one and Vijayarāghava, it is gathered from the Jesuit accounts, seemed to have determined to defend it with all his energy. Proenza again says 'when the hour of peril was rung, he had no more faith in his courage than in the fidelity of his subjects; he sacrificed his dearest and fled to the forests of Talavarāyan,[48] his vassal. The army of Idal Khan (Adil Shah) was not even put to the trouble of attacking this third citadel. Those who defended it, frightened by the capture of the two principal towns despaired to resist an enemy so formidable. Besides, actuated only by the feeling of self-preservation, without any kind of devotion for a king who deserved so little of them, they believed that they would be safer in their impenetrable forests than behind their ramparts. As soon as night came, to cover them, they escaped one after

47. Bertrand III, p. 270. Proenza's letter from Trichinopoly dated 1659. *The Nayaks of Madura*, pp. 270-271.

48. Who this vassal was that gave Vijayarāghava shelter is not easy of identification.

another, without noise and with such perfect agreement, that, at day-break, the commander found himself in a deserted town with only a few faithful followers. They themselves made up their mind to follow the fugitive; but when going off, they wished to take their share of the treasures which they abandoned to the enemy; they opened the coffers of the Nayak, took what they could carry of the most precious in gold, pearls and precious stones, and fled to the most inaccessible forests. 'Their strength was not in proportion to their greed.' When the commander himself fled in a panic, the Kaḷḷans (wild tribes) of the neighbourhood visited the fort before it was surrounded by the Muhammadan forces and took possession of the 'fabulous treaures which till then were not counted but in measuring them by the bushal.' The fort was emptied of its riches and was thus saved 'from the rapacity of the Muhammadans.' The thieves while searching for the treasures came across the prisons which they threw open and thus set free a large number of prisoners. Proenza calls this 'the happiest episode of this war' and adds that those treasures which were the fruits of the greedy kings and the labour of the poor, when removed gave to all people an honest life. By the time the Muhammadan armies arrived at Vallam the palace was left barren. 'Sagosi' and 'Mula' finding the fort empty and evacuated and bereft of all riches, is said to have put a small garrison in charge of it. Proenza writing sometime after this event (March 19, 1659) says that the Muhammadans have already been 'for several months in possession of this beautiful and fertile country' and adds that at the time of his writing it was not possible for him to say definitely whether they would remain there or go back to their country collecting the riches. In another letter dated 1662, he again says that 'Mula' and 'Sagosi' had occupied the kingdoms of Gingee and Tanjore 'since two years' and 'seemed determined to fix their dominions there.' From the same letter it is also gathered that they had to abandon their project of colonisation, when a famine broke out as a consequence of this invasion and havoc done, to human life. Proenza says that the famine was severe in all this country and was followed by the migration of the people to the neighbouring places like Madura and Satyamaṇgalam, where the ravages were less felt. The Muhammadans themselves suffered much from this pestilence. Their exposure in the open air of dead bodies without burying them, soon developed an epidemic disease resulting in increased mortality. To this was added the disunion among the officers and generals of the army. 'Mula' reduced to this sad plight, tried negotiations with the Nayaks of Tanjore and Madura by saying that he would leave the land if they should agree to advance him the tribute of three years. Vijayarāghava Nayaka, having lost everything already and with nothing more to lose betook himself in the forests, while Madura paid no heed as she was confident of her strength. And both of them realising the adverse circumstances under which the Muhammadan army was suffering remained quiet. 'Mula' finding that further delay would mean additional loss of men and lives, left Tanjore and laid siege to the fort of Trichinopoly, where again he found the task quite beyond his skill and resources. Bands of Kaḷḷans (robber chiefs) caused considerable havoc and further damage to the misfortunes of 'Mula,' who at-last finding it very hard to continue the siege for long retired on receiving a moderate sum from the Madura ruler, Muttu Virappa Nayaka.[49] Thus, for the fourth time, we find Vijarāghava Nayaka being attacked by the Muhammadan forces and on this occasion he seemed to have suffered much on account of his cowardice and want of popularity with his subjects. Proenza speaks of the Tanjore people, who were left unprotected by the Nayaka 'as those who had no devotion for a king who deserved so little of them.' Even the army was tired of his rule and it did not co-operate with him fully at times of danger. And Vijayarāghava could not even continue his self-made policy ot submission and surrender to the enemy, as a result of these frequent invasions and hence we find him adopting a new policy of moving with his men and money from one place to another and thus avoiding the enemy. Vijayarāghava's extreme piety and devotion to God and his intense religious zeal stood by him as a great consoler and he, a philosopher king understood success or failure as only a manifestation of the Supreme Will.

However, Vijayarāghava soon after the departure of 'Mula' to Gingee, occupied Tanjore. Referring to the miserable life led by him, Proenza mentions that the robbers, the former plunderers of the Nayak's treasures in the Vallam fort, took pity on him and restored to him a part of his riches, saying that they plundered it only to preserve it safe.[50] Thus with the active aid of the Kaḷḷans, Vijayarāghava succeeded in re-establishing his authority in the land but as misfortune would have it, he was not destined to rule peacefully even for a short time.

Muttu Vīrappa Nayaka of Madura died shortly afterwards after a rule of about six months and he was succeeded by Chokkanatha in July 1659. His accession saw the revival of the old long-standing animosities between Tanjore and Madura and also the beginning of internal trou-

49. For an account of the expedition of 'Sagosi' (Shahji) and 'Mula' (Mustafa Khan), see 'A Great Maratha Service to South India in the Pre-Shivaji Epoch' by Rao Saheb C. S. Srinivasachari—*Sardesai Commemoration Volume*, pp. 76-77.

50. *La Mission Du Madure*, Vol. III, p. 53.

bles. As he was only sixteen at the time of his accession, he left the administration in the hands of his Pradhāni, Rāyasam and Dalavāy, who, forming a close association among themselves, were bent upon furthering their own selfish interests. The Jesuit evidence[51] says that Chokkanatha declared a policy of conquest on the advice of his ministers in order to drive away the Muhammadans. With this object, Liṇgama Nayaka was despatched with forty thousand men to attack 'Sagosi,' who was then encamping at Gingee. Liṇgama is said to have received bribes from the Muhammadan general and prolonged the campaign, while in Madura, the Pradhāni and the Rāyasam were conspiring together to put an end to the life of Chokkanatha and to instal his brother on the throne. The news of this projected plot was revealed to the Nayak by a lady of his court and he lost no time in taking a bold action. The eyes of the Pradhāni were pulled out and the Rāyasam was murdered and Chokkanatha captured the power from them. Too weak to oppose Liṇgama Nayaka, he pretended friendship with him only to take him captive at a suitable opportunity and punish him accordingly. But Liṇgama, whose conscience rendered him suspicious, escaped from Trichinopoly and joined 'Sagosi.' Proclaiming hostility towards Chokkanatha, he besieged Trichinopoly with twelve thousand cavalry. According to the Jesuit evidence,[52] Vijayarāghava held out assurances to Liṇgama of his help in his attack upon Madura. The beginning of the siege was favourable to the allies and Liṇgama thought of capturing Chokkanatha alive. The latter given to understand that the failure of his men was due to the vile and treacherous Pradhāni, soon assumed the command of his army in person and made strong efforts to repulse Liṇgama and 'Sagosi.' Soon victory was on the side of Madura and the enemies withdrew to Tanjore. Chokkanatha encouraged by the victory, ordered his troops to advance upon Tanjore and attack Vijayarāghava Nayaka for co-operating with 'Sagosi' and Liṇgama. Vijayarāghava again helpless surrendered to the enemy, while his allies fled to Gingee. Since these events are recorded in a Jesuit letter[53] dated A.D. 1662, the invasion of Madura upon Tanjore in order to punish Vijayarāghava for helping Liṇgama, must have happened between 1660

51. *La Mission du Madure*, Vol. III, p. 121; and '*The Nayaks of Madura*,' p. 155. Prof. Sathianatha Aiyar says that Chokkanatha was not responsible for this policy of conquest, since the whole project was worked out by the three officers in order to create confidence in the people. And when Liṇgama, the Daḷavāy, heard of the Nayak's activities he turned an enemy, when the Nayak wanted to deal with him severly.

52. *La Mission du Madure*, Vol. III, p. 123.

53. *La Mission du Madure*, Vol. III, p. 119. Letter of Proenza, dated 1662.

and 1661. This victory of Madura over Tanjore proved to be the first of its kind, ever since the foundation of the Tanjore Nayakship.

The Jesuit letter speaking on the troubled political conditions of this period, says that Tanjore suffered serious consequences on account of these frequent attacks. 'The people abandoned their homes and took refuge in Madura and some at San Thomé. The excessive and fatal religious zeal of Vijayarāghava made him culpably negligent of his subjects' sufferings. To all the mishaps due to the Muhammadan scourge and famine, was added the 'inhuman exploitation of the situation by the Dutch, prompted by mercenary motives.'[54] A Jesuit writer[55] says, 'shame, eternal shame to the Dutch, who cruelly speculated on the misery of the Indians. They enticed them to the coast by the bait of abundant food; then, when their number became pretty large and their strength a little recouped, they piled them up in their ships and transported them to other countries to be sold as slaves.'

The retirement of Chokkanatha from Tanjore after Vijayarāghava's abject surrender gave the land some sort of nominal peace. In this short period nothing seems to have happened in Tanjore except the preparations of Vijayarāghava to wreak vengeance upon Madura, as he could not reconcile himself with his submission to Chokkanatha. The recent invasion was so significant, as to induce him to action. But as he found that by himself he could not face Chokkanatha, he was waiting for an opportunity to display his enemity openly. Soon the longed-for opportunity came in A.D. 1663 when 'Vanamian' the able general of Bijapur came to the south on an expendition and laid siege to Trichinopoly.[56] The Jesuit evidence again tells us that 'Vanamian' was helped by Vijayarāghava of Tanjore, who is said to have been the enemy and opposed Madura 'against the fidelity of treaties.' The Bijapur general laid waste the neighbouring territories but finding that his threats and show of power as well as his several attacks were of no avail, he opened negotiations with Chokkanatha and asked for a ransom as a condition of his leaving his kingdom. The latter availed himself of this and purchased peace by paying a large contribution in money and thus saved himself for the moment from the horrors of war. But he could not

54. *'The Nayaks of Madura'*, p. 157.

55. *La Mission du Madure*, Vol. III, pp. 124-5.

56. The causes for this expedition are not known for certain. Perhaps the news of the defeat of Sagosi and Lingama at the hands of Chokkanatha, might have induced the Bijapur Sultan for further action. The co-operation of Vijayarāghava of Tanjore with 'Vanamian' and the Jesuit reference to Tanjore's betrayal also admit the probability of Tanjore seeking the help of the Sultan as against Madura.

allow Vijayarāghava unpunished for his betrayal in joining 'Vanamian' in his siege of Trichinopoly, by breaking his treaty with Chokkanatha made recently. Accordingly, the Nayak of Madura marched upon Tanjore for a second time with a large army and soon captured the fort of Vallam which 'by its position and by the rich lands which depend on it' was efficiently garrisoned. Vijayarāghava was forced to surrender and he made peace by agreeing to the timely conditions imposed by the victor. The fort of Vallam which formerly belonged to Madura, but which was transferred to Tanjore by an order of Achyutha Raya at the commencement of the rule of the Tanjore Nayaks in exchange for Trichinopoly, was now lost to Madura by Vijayarāghava as a consequence of this defeat. Chokkanatha Nayaka's annexation of the Vallam fort is confirmed by the Jesuit evidence, which speaks of his return 'after leaving a good garrison in the fortress of which he has just made the conquest.'[57] The loss of Vallam must have happened in A.D. 1663, since John Nieuhoff speaks of Vijayarāghava's recapturing it in A.D. 1664.[58] Nieuhoff says "the Nayak of Madura had been for a considerable time in war with the Nayak of Tanjore and taken many places from him; at my time the war was renewed with more vigour than ever; and the Nayak of Tanjore having gathered a great army attacked the Nayak of Madura so briskly that he took from him, in a few days, all the places he had conquered from him before. The army of the Nayak of Madura being much disheartened by the victories of their enemies, the Nayak of Madura sent to me to Koylang his chief governor desiring assistance from the Company; but as it was not our interest to engage on any side, I excused it as handsomely as I could."[59] And from this it is known that Vijayarāghava recaptured the fort of Vallam and that the latter remained under Chokkanatha only for a very short time. Mr. K. Sitaramayya says that this was the first victory won by Vijayarāghava Nayaka. As Chokkanatha Nayaka was engaged with the reorganisation of the affairs of the Sētupatis of Ramnad and also with the preparations for an attack on Mysore,[60] and as he was not able to enlist the co-operation of the

57. Proenza in his letter dated 1665 speaks of Vijayarāghava as having been 'defeated and fleeced by Sokkalinga', whom he had notoriously betrayed. *La Mission du Madure*, Vol. III, pp. 164-5. Since the letters were written at a regular interval of three years, the reference to this war will have to be placed in 1663. However the reconquest of Vallam is not mentioned by him.

58. *The Nayaks of Madura*, p. 159.

59. John Nieuhoff: *Voyages and Travels into Brasil and the East Indies*, II, 1703, p. 297.

60. For an account of these wars, see *the Nayaks of Madura*. pp. 159-162.

Dutch,[61] he perhaps allowed Vijayarāghava without opposition, to re-occupy his fort. However, as subsequent events would show, he was preparing for a big offensive against Tanjore.[62]

From A.D. 1664 to A.D. 1673 there was comparative peace and calm in the country[63] and the Nayaks of Madura and Tanjore were busy preparing for their mutual war. The *Tanjāvūri Andhra Rājula Charitamu* says that Vijayarāghava fortified the forts of Tanjore, Arantāṇgi, Pattukkōttai, Tirupattur and Rēlatalli.[64] The enemity between Tanjore and Madura grew violent and each wanted to get rid of the other. And Madura was the only insuperable enemy of Vijayarāghava. Though his policy was one of submission towards the Muhammadans, yet he could not think of adopting the same towards Madura, as she was also a former feudatory of Vijayanagar like himself. Ever since the foundation of the Tanjore Nayakship as a dependency of Vijayanagar, the Nayaks of Madura had entertained a policy of distrust and hatred towards her. And the latter's interest in the affairs of the empire and her loyalty and the wars waged by Achyutappa Nayaka and Raghunātha Nayaka on behalf of the Vijayanagar emperors against Madura, all these were looked upon by Madura with hatred, since they were not quite in agreement with her idea of independence. The recent help given by Vijayarāghava to 'Sagosi' and 'Mula' and also to 'Vanamian' in their attacks on Trichinopoly, only added momentum to the already existing indignation of Madura. The absence of strong and powerful rulers on the Tanjore throne and the inability and helplessness on the part of the empire to take up her cause, gave Madura an opportunity to wreak vengeance upon Tanjore.

61. Nieuhoff's reference to his refusal of Chokkanatha Nayaka's request in A.D. 1664 was perhaps due to the friendly relations that existed between the Dutch at Negapatam and Vijayarāghava Nayaka. The Dutch took Negapatam from the Portuguese in A.D. 1658 and in that year the Dutch got a deed from the Nayaka (Nammikka Śāsanam: deed of assurance) through one Cinnaṇṇa Chetty by which their claim to Negapatam was recognised. One of the clauses of the deed required the Dutch to entertain feelings of friendship and loyalty towards Vijayarāghava. (Two Negapatam grants from Batavia by Prof. K. A. Nilakanta Sastri *Proceedings of meetings of The Indian Historical Records Commission*, Vol. XIV, p. 39).

62. The change of capital from Madura to Trichinopoly in A.D. 1665 and the fortifications carried out at the latter place were all undertaken with a view to attacking Tanjore. *The Nayaks of Madura*, p. 160 and *The La Mission III*, pp. 181-2.

63. Andre Friere in his letter dated 1666 refers to a prospective Bijapur invasion of the South, to collect the promised contributions from the Nayaks. But it is not known what became of this intended invasion. *La Mission* III, page 203.

64. *Sources of Vijayanagar History*, p. 324. Dr. S. K. Aiyangar identifies Rēlātalli with Kīlānilai on the road between Arantangi and Tiruppattur. Even though there is nothing to show that the above fortifications were made in this period, yet the history of his reign shows that he must have been busy with this work only about this time.

II

(a) *The Fatal War with Madura.*

As was expected the storm broke out in A.D. 1673, when Chokkanatha ordered his troops to march upon Tanjore. Vijayarāghava put up a strong and gallant defence and died a glorious death on the field of battle. The immediate causes for this war are not clear. The chronicles say that Vijayarāghava's refusal to give his daughter in marriage to Chokkanatha and the bad treatment meted out to the Madura ambassadors, who brought the proposal for the marriage alliance were the immediate causes of this war.[1] Whether the marriage proposal was the real cause of this war is not known for certain and unfortunately Andre Freire's letter dated 1673, in which he claims to have written about this war, is not available to us. However, Mr. Nelson, in his *Madura Manual*, has accepted the account of the chronicles and finds fault with Vijayarāghava for rejecting the offer and consequently bringing about his own ruin. He says:—'one would naturally have supposed that the offer of marriage would have been gladly accepted, more especially as the two kings......were Nayakkans, descended probably from common ancestors.'[2] Dr. S. K. Aiyangar further gives credence to the account of the chronicles by referring to Raghunātha Nayaka's marriage with a Pāṇdyan Princess. He thus writes, 'there is also nothing improbable in Tirumala's having married the Tanjore princess, whether she was actually stabbed to death in the manner described or not. In view, therefore of these previous alliances it is extremely likely that Chokkanatha sought an alliance and the refusal to comply must both be considered solely from the point of view of political relationship between the two families.'[3] He further adds that the cause for Chokkanatha's proposed alliance was his desire to gain the support of Tanjore against his own enemy Mysore.[4] However, he concludes that the rejection of the proposal alone was not 'the sole cause of the war between the two.' Mr. Sathianatha Aiyar thinks that Chokkanatha's demand of the Tanjore

1. Taylor: *Oriental Historical Mss*, II, pp. 185 and 191-5; *Catalogue Raisonnée* III, p. 177. Also the *Tanjāvūri Añdhra Rājula Charitam*. Also *Sources*, p. 324.
2. *The Madura Manual*, p. 191.
3. *The Nayaks of Madura*, p. 164, Note 33.
4. If Chokkanatha was for real peace and a strong alliance, he need not have precipitated a war immediately on Tanjore. Moreover he had nothing to fear from Mysore by way of an invasion soon after the recent battle of Erode in 1670 which went against him.

21

princess was only an alleged reason for his intended war.[5] But he controverts Nelson's view that 'both were Nayakkans descended probably from common ancestors', by saying that this could not have been possible since the ancestor of the Tanjore Nayaks was connected by marriage with the ruling house of Vijayanagar, while those of Madura could not boast of such royal relationship. He adds in further support of his statement, that even though there had been marital alliances between the Nayak families of Tanjore and Madura, yet 'Vijayarāghava may have thought differently of the matter.'[6] Mr. K. Sitaramayya casts a doubt regarding the truth of this proposed marriage alliance. He says that mutual hatred and enmity between the two lines had been manifest from the year 1616 and so no marriage would have been possible in 1672 or in 1673 or even earlier,[7] in view of their hostilities. Secondly the higher status, due to their connection with the royal house, of the Tanjore Nayaks, is pressed into service to disprove the possibility of this proposal. He even says that Tirumala Nayaka's marriage with a Tanjore princess is not supported by any reliable testimony as there is no evidence as to its having been a fact found in the Tanjore literature; he adds that Raghunātha Nayaka, who was opposed to the Madura Nayaks in general and to Muthuvirappa Nayaka I in particular, would not have consented under any circumstances to give his daughter in marriage to Tirumala. Even granting that he had made this alliance and that Tirumala murdered his Tanjorean wife, he asks pertinently, whether Raghunātha, the most powerful of all the Tanjore rulers could have kept quiet without revenging himself on his brutal son-in-law for his daughter's death. There is no evidence even in the chronicles to show that Tanjore was at war with Tirumala. And he therefore concludes that Tirumala Nayaka's marriage with Achyuta Raghunāthamma of Tanjore as recorded in the *Tanjāvūri Āndhra Rājula Charitam* is not only improbable, but highly impossible. Moreover, none of the literary works of Tanjore mention the existence of a daughter of Raghunātha Nayaka and even the *Raghunāthābhyudayam* of Vijayarāghava, which contains a genealogy of the Tanjore Nayaks, does not speak of a sister of Vijayarāghava. The Jesuit evidence, which speaks of a son-in-law of Vijayarāghava in A.D. 1659, re-

5. *The Nayaks of Madura*, p. 163.

6. *The Nayaks of Madura*, p. 164. He seems to accept the statement of the *Raghunāthābhyudayam* that Raghunātha married a Pāṇḍyan princess; but rejects the marriage of Tirumala with a Tanjore princess and his murdering her on the ground that this statement of the chronicles is not confirmed by any other evidence.

7. *The Tanjore Andhra Nayaka Charitam*, pp. 321-2.

mains silent on this matter.[8] The chronicles of Madura also make no reference either to this marriage proposal or to Tirumala Nayaka's marriage with Raghunātha Nayaka's daughter. Hence it is difficult to give any credence to this fanciful story that has gained so much currency; and so, the truth of Chokkanatha Nayaka's proposed alliance with Tanjore will have to be discountenanced, until it is supported by further evidence and even then, the refusal of Vijayarāghava could not have brought about an immediate crisis.[9] If the statement were to be supported by future evidence, then the observation of Mr. Sathianatha Aiyar that the Madura Nayak's demand of a Tanjore princess in marriage was made as a subterfuge will remain good. Until then, the question of a marriage alliance as a cause for this war, will not hold good. Hence, the necessity arises of making further enquiry on this question.

The immediate event that preceded this war was the reconquest of Vallam by Vijayarāghava about A.D. 1664.[10] Nieuhoff says that the Nayak of Tanjore attacked the Nayak of Madura and took from him in a few days all that he had lost. This conquest might have encouraged Vijayarāghava to entertain hopes of recovery and revival and he perhaps refused to pay the agreed tribute to Madura.[11] Mr. Sathianatha

8. *La Mission*, III, p. 51. If the reference is correct, then, it means that Vijayarāghava had at least a daughter who had been married already by 1659. But the internal evidence does not mention even a daughter of Vijayarāghava, not to speak of two, as mentioned in the Jesuit letters.

9. The view that Vijayarāghava's refusal to comply with the request of Chokkantha, was due to his nobility and high birth, does not seem to be quite secure. Of course, the Tanjore Nayak, Śevappa, was related to the imperial house of Vijayanagar by his marriage with a sister of one of Achyutarāya's courtesans. That Tirumalāmba herself was not Achyutarāya's queen is stated by her in her *Varadāmbikāparinayam*. But both Nāgama Nayaka, father of Visvanātha Nayaka and Timmappa Nayaka, the father of Śevappa, were brother officers under Krishnadēvarāya and both hailed from the Toṇḍaimaṇḍalam country. And Nāgama Nayaka became the Raya's favourite and that was the reason for his coming down to the South to settle the affairs of the Pāṇdya. Both of them were Nayaks and Achyutarāya showed his regard for Viswanātha Nayaka, by making a gift for his merit. Apart from this, there is nothing to show that the Tanjore Nayaks were of a higher caste status than the Nayaks of Madura. Both of them were obliged to pay tribute to Vijayanagar according to the Jesuit letters.

10. *The Nayaks of Madura*, p. 159.

11. Vijayarāghava's failure to pay the tribute and his breaking the treaty concluded with Madura are already referred to in the Jesuit letters in connection with Vijayarāghava's help given to 'Vanamian'. Chokkanatha Nayaka's terms, soon after his capture of Vallam would have also contained a reference to Tanjore's tribute.

Aiyar also says that 'it is likely that the loss of the latter's (Madura) conquest in Tanjore referred to by John Nieuhoff was the governing consideration.' And it is also held that Tanjore's part in the struggle of Chokkanatha waged against the Mysore ruler, Dēvaraja Udaiyar (1659-1672) at Erode and the disagreement between the two powers as a result of their defeat; formed the causes for this invasion by Madura. Dr. S. K. Aiyangar[12] says that Dāmarla Aiyapēndra or Aiyappa, a half-brother of Aṇka, the son of Cheṇṇa, and the founder of Chennapatnam exhibited his loyalty towards Sriranga III in a battle at Erode where a confederacy composed of Chokkanatha Nayaka of Madura, a general of the Tanjore Nayaka, Aiyappa and one of the officers of Bijapur, was formed to uphold the claims of the fugitive Emperor, Sriranga III. In this battle Aiyappa fell and the imperial allies were completely defeated. Mr. Sathianatha Aiyar says[13] that 'it is likely that disagreements rose between Chokkanatha and the ruler of Tanjore as a result of this defeat, which probably precipitated the former's war against the latter in 1673.' This view is untenable in the light of our knowledge of the then existing political relationships between these two houses; and Vijayarāghava's sending his general, to participate in the battle of Erode, in which Madura, his enemy, played a prominent part, will have to be supported by further evidence. And hence a clear analysis of all the sources and other statements can only support the view, that the reconquest of Vijayarāghava Nayaka of his lost territories and the old animosities between Madura and Tanjore, constituted the main causes for a war in A.D. 1673.

Chokkanatha despatched a large army under the command of his Dalavāy Veṇkatakrishnappa Nayaka with Pēishkār (Revenue Officer or treasurer) Chiṇṇatambi Mudaliar as next in authority. Chiṇṇa Kattiri Nayaka, the poligar of Kaṇṇivādi is also said to have accompanied them with his troops.[14] Vijayarāghava, on the receipt of the news of the

12. *Sources of Vijayanagar History*, Introduction, p. 21. Also the *Ushaparinayam* by Damarla Aṇka:—*Ibid.*, p. 308. The battle of Erode must have taken place in or about A.D. 1670 since the Mysore account says that Chikkadēva Udaiyar (*acc.* 1672), while yet a prince, offered to attack Madura, when negotiations failed. This is further confirmed by the statement that Dāmarla Aiyappa waged a war with him and the latter in his epigraphs dated A.D. 1679 and 1686 claims to have defeated Chokkanatha of Madura and to have taken Tripura (Trichinopoly), etc. See also 'Sriranga III of Vijayanagar' by Mr. R. Sathianatha Aiyar—*Prroceedings of the All-India Third Oriental Conference, Madras,* 1924. The reference to the part played by a general of Tanjore is also vague.

13. *The Nayaks of Madura*, p. 173.

14. *The Nayaks of Madura*, p. 165.

advance of Madura troops, is said to have despatched an army to meet them on their way and offer battle, before they could reach Vallam. Dalavāy Veṇkatakrishnappa Nayaka defeated the Tanjore army and captured the fort of Vallam and soon arrived near the outskirts of Tanjore. Vijayarāghava, learning of the defeat of his army near Vallam, soon collected a large force and came out to fight, along with his Senapati, Dalavāy Veṇkatādri Nayaka.[15] In the fierce battle that ensued, the Tanjore army sustained serious losses. It is said that the Madura Dalavāy proposed peace terms in vain to Vijayarāghava Nayaka, who ordered his men to march forward for battle, himself marching at their head. His son, Maṇṇārudās, who had been kept in confinement[16] was also released and he was left behind along with another person, called Akkirāju, to be in charge of the ladies of his family and to blow up, the Zenana quarters, if the fight should go against Tanjore. It is said that Vijayarāghava, despairing success, gave the fateful signal, by which the Zenana quarters in the palace were blown up and Maṇṇārudās after this, entered the thick of the battle. Shortly after this happening, both Vijayarāghava and his son rushed forward in the battle and fell. Veṇkatakrishnappa Nayaka proclaimed his victory and returned to Trichinopoly leaving a garrison behind at Tanjore.[17] This battle, which was fatally disastrous in its results to the Nayak's rule in Tanjore, also proved to be the last of the wars of Madura upon Tanjore. Vijayarāghava finding that he could not escape death, faced it with all courage and died gloriously. And Tanjore was annexed by Chokkanatha Nayaka, who put it in the charge of his foster-brother, Aḻagiri Nayaka, who was appointed Viceroy, according to the evidence of the Jesuit letters.[18]

15. The chronicles mention one Raṇgappa Nayaka as the Dalavāy of Tanjore. Also the *Tanjāvūri Āndhra Rājula Charitam*. But an inscription coming from Tirukkoshtiyur (309 of 1923) mentions one Dalavāy Veṇkatādri Nayaka. Mr. K. Sitaramayya also says that Veṇkatādri Nayaka was his general as he is mentioned in a *Kuravaṇji Nātakam* and also in the *Ushāparinayam*.

16. The reason for his imprisonment is not known. Tradition has a fanciful story to tell. It says that he advanced his love to one of the daughters of Gōvinda Dīkshita and when this was brought to the notice of the Nayaka by the minister himself, he ordered him to be put into prison. The *Dakshina India Charitam* by Narasimhalu Naidu, Vol. II.

17. An account of this battle is given in Taylor's Mss. II, pp. 191-203. Also the *Tanjāvūri Āndhra Rājula Charitam, Sources*. Mr. V. Rangacharya gives a detailed account of this war. *Indian Antiquary*, 1917, pp. 58-62.

18. *La Mission*, III, p. 247. The Tanjore chronicles also refer to his appointment.

The reign of Vijayarāghava thus came to an end in A.D. 1673 (the date of this disastrous battle).[19]

(b) *The Nayak's relations with the Europeans.*

Vijayarāghava Nayaka's relations with the Portuguese were generally friendly except for a short time. The latter continued to hold the port of Negapatam till the middle of A.D. 1658 when it passed into the hands of the Dutch. Speaking of the Portuguese trade on the Eastern Coast and the patronage shown by the Nayaks to them, Mr. Danvers says that in A.D. 1638 both the Nayaks of Gingee and Tanjore were on friendly terms with the Portuguese.[20] However, in the keen rivalry between the Portuguese and the Dutch on the question of Eastern trade the Dutch contrived to gain some advantage over their rivals by 1638. In 1636 the Portuguese Viceroy wrote to Lisbon that trade had generally fallen into the hands of the Dutch, who were making attempts to capture San Thome de Meliapore (Mylapore).[21] The Portuguese, on account of this competition, suffered serious losses not only on the coast but also in Ceylon, where their power was slowly declining, yielding place to the rise of the Dutch power. The Danes of Tranquebar were friendly towards the Portuguese; and about 1638 the President of the Danish East India Company, getting intelligence of a projected attack on the Portuguese in Gao and Ceylon by the Dutch, offered his help to them in their defence of Negapatam and Tranquebar, if they were to allow him to establish a factory in Ceylon. When this request was turned down by the Portuguese authorities, the President made another request with a repetition of his offer of help, and this time the request was to allow the Danes to purchase cinnamon, elephants and arecanuts from Ceylon. Nothing came out of this and the Portuguese lost their fort at Batticalova in Ceylon to the Dutch in 1638. The latter were good enough to permit the Portuguese inhabitants to set sail for Negapatam. The Dutch continued to harrass the Portuguese and attacked Goa in 1639 and Malacca in 1641. About this time the Portuguese seemed to have suffered

19. Unfortunately Andre Freire's letter dated A.D. 1673, in which, he says he had given an account of this war is lost to us. Since his subsequent letter dated 1676 begins with a reference to this war and the occupation of Tanjore by Alagiri, the battle must have come to a close by the end of 1673. Lespinay has two dates as he once records the events under July 1672 and elsewhere places them in 1673.

20. *The Portuguese in India*, Vol. II, p. 252.

21. *Ibid.*, Vol. II, p. 257.

from an attack made by Vijayarāghava of Tanjore.[22] The causes for this attack are not known, but it is known that nothing serious had happened as the Records say that the Nayak of Tanjore soon concluded peace with them. However, they began to decline and Conte de Avieras, writing home in December 1643, informed the king of Portugal that all the rulers of South India were against the Portuguese. In 1658, the Dutch under Major Van der Lean captured the settlement of Negapatam without a shot being fired and the Portuguese surrendered completely. According to the terms of surrender, the Portuguese were to be at liberty to leave the town and take with them all their possessions and goods, as well as their church ornaments, and the Dutch should provide them with the means of conveyance in the transportation of goods.[23]

From A.D. 1658 onwards Negapatam was held by the Dutch. From the Dutch Records,[24] it appears that Vijayarāghava was at first not favourably disposed towards them and even did not recognise their hold of the town; but subsequently he had to acquiesce in their possession when an army sent by him to oppose them was defeated.[25] At the instance of Chinnaṇa Chetty, *alias* Mallayya, of whom we have read above, Vijayarāghava gave the Dutch a charter offering them valuable trade concessions on 15th September 1658.[26] The deed given by Vijayarāghava begins with a reference to Cinnaṇa Chetty, who submitted to him that the Dutch were desirous of carrying on trade operations in the port of Negapatam and says that the Nayak gave the fort, the houses and the yards that were in possession of the Portuguese along with ten

22. That Vijayarāghava besieged the town of Negapatam about 1642 is mentioned in a letter dated January 4, 1643, which says that at Negapatam 'the Portuguese have been put to a great strait, for the Naik of Tanjore hath besieged them now upwards of seven months' Foster: *The English Factories in India*, 1640-45, p. 81. Danvers says that Pedro Boreel, a Dutch Commissioner arrived at Tranquebar and endeavoured to persuade the Naik of Tanjore to continue the war with the Portuguese and to besiege Negapatam, offering him to bring another force to aid him in his capture of the town. The Naik, however, refused to act on this and soon made peace with the Portuguese. Vol. II, p. 284.

23. *The Portuguese in India*, Vol. II, p. 324.

24. The two grants from Batavia by Prof. K. A. Nilakanta Sastri. *The Indian Historical Records Commission*, Vol. XIV, p. 39.

25. *The Cambridge History of India*, Vol. V, p. 127.

26. The first grant is dated 15th Mārgaḷi of the Cyclic year Vilambi, corresponding to 15th September 1658. The deed is called a Nammikka Śāsanam (deed of Trust).

villages to the Dutch who were asked to pay to the state an annual tribute as tax thereon. The same charter was renewed for a second time on June 5, 1662 by Vijayarāghava, who now gave them the additional privilege of setting up their own mint for the coinage of gold, silver and copper, the profits of which were to be shared between the Company and the Nayak.[27] About 1666 the Dutch got from Vijayarāghava Nayaka the port of Trimelipatam (Tirumalairājanpatnam in the Nannilam Taluk of the Tanjore District) and some other places in its neighbourhood on lease, for a period of three years 'for a sum of 2,800 parados, on condition that the Company were neither to fortify the places nor to disembark any merchandise or cloth in these places.' The Company wanted the lease in order to be able to regulate their dealings with the local dyers and also to be free from the molestation of the Nayak's officers. The issue of these charters shows that Negapatam had definitely passed on from the Portuguese into the hands of the Dutch and that Vijayarāghava, who was opposed to the latter at the beginning, had to reconcile himself with them. The grant of additional villages on lease shows further, that Vijayarāghava became more friendly towards them as years passed on.

The Danes at Tranquebar continued to enjoy their privileges unmolested and free from the Nayak's intervention. However, they do not seem to have fared well at all, for want of regular supply of money and ships from home. President Muschamp wrote to London on October 28, 1629[28] that the Danes for want of stock and shipping have finished their trade and by report, their general had gone to surrender their castle to the Dutch for 15,000 rials, but it is supposed that the Naik will not suffer them to enjoy it peacefully, unless upon a new composition which will cost them dear. A Dutch letter from Masulipatam dated September 24, 1628, speaks of the possibilities of the Dutch obtaining Tranquebar should the Danes decide to leave, adding that in the event of their refusing it, "Malaya, (Malliah) the Cōmati, would take it as he had a great trade on the Coast and was afraid of being plucked by one or another of the Naiks." In December 15, A.D. 1629, the Dutch Governor-General at Batavia reported to the Company that Roelant Crape, the Danish Admiral of Tranquebar,, had proposed that the Dutch should buy the port of Tranquebar for 12,000 or 15,000 rials of eight and that they had refused it. Another letter dated December 2, 1629 contains a reference

27. *Tijdschrift*, Batavia, Deel LXXIX, A flevering I, p. 7.
28. Foster: *The English Factories in India*, 1623 to 1629, p. 347.

to the Danish proposal made to Malaya (Malliah Chetti) to occupy the port, paying the stipulated rent of 3,000 parados per annum to the Naik of Tanjore. It was also made clear that the Danes might claim the place within three years 'on reimbursing Malaya, all his outlay.' The Hague Transcripts refer to the proposals made to the Dutch and Mallaya Chetty and add that these fell through. owing to the opposition of the Nayak of Tanjore. From William Bayley's account of the voyage in A.D. 1637, it is clear, that the Danes were still in occupation of Tranquebar. However, the sad plight to which the Danes were subjected to, by the absence of regular supplies of ships and money from home, did not seem to have improved the situation and the Danish authorities of Tranquebar were still entertaining the idea of either selling away the settlement or of leasing it out. In the beginning of 1640, the English Council at Surat suggested that Tranquebar should be acquired from the Danes 'if their poverty should induce them to part with it.' Another letter dated January 28, 1644 from Fort St. George refers to the miserable condition of the Danes at Tranquebar. The Dutch were, however, negotiating with the Danes for the purchase of Tranquebar, as they were anxious to prevent it from falling into the hands either of the English or the Portuguese. The Danes also seemed to have promised the Dutch to give them their first offer.[29] That Paul Hauseene, the Danish Chief at Tranquebar, had offered to deliver the fort to the Dutch on condition that the latter should pay the debts incurred by the Danes on the Tanjore coast and should restore it to the king of Denmark on demand is contained in a letter dated October 19, 1653. In 1654, a Danish ship containing cargo was captured 'by the Brahmans.' Since nothing more is known of Tranquebar, it is certain that it continued for sometime more under the Danes themselves. In 1669 after a lapse of twenty years a ship is said to have arrived at Tranquebar from Denmark.[30]

The English after their first attempt to found a settlement at Karikal in A.D. 1624, and which ended in a failure, seem to have given up altogether the idea of making further attempts to establish a factory in the dominions of the Nayak of Tanjore. However, their trade with the Danes at Tranquebar is recorded in their records, where it is mentioned that in 1643, ships loaded with arecanuts and calicoes had arrived from Tranquebar, about the middle of the same year. In that year the English

29. Foster: *The English Factories*, 1651-53. Introduction, p. 28.

30. Foster: *The English Factories*, 1668-69. Chokkanatha Nayaka's negotiation with Francois Martin in 1675, offering him both Negapatam and Tranquebar in return for his help in driving away the Dutch and the Danes from the kingdom of Tanjore, shows that Tranquebar was still under the Danes. Tijdschrift, p. 11. Cited above.

are said to have sent Mr. Greenhill to Tranquebar with 3,500 rials in money and coral to be invested in commodities. The fact that the English made a further attempt to found a factory at Dēvikōttah (at the mouth of the Coleroon) in 1664 and that they were again refused permission by the Nayak of Tanjore, is mentioned in a Dutch letter.[31]

(c) *The Condition of the Kingdom under him.*

The long reign of Vijayarāghava from A.D. 1633 to A.D. 1673 was full of troubles and costly wars which impoverished the land and denuded it of men and wealth. The Nayaka comparatively speaking, may be said to have had a peaceful reign till A.D. 1642 and for the rest of his period, he had to struggle hard to maintain his position and dominion in tact. He was the last of the Tanjore Nayak line. His epigraphs do not take him beyond A.D. 1656,[32] and from the provenance of these it may be said that he succeeded in keeping intact the territories left by his father Raghunātha Nayaka ; but in the later years of his reign, his territories suffered a diminution on account of his wars with Madura. In the east, the ports of Negapatam and Tranquebar were held by the Portuguese, the Dutch and the Danes respectively, while on the south-west his epigraphs and the chronicles support his authority over a part of the modern Ramnad District.[33] An inscription coming from Neduṇguṇram[34] in the North Arcot District shows that the place had continued to be under the Tanjore Nayaks and also under Vijayarāghava Nayaka in A.D. 1643.

Like his predecessors, Vijayarāghava also had numerous agents, who assisted him in the administration of his kingdom. A record coming from Ōlayāmputtur[35] and dated in the cyclic year Sarvadhāri corresponding to A.D. 1648, mentions one of such agents, who was called Vaidyanātha Aṇṇagal and who is said to have effected a *parivartana* (exchange of property) with the people of that locality. Another agent is mentioned in an inscription coming from Mudigondanallūr.[36] Nainiappa Nayanar, the agent referred to, made provisions for the maintenance of daily worship and festivals in the temple of Mudigondanallūr in lieu of the old right of the temple in collecting donation from

31. Foster : *The English Factories*, 1661-1664, p. 365.
32. 10 of Appendix A of 1921-22.
33. There is an inscription of his to be found at Tirukkōshtiyur in the modern Sivaganga Zamindari
34. 709 of 1904.
35. 543 of 1918.
36. 166 of 1925.

the villagers for that purpose. A third agent is mentioned at Neduṇguṇram, but his name is not known. Vijayarāghava Nayaka was tolerant of all religious faiths, but he specially favoured Vaishnavism by his liberal patronage. His inscriptions as well as the literature of the period show that he was a staunch Vaishnava devotee and this extreme devotion was due to the presence of Kumāra Tatācharya, the great Vaishnava scholar, at Tanjore. Vijayarāghava made him the royal preceptor.[37] And speaking of the Nayak's regard and veneration towards his spiritual master, a Jesuit letter dated 1659 says 'that every December the then Nayak (Vijayarāghava) of Tanjore used to cause his *guru* to be carried several times round and round the town in a gorgeous palanquin borne by the ladies of the palace and preceded by another palanquin containing the guru's slippers and used to walk himself in front of the procession swinging a censer and making repeated obeisances to his spiritual master'.[38] The *Tanjāvūri Añdhra Rājula Charitamu* says that he used to feed daily about twelve thousand Brahmans and it is said that he himself partook of his food only after seeing that this feeding was actually over. It is also claimed in the chronicles that Vijayarāghava paid daily visits to Srirangam to offer worship to Lord Raṇganatha and that, when hostilities between Tanjore and Madura became intense he stopped going to Srirangam but, instead, erected a big tower in his own capital so that by climbing to its top, he could have a view of the towers of Srirangam. He is also said to have made large benefactions to the tutelary God, Rājagōpālaswami at Mannārgudi. The *Raghunāthābhyudayam*[39] says that he presented the God, Rājagōpāla, with an armour studded with precious stones. He also built the *prākāras* of the same temple and added flower gardens and tanks to it. He founded an agrahara and named it after his father Raghunātha Nayaka. The present Rājagōpālaswāmi temple at Tanjore was also built by him. Mr. K. Sitaramayya says that even though he was a staunch Vaishnava, yet he was tolerant of other religions and built several maṇtapas to Siva temples in the land.

According to the evidence contained in the *Maṇṇārudāsavilāsam*[40] of Raṇgājamma, Vijayarāghava married Kāntimati, the daughter of one

37. The *Maṇṇārudāra Vilāsam* of Raṇgājamma. The work bears evidence to the close association of the Nayak with his master, Tatācharya.

38. *The Madura Manual*, p. 160.

39. *Sources of Vijayanagar History*, p. 255. The same work gives an account of the decorated halls and royal mansions within the palace, p. 265.

40. Since the works refer to Vijayarāghava's marriage in Subhakrit, corresponding to A.D. 1662, the work must have been written about that time.

Rājachaṇdra, who is said to have given away as dowry, ten lakhs of villages to his daughter. This marriage with Kāntimati appears to have taken place at the instance of his master Tātācharya. That Vijayarāghava had more than one wife is supported by the evidence of the Jesuit letters and Maṇṇārudās in his *Hēmābja Nayika Swayamvaram* says that he was the son of Vijayarāghava by his another wife called Rājagōpāla Kaṇchika. The Nayaka was also a great patron of learning and man of letters. Numerous poets and poetesses lived and flourished in his court. Among his poets, Kāmarāzu Vēṇkatapati Sōmayāji, the author of *Vijayarāghava Chaṇdrika*, Kōnēti Dikshita, the author of *Vijayarāghava Kaḷyānam;* were the important poets of his court. The *Tanjavūr Añdhra Vāṇgmaya Charītam*, which forms the basis for a study of South Indian Telugu Literature, says that Cheṇgalvala Kālakavi, the author of *Rājagōpāla Vilāsam* and Purushōṭṭama Dikshita, the author of *Annadāna Nātakam;* were also his poets. Kshētragña, the great South Indian musician and composer is said to have adorned the court of Vijayarāghava and flourished in that period. Maṇṇārudāṣ himself was an author and he wrote *Vijayarāghavābhyudayam* and *Hēmābja Nāyika Swayamvara Nātakam.* The name of Raṇgājamma figures prominently among his numerous poetesses.[41] She calls herself a wife of Vijayarāghava and prides herself as being able to compose a hundred verses at a time.[42] She was the daughter of Pasupulēti Vēṇkatādri and Mangamāmba and wrote the *Rāmāyana* and the *Bhāgavata sāram.* Vijayarāghava, in appreciation of her scholarship and versatile learning, is said to have honoured her by performing a *kanakābhishēkam* (bathing in gold) on her. The reference to a number of Telugu poets in the Tanjore literature of this period, shows clearly that Vijayarāghava patronised them more and more. Sanskrit also received its due share and Vēṇkatamakhi's *Chaturdaṇdiprakāsika* was written during his reign. Vijayarāghava himself was an accomplished poet in Telugu and the *Tanjavūr Añdhra Vāṇgmayam* says that he wore an anklet called Sāhitya Rāya on his left leg and had a banner containing the image of Sri Sarada as indicative of his patronage of learning. He bore the *birudas* of Sāhitya Bhōja, Sangīta Vēdi and *Lakshavipra aṇṇadāta.*[43] All his works refer to his interest in theatricals and the palace itself contained a big theatre

41. The *Maṇṇārudāsa Vilāsam* mentions Chaṃpakavalli, Kastūri, Sasirēka, Mōhanamūrti, Krishnāji and others besides Raṇgājamma.

42. The *Maṇṇārudāsavilāsam.* Satalēkhini and Achyuta Vijayarāghava sārvabhauma Dharmapatniyāha Raṇgājamma.

43. The *Maṇṇārudāsavilāsam.* Published by the Andhra Sahitya Parishad, Coconada.

(*ranga*), where numerous plays were enacted to the satisfaction of the Nayaka. Speaking of his reign, Jayanti Ramayya Pantulu[44] says that 'the Telugu Prabhanda Literature inaugurated by Allasani Peḍḍaṇṇa, reached its glory under the careful nourishment and patronage of Vijayarāghava.' And the important contribution made to the southern school of Telugu literature during his reign, was the impetus given to the dramatic form of literature.

The internal evidence shows that his reign was noted for its literary activity and it is well known that he was loved and respected by his subjects for his pious and charitable works. In spite of all these finer shades of his character which represent him as a patron of the fine arts and a lover of music, the foreign evidence contained in the Jesuit letters shows that his later years were full of troubles and wars and also paints a black picture of him, charging him with neglect of duty, want of courage and oppression of his subjects. His lack of leadership and short-sighted policy are all portrayed in them. The frequent departure of a number of his subjects from the realm and their migration to Madura and Mysore are ascribed to his neglect of duty in protecting his subjects from danger and to the oppression to which his people were subjected to by the cruel exactions of the Pradhāni. On account of this, 'the artisans suspended their work; the merchants closed their shops; most of the people left their homes and the kingdom showed the appearance of a desert.' From the letter of Andre Freire, it is known that Vijayarāghava soon remedied the sufferings of his people 'by giving him (Pradhāni) up to the people's anger about A.D. 1666.[45] Even though his exactions can be justified by his purchasing peace with the Muhammadans at a heavy price, yet his weak character and lack of courage cannot be adequately explained and the extremely religious policy of Vijayarāghava only hastened the downfall of the Tanjore Nayaks.

44. The Southern School of Telugu Literature. *Journal of the Andhra Historical Research Society*, Vol. II, Parts 3 and 4.

45. *La Mission III*: pp. 201-2.

CHAPTER IX

CHENGAMALDĀS (A.D. 1674 to 1675)

Soon after the fall of Tanjore and the death of Vijayarāghava and his son Maṇṇārudās in the tragic battle of A.D. 1673, Chokkanatha Nayaka of Madura appointed Aḻagiri Nayaka his foster-brother, to the governorship of Tanjore. Aḻagiri assumed charge of Tanjore in A.D. 1673 and soon restored peace and order and reorganised the administration of the kingdom on a strong basis. As viceroy, he had to remit the surplus revenues to the Madura Nayaka, and he seems to have done so only in the first year of his rule. But in the succeeding year his ambition increasing with his power, he neglected to remit this sum in time to the court of Madura and even assumed a tone of equality in his correspondence with Chokkanatha Nayaka.[1] The chronicles mention that he took among his officers one Veṇkaṇṇa, a Niyogi Brahman, who had served the late Vijayarāghava Nayaka as his Rāyasam (secretary). And it is said that it was his mischief that was responsible for Aḻagiri Nayaka's independent and indifferent attitude towards his suzerain. However, Chokkanatha did not think of punishing Aḻagiri for his impudence, on account of his close relationship and liking for the man and so Aḻagiri was left alone. In the interval news was received that the old Nayak family was not totally extinct and that a boy of the late Nayak's family, who was saved from the catastrophe that befell Vijayarāghava and his family, was being brought up by a merchant at Negapatam.[2] And Veṇkaṇṇa, who was probably 'discontented with

1. The Jesuit letters do not refer to these incidents but say that Alagiri was ruling over Tanjore under Chokkanatha. Taylor's Mss. and the *Tanjāvūri Āndhra Rājula Charitamu* speak of his independence. Also see *The Nayaks of Madura*, pp. 164-170.

2. The *Tanjāvūri Āndhra Rājula Charitamu* says that Chengamaladās, at the time of his rescue, was a boy four years old and he is called as the younger son of Vijayarāghava. It adds that he was brought up by a wealthy merchant. *Sources*, p. 325. Another chronicle (Taylor's Mss. 11, p. 200) says that he was a petty merchant and that Chengamaladās was a child aged only two years, at the time of his rescue and that he was the son of Maṇṇārudas (child of Maṇṇārappa). Mr. Sathianatha Aiyar says that Chengamaladās must be a son of Maṇṇārudās and not of Vijayarāghava, as the latter is described as an old man aged eighty at the time of his death. The *Nayaks of Madura*, p. 167, Note 38. Mr. K. Sitaramayya. (p. 338 to 340) is also of the same opinion. He says that Chengamaladās was a grandson of Vijayarāghava and adds that he must be at

his position and influence in the new regime,' thought of taking advantage of the presence of a member of the old family and also the feud between Aḻagiri and Chokkanatha, by working out a scheme, in order to restore the old dynasty and to bring about the downfall of Aḻagiri. Organising the necessary measures to 'facilitate his *coup-d-etat,* he hastened to Negapatam.[3]

Joining Cheṇgamaladās (also known as Cheṇgamala Nāyaka) Veṇkaṇṇa made his way to the court of Bijapur and sought the sultan's help for re-establishing Cheṇgamaladās on the Tanjore throne.[4] Veṇkaṇṇa was successful and the Bijapur Sultan, who was led to believe that Cheṇgamaladās was the legitimate heir to the Tanjore throne, sent an army under his general Ekōji, *alias* Vyankoji, to assist Cheṇgamaladās in his attempt to recover back his crown and patrimony and also to drive away the usurper, Aḻagiri. Capturing the fort of Ārni on his way, Ekōji marched on towards Tanjore.[5] Aḻagiri being informed of Ekōji's advance, appealed in vain to Chokkanatha for help: and the latter bearing in mind Aḻagiri's past conduct refused to send any help. In the meanwhile Ekōji had entered the kingdom of Tanjore and was advancing towards the capital. Collec-

least twenty to twenty-five years of age since both Maṇṇārudās and Cheṇgamaladās are mentioned in the *Ushāparinayam.*

3. *Taylor's Ms.* says that Veṇkaṇṇa stayed at Negapatam till the boy was ten or twelve years of age, i.e., for about eight years. But the reference to Alagiri's fall in A.D. 1675 in the Jesuit letters disproves the statement of the chronicles. The *Tanjāvūri Āndhra Rājula Charitamu* does not speak of his stay at Negapatam. Moreover as Mr. Sathianatha Aiyar says (p. 167) 'Veṇkaṇṇa was too much of a politician not to realise that a moment's delay, would be dangerous to the success of his plans.'

4. Nelson (*The Madura Manual,* p. 194) says that 'Cheṇgamaladās escaped from the palace during the confusion which ensued upon its destruction and fled to the court of Idal Khan (Adil Shah), who received him kindly and promised to assist him.' But he does not mention the source of this information.

5. Andre Freire's letter dated 1676 refers to the expedition led by Ekōji, but it differs from the native chronicles in more than one respect. (*La Mission* III, pp. 247-249). The letter says that Idal Khan, informed of these events sent an army under Ekōji to re-establish the son of the defeated king on the Tanjore throne. According to it, Ekōji fought with the Madura troops sent under Alagiri and defeated them. The *Tanjāvūri Āndhra Rājula Charitamu* and the chronicles say that Ekōji arrived at Ayyampēt and fought with the troops of Alagiri. As it is known for certain, that Cokkanatha did not send any help to Alagiri; the statement of the chronicles seem to be more probable. See also *The Nayaks of Madura,* pp. 167-170. Moreover the chronicles refer to the crowning of Cheṇgamaladās and then only speak of Ekōji's usurpation, but do not refer to the circumstances that led to it.

ting all the available forces, Aḻagiri met Ekōji near Ayyampēt and offered him battle. The defeat of the Tanjore army disheartened him and he is said to have fled to Mysore by way of Ariyalur to save his own life. And Ekōji entered Tanjore soon after and crowned Cheṇgamaladās as the rightful king of Tanjore. The native chronicles speak of the lavish and munificent gifts and presents made to Ekōji by Cheṇgamaladās; and it is said that Cheṇgamaladās was also shown the place where the treasures were buried and that he unearthed a sum amounting to twenty-six lakhs of pagodas. Ekōji was also given the revenues of the districts of Kumbakonam, Maṇṇārkōil (Mannargudi) and Pāpanāsām, to cover the expenses of his expedition. The chronicles again speak of Ekōji's stay at Kumbakonam for some time.[6]

Cheṇgamaladās was proclaimed ruler of Tanjore and he began to rule about A.D. 1674. According to the account of the chronicles, he was not allowed to rule peacefully even for a short time as there were internal dissensions among his followers. Cheṇgamaladās acting on the advice given by his foster-mother who had rescued him from the tragedy in 1673 and brought him up faithfully, is said to have appointed the Chetti merchant of Negapatam, who had protected him in his exile, as his Pradhāni and Dalavāy instead of giving it to Veṇkaṇṇa, who was eagerly expecting to be raised to those offices. And the latter dissatisfied with his master's arrangement and 'displeased at the loss of his coveted prize,' approached Ekōji and induced him to take possession of Tanjore for himself.[7] Emboldened by the co-opera-

6. *The Madura Manual*, p. 197. Mr. Nelson following closely the Jesuit evidence says that Ekōji instead of placing Cheṇgamaladās on the throne, had himself usurped it and became an independent ruler. But all the chronicles are agreed that Ekōji's usurpation happened only some time later and was not immediate. Wilson gives a different account. *The Historical Sketch of the Kingdom of Pāṇḍya*, pp. 55-56.

7. Mr. K. Sitaramayya says that Ekōji and Veṇkaṇṇa conspired together against Cheṇgamaladās and adds that the former's stay at Kumbakonam was perhaps due to his ambition to conquer and annex Tanjore. Mr. Sathianatha Aiyar following the chronicles (*The Nayaks of Madura*, p. 170) says that Ekōji though ambitious, at first refused to invade Tanjore as he feared his master, the Sultan of Bijapur but the receipt of the news of the death of the Sultan emboldened him to take action. Mr. Sitaramayya says that the statement in the chronicles that he feared his master is not trustworthy since, there is nothing to support the death of the sultan of Bijapur in 1675. Adil Shah II died in 1673 and was succeeded by Sikander Shah who ruled from 1673 to 1686. He adds that Ekōji himself must have been sent by Sikander Shah and Ekōji stayed at Kumbakonam only to give effect to his ambitious policy of conquest. Hence the death of a sultan and the determination of Ekōji to march against Tanjore have no basis of authenticity and the latter must have acted of his own accord.

ion of Veṇkaṇṇa, Ekōji advanced upon Tanjore; and Cheṇgamaladās informed of the advance of Ekōji, the Maratha general, escaped to Ariyalur.[8] Tanjore now fell into the hands of Ekōji without any difficulty; Ekōji's occupation of Tanjore marks the beginning of the Maratha rule in the South. He restored peace and order and tried to make amends for the defect in his title by increasing the material welfare of his subjects. Fr. Andre Freire adds (in his letter dated 1676) that 'justice and wisdom of his government begin to heal the wounds of the preceding reign and develop the natural resources of this country . . . . .'.

The Maratha occupation of Tanjore must be deemed to have taken place in the beginning of A.D. 1675 as it is mentioned that Ekōji took Tanjore in the month of Māgha of Saka 1596 corresponding to February-March A.D. 1675.[9] Fr. Andre Freire's letter dated 1676 after men-

8. About this time Rāja Sūrya, the nephew of Tirumalai Sētupati of Ramnad, is said to have supported the cause of Cheṇgamaladās. What became of this coalition is not known. But Rāja Sūrya was imprisoned and put to death subsequently. *The Nayaks of Madura,* p. 184. H. H. Wilson's reference to a Sētupati called Sūrya Dēva, who is said to have taken part in the fight along with Vijayarāghava in 1673 perhaps has reference to this Rāja Sūrya. *The Historical Sketch of the Kingdom of Pandya,* 1838, p. 55.

9. *Inscriptions of the Marathas* by Mr. T. Sambamurthy Rao. Nelson says that Ekōji marched upon Tanjore in the early part of 1675 and established his authority. *The Madura Manual,* pp. 194-5.

Additional Note by the Editor.—

"A statement given in the Marathi language by an old servant of the Tanjore palace, sometime before 1787 and of which a translation is printed in Appendix VI of Fullarton's *A View of the English Interests in India* mentions it as the 17th February 1675." The account was given by a writer under the Dabir and Manoji in the time of Pratap Singh and was given in its literal translation from the Marathi. It runs thus:—"The Yacojee Rajah was the first man who took possession of the fort and country of Tanjore from a Gentoo (Telugu) king; this event happened on the 7th day of February 1675, dated in Gentoo, Rauchina Nama Sumvacharum, Magah Suddha Septimee. It appears, from the books which are kept in the palace, that there were 5753, which said villages were divided into the five following *subahs* or districts; *viz*:—

Subah Trivady,	Subah Mannargoody,
Subah Combeconum,	Subah Pattacotah and
Subah Mayavaram,	Subah Valumputt.

The country produced, in the year 1675, under the Yacojee Rajah, paddy cullums—32,050,000 (pp. 317-8 of *A View of the English Interests in India,* by W. Fullarton, London, 1781). Vyankoji Raja went from Tanjore to meet Shivaji in his camp to the north of the Coleroon in 1677 (September)=Shravan, Pingala, 1599 (Saka) according to the *Jedhe Chronology,* and after mutual greetings and

tioning the occupation of Tanjore by Ekōji, also supports this date. Thus Ekōji, who was sent out to assist Cheṇgamaladās and to re-establish him on the throne, had himself usurped the throne and thereby brought to an inglorious end the Nayak dynasty of Tanjore, the last Nayak himself taking refuge in the west. What became of him is not known; and the traditions, varied as they are, do not admit of any verification. It is claimed by some that Chokkanatha gave Cheṇgamaladās asylum and protected him.[10] Kavitvavēdi says that the descendants of the Tanjore Nayaks continued as jaghirdars under the Madura Nayaks and that a grand-daughter of Cheṇgamaladās was married to Vijayaraṇga Chokkanatha Nayaka of Madura.[11]

fraternising for eight days, Vyankoji got suspicious of the intentions of his brother and fled on a catamaran, across the river, without taking leave of his brother. Thereupon Sivaji seized his lands, 'Jagdeogad and the surrounding territory, and the whole province of Chidambar, and Vradhachal;" (See the *Sabhasad* of Krishnaji Anant. (cir. 1694) tr. of Mankhar).

A Tamil chronicler, Narayana Kone who wrote a detailed account of the history of the Carnatic with particular reference to the Gingee country and whose account was deemed to be fairly authentic and reliable, thus speaks of Vyankoji's usurpation at Tanjore:—"It is true that Shahji before his death had given to his younger son, Vyankoji (Venkoji), his jaghir of Bangalore. He had confided his son Venkoji to his Brahman minister, Raghunath Narayan Hanumante. For his part the latter considered Venkoji as his own son."

"Fired by ambition, Venkoji unjustly took possession eventually of the kingdom of Tanjore by force of arms. To pacify the country and make the population admit his authority, he had spent all the wealth amassed in the royal treasury (of Tanjore) by the previous king, Vijayarāghava Naicker. Far from suceeding, this subterfuge only seemed to alienate the neighbouring chiefs. He had to fight them incessantly and raise armies; which could not be done without enormous expenditure."

"Then famine having taken its part, it was not possible for him to levy heavier imposts on the inhabitants. Having deliberated he determined to confiscate the wealth of the temples which drew on him the hatred of Hanumante. He therefore took leave of his king under the pretext of making in his old age the pilgrimage to Benares. Really he went to see King Sivaji to inform him of the rapines and pillage (plunderings) of his brother." (Tamil Ms. *Karnātaka Rājākkal Savistāra Charitam* (in the Mackenzie collection)—Section VIII—and Guana Diagou's French rendering of the above—"Historie Distaillēē des Rois du Carnatic" par Narayanam Poulle—1939).

According to this chronicler, Vyankoji should have harried the whole country into poverty within a little over a year since Hanumante had left Tanjore even in the middle of 1676.

10. *The Tanjore Manual*, p. 753.

11. *The Añdhra Vāṇgmayam*, p. 214. Quoted also in Mr. Sitaramayya's work.

He further adds that Cheṇgamaladās had a son called Vijayarāghava and a grandson by name, Vijaya Maṉṉārappa. Still another view is that Cheṇgamaladās went over to Ceylon along with his daughter, who was given in marriage to a Kandyan King.[12] Mr. Nelson gives some information apart from these traditional stories; but they are also not supported by any other plausible evidence. He says that Kiḻavan Sētupati, enlisted the co-operation of Cheṇgamala Nāyakkan of Tanjore, who, it is said, was living then in perfect amity with the usurper Ekōji, against Madura.[13] However, an attempt was made by Kumāraiya, the Mysore general, to restore the old line of the Tanjore Nayaks, but it fell through for want of support and co-operation on the part of Chokkanatha of Madura.[14]

Cheṇgamaladās was the last known member of the Tanjore Nayak line and with his flight, the rule of the Nayaks came to an end. The Nayaks of Tanjore, who rose to power and prominence under the powerful protection and patronage of the Vijayanagar Empire did not long survive the decline of that Empire. Ever since the accession of Sriranga Raya III in 1642, the fortunes of the Empire as well as that of Tanjore entered on a definite phase of decline; and the subsequent troubles caused by the invasions of Bijapur and Golconda ruined the life of the Tanjore kingdom. Tanjore could not continue for long, single-handed and unaided against these great odds, and so exhausted, she fell. The frequent depradations of the Muhammadan force dried the land of its resources. Besides, the traditional loyalty of Tanjore to the Empire made her an irreconcilable enemy to the neighbouring Madura Nayaks, who were always in a hostile attitude towards her. To these was added the succession of weak and feeble rulers like Vijayarāghava and Chengamaladās. And Vijayarāghava was to a large extent responsible for allowing the kingdom to drift away by his extreme piety, neglect of duty, and want of statesmanship. All these causes acting in unison and favoured by the political circumstances of the times brought about the downfall of the Nayak rule in Tanjore.

12. *The Tanjore Manual*, p. 763. Mr. Sitaramayya thinks that this is probable on the ground that a member of the Kandyan Royal family told him the same story. *The Andhra Nayaka Charitam.*

13. *The Madura Manual*, p. 213. Mr. Sathianatha Aiyar in his work makes no mention of this. Pp. 104-185.

14. *The Nayaks of Madura*, p. 182.

CHAPTER X

GENERAL FEATURES OF THE NAYAK RULE

The Tanjore Nayaks were technically and formally tributary vassals of the Vijayanagara Rayas and their vassalage is proved by their title Nayak which signifies a captain or governor. That Tanjore was a tributary fief of the Empire is testified to, clearly by the Jesuit evidence. The present custom of appointing a governor only for a term of years was not then in general vogue and when once an appointment was made, it was continued without any break or change so long as the appointee remained loyal and faithful to the suzerain power. Thus gradually the system of hereditary succession began to take root even with respect to provincial governorships. Hindu kingship was never elective in practice and the appointment of Śevappa Nayaka as the governor of Tanjore by the Emperor Achyutarāya began practically a hereditary line. The Nayaks thus appointed, carried on the administration of the government as the Raya's deputy. As tributary rulers, they were obliged to pay an annual tribute to their overlords and to maintain an army. Whenever their help was requisitioned by the emperors they had to render necessary assistance and help and play their part as became loyal feudatories. As subordinates, the Nayaks had only limited powers regarding their relations with outside powers and neighbouring rulers. Above all, their subordination meant their comparative security from foreign aggression since the suzerain power looked after their interests and it also meant less expenditure on defence.

Though the Nayak was technically only a vassal, yet in his own jurisdiction he was the supreme and practically the uncontrolled head of the government and he enjoyed almost sovereign powers. The people looked upon him as God's nominee and there was always exhibited an affectionate reverence for his position. His words were final and none dared to find fault with his actions except on rare occasions, as it was believed according to the Hindu conception of state ideals, that the ruler could do no wrong. Even though the Nayak's power was not checked by any council of ministers or popular assembly, yet it could not be deemed to have been an autocracy or an irresponsible power. He had the usual checks and restrictions in the form of *Dharmaśāstras*, conventions and the traditional moral code as enjoined in the Hindu text-books on *Rājanīti* and *Daṇḍanīti*. These were his guides and binding limitations in his work as administrator. Besides, customary law, such as was embodied in the *āchāra* of the *sishtās* (conduct of the good) was much respected in the actual dispensation of justice; though it did not claim the same superiority as Dharma. As these laws were only to ensure a proper and good administration of the government and to put the king in the right path of Rājadharma, they were generally looked upon as inviolable checks upon the king's arbitrary power. The Nayak ruler, like other Hindu rulers, was a secular ruler as well as the protector of religion. The Nayaks in general, do not seem to have transcended the limits imposed by the traditional moral code and the good and welfare of the people were never sacrificed for any selfish interests or motives. And since the Hindu polity never comprehended a constitutional monarch of the modern type, the welfare of the people depended in practice largely on the individual character of the ruler and hence sometimes good government was followed by grave misrule. In case of tyranny and oppression the subjects had no legal means of getting their grievances redressed and the idea of rising up in open rebellion was never thought of by the people except on very rare occasions of intolerable oppression. Under such circumstances, the people resorted to migrations to places beyond his jurisdiction. According to the Jesuit evidence, such migrations took place in the reign of Vijayarāghava Nayaka on account of his heavy exactions to pay off the Muhammadan enemies. So also, in epochs of benevolent rule there were immigrations from other places into the country.

Practically the ruler's powers were limited by the prevailing moral codes; and the Nayak's rule was a benevolent despotism. Succession to the Nayakship was hereditary and the heir apparent called Yuvarāja, was given proper education and military training and was prepared in the art of government. The *Raghunāthābhyudayam* and the *Sāhitya-ratnākaram* refer to the early education of Raghunātha Nayaka in *Rājanīti* and in the art of handling the various weapons of warfare. Practical administrative training was also given to him by associating him in the working connected with the affairs of the administration. The ruling Nayaks gave abundant opportunity to their heirs, to get themselves fully acquainted with the functions of administration either by installing them on the throne openly or by associating them in rule. Such abdications to give full powers to the heirs and co-regencies, were resorted to when the ruler felt it was impossible for him to carry on the government, either on account of age or because of any crisis.

The Nayak was helped in the discharge of his duties by a number of officials, who formed a small council of advisers. Among them, the minister was the most important person. The office of 'Mantri' or 'Sachiva' was always held by men of great learning, integrity and inde pendence. According to the Hindu political idea the good of a state depended largely upon the king and his minister. And a king without a minister was compared to an elephant without its trunk. The Nayaks of Tanjore had a council of ministers and the chief minister was called the *Pradhāni*.[1] Under the Nayaks this office was always held by Brahmans. Gōvinda Dīkshita was minister to both Achyutappa Nayaka and his son Raghunātha and the epigraphs tell us that he was the Pradhāni as well as the agent (viceregent ?) of the Nayaks. The *Sāhityaratnākara* says that when Raghunātha started from his capital on his famous expedition against his enemies, he entrusted Gōvinda Dīkshita with the entire charge of the state. The powers enjoyed by the Pradhāni and his influence, were second only to those of the king in importance. In his political status he was more even than the average Diwan and Prime-minister of the Indian States. The Nayak had great confidence in him and his advice was sought on all occasions. The Pradhāni was largely responsible for the shaping of the internal as well as the foreign policy of the state. Yagnanārāyana Dīkshita refers to the war council held by Achyutappa Nayaka and to the momentous part played by Gōvinda Dīkshita therein.

Next in importance to the Pradhāni was the *Dalavāy* or the commander-in-chief of the forces. He was also called the Sēnāpati; and he was responsible for preserving the internal peace and safety of the kingdom and also for defending it against external troubles and aggressions. The Dalavāy seems to have combined in him the office of Pradhāni and commander also under the Nayaks of Madura. But in Tanjore, the Dalavāy was only in charge of the army and its management. He also tended advice to the king on the problem of defence of the land as well as on war. The *Rayasam* or Chief Secretary, corresponding to the *Tirumandira Ōlai* of the Chōlas, was also an important officer under the Nayaks. He seems to have been the chief administrative officer, but did not enjoy the same importance and status as the Pradhāni or Dalavāy. He was the recorder and the executor of royal orders and was held responsible for the proper working of the civil departments of the state. Next in importance among the hierarchy of officials, was the officer called *Aṭṭavaṇai* or the chief

1. The Pradhāni is sometimes called the minister in charge of revenue. (*The Nayaks of Madura*, p. 237). Since the officer called *Aṭṭavana* is said to have been also in charge of this department, it is not possible to assign the portfolio of revenue to the Pradhāni of these times. See also, *Studies in the Third Dynasty of Vijayanagara*, p. 111.

accountant of the Revenue Department. He was the head of all the revenue officials who were called *Śampratīs* and *Kaṇakkans* (accountants). The Śamprati had under his jurisdiction a number of *Kaṇakkans*, the accountants of individual villages. The head of the *bhandāram* (treasury) was called the *Tōshikāna adhikāri* and he was also an important official connected with the king's council of ministers. The Nayaks did not seem to have paid regular salaries or fixed amounts of remuneration to these officials and their establishments; their services were secured to the state by gifts of land known as *mānya*.

Yagnanārāyana Dikshita also refers to the system of espionage working under a regular department, then prevalent in the court of the Nayaks. The spies had to make secret enquiries into the affairs of the people and study their disposition towards the state and other officials and also to report on the happenings in the neighbouring states. It is said that the news of the death of the emperor Venkatapati Raya I and the outbreak of the war of succession and the consequences thereof, were all quickly communicated to the Nayaka by these royal spies, who were men of great intelligence and skill. The reference in the Portuguese chronicles and in the English Factory Records to the Nayak's warm reception of foreign ambassadors, shows that foreigners were treated with much friendliness and cordiality by the Nayaks. Father Nicholas Pimenta,[2] a Jesuit observer, tells us how cordially he was received by the Nayak of Tanjore. He says:—'He (the Nayak) entertained us kindly and marvelled much that we chewed not the leaves of betel which were offered to us and dismissed us with gifts of precious clothes wrought with gold desiring a priest of us for his new city which (he) was building'. Captain John Bickley's account of the English voyage made from Bantam to Tanjore also contains references to the royal reception given by the king and his noblemen, to the English envoys at Tanjore.[3]

In the early part of their rule the Nayaks spent comparatively little on the defence of their kingdoms; but they always maintained an army. In course of time when the country was threatened by foreign invasions they had to devote more attention to defensive measures in order to ensure their own safety by erecting forts at places of strategic importance on the borders of the land. Thus the capital of Tanjore had first of all to be well fortified by the erection of a strong fortress with a deep moat full of water running round it. On the west of the

2. *Purchas: His Pilgrims*, Vol. X, p. 205.
3. *The English Factories*, Vol. III (1624-29), pp. 13-14.

capital, Vallam was likewise fortified against the possible attacks of Madura rulers, and it was deemed to be a first line of defence for the capital. Under Vijayarāghava these fortifications were further strengthened and new fortresses were built at Paṇdanallūr in the north-east, Araṇtāṅgi on the south and at Pattukkōttai and Tiruppattur on the south-west in order to prevent the sudden and unexpected attacks upon Tanjore by the Muhammadans, who had extended their power in the lower Carnatic and the Nayaks of Madura who always threatened the Vallam line of defence. As the safety depended upon the defence of these forts, considerable care and trouble were taken to maintain them in good order. Each fort was placed under the command of a loyal and trusted captain and was equipped with up-to-date weapons of offence and defence. The Jesuit letters speak of the artillery that were installed in these forts. Huge quantities of provisions also were stored up in these forts for the garrisons in case of siege. The Dalavāy was the commander-in-chief and the commanders of these forts were his subordinates.

The Tanjore army was composed of infantry, cavalry and elephantry. Foreign mercenaries were also employed at times of need. The *Sāhityaratnākara* speaks of a camel corps forming a part of the Nayak's forces.[4] The foot-soldiers carried with them long spears, broad swords, bows and arrows and the reference to *agniyantrās* is evidence to the soldiers using firing guns. The use of muskets and cannon had become general in India in the sixteenth century, and had been familiarised by the Muhammadan powers of the Deccan and the European settlers of the coast. The soldiers wore armours and helmets. The cavalry and the elephantry were all well caparisoned and were manned by trained soldiers. Each elephant was equipped with a howdah of iron-plates on its back. As these two arms formed important elements of the Nayak's forces, much attention was paid for their proper upkeep and maintenance. The Portuguese accounts speak of the heavy prices which the Nayaks paid the Moors for good cavalry mounts. Elephants were mostly bought from the Portuguese who imported them from Ceylon. According to an arrangement made by Antao Vaz Fereira in 1607, the Portuguese were allowed to sell the elephants captured in the forests of Ceylon, only to the Nayak of Tanjore; and we find it stated 'according to the existing custom, the best purchaser being the Naik of Tanjore' in their records.[5]

4. *Sāhityaratnākara,* Chapter XIII, Sloka 5.

5. *The Portuguese in Ceylon,* Dr. Pieris. Also J. R. A. S., Ceylon Branch, Vol. 21, p. 102.

Nothing more is known of the way in which this huge army was officered or maintained. The king himself sometimes led the army to battle and took the field in person. Yagnanārāyana Dīkshita gives details of the materials required for erecting tents and also the other provisions that were carried by the soldiers. Reference has already been made to the soldiers taking with them a medicinal herb which had healing properties. No definite information is available from the sources regarding the navy of the Nayaks; however, the reference to small *dhonies* or junks in the Portuguese chronicles and which were used in the fighting on the Jaffna coast support the view that the Nayaks of Tanjore had small ships equipped with guns and soldiers with the aid of which they seem to have transported their troops to the coast of Ceylon and carried on their oceanic warfare.

Unlike the Madura Nayaks the Nayaks of Tanjore had no *pālaiyams** (i.e., feudal estates let out on condition of military tenure and with wide power of administration given to the holders) under them but there were numerous agents of the Nayak, who were in charge of small administrative divisions.[6] They were the official representatives of the Nayak and the collector of royal dues and taxes. The kingdom was divided into a number of divisions called *nādus*; and each *nādu* was further divided into several *māhānas* or *sēēmé*. Each *sēēmé* was composed of numerous villages, which were called by several names such as *ūr, kudi, maṇgalam, grāmam, kurichchi* etc. The village was the smallest administrative unit of the state and it was governed by village officials. Each village had a headman, a *kaṅakkan* (accountant) and a *talayāri* or watchman. The local needs of the village were attended to by these officials with the aid of representative householders, who formed a small council akin to our modern Panchayats. As the Nayaks did not seem to have introduced any change with regard to the village administration, it may be held that the old Chola system of rural administration was continued. John Neiuhoff says that 'each village has two judges, who are much respected by the inhabitants.'

*Definite conclusions on this point are not possible in the present state of our knowledge. Nayak rule, being feudatory in its origin; naturally tended to promote sub-infeudation of a kind. In the other Nayak states of Madura and Gingee, the grant of fiefs on a quasi-military tenure formed the general rule. The existence of fiefs like Papanad, etc., in Tanjore may point to some degree of prevalence of the same tendency, though it was largely limited by the nature of the village organisation.

6. The epigraphs mention a number of agents. One of such agents at Karaikal is called in the English Records, as the local governor.

The administration of justice was not based upon any elaborate establishment. In the villages, justice was administered by the village officials themselves with the aid of learned men and selected boards of arbitrators. Arbitration, however, was largely in vogue. Even disputes regarding ownership of property, were settled by the arbitrators. Dispute of a general nature involving social and religious rights were heard by the king, who was believed to be the fountain of justice. The Nayak was helped in his capacity as the final appellate authority by the *Pradhāni* and other learned men, who were summoned by the king on those occasions. In the absence of the ruler, the Pradhāni took his place and presided over the court generally called *Dharmaṣāla*. Trials were held in public in the sense that people were allowed to attend and to witness the trail but not to offer their opinions. An inscription from Pattīswaram refers to a settlement made by the Pradhāni of a dispute in which the Paṭṭunūlkārars (weavers) and the Chettis (merchants) were involved. The petition or Vaḻakkumuṛai made to the Pradhāni was the result of a dispute regarding the procedure in the receipt of betel leaves and arecanuts during marriages. The exact details of the settlement are not available to us, but the reference to the vow made by both the parties to supply a new cloth worth five panams to the goddess of the local temple in case of transgression of the terms of this settlement, shows that the dispute was settled in a manner that was satisfactory to the contending parties.[7] Generally, punishments took the form of a fine or penalty but in extra-ordinary cases involving criminal offences, the culprit was put into prison where he was detained. The Jesuit letters refer to the prisoners, who were detained at the Vallam fort.

The coastal region was, at the several ports, in the hands of foreigners like the Portuguese, the Danes and the Dutch. The Nayaks do not seem to have possessed any control either fiscal or judicial over them. The Nayaks cared only for their revenue-returns from their trade operations, the regular payment of which maintained happy relations between them and the rulers of the land. A *cowle* given to the Dutch contains provisions by which Vijayarāghava Nayaka was obliged to hand over back to them such offenders, who might have escaped from their settlements in fear of punishment.

The main source of revenue was the land tax, besides taxes on various articles of merchandise. There were also taxes levied on different professions like the goldsmith's tax and the grazing tax.[8] According

7. 257 of 1927.

8. 22 of 1897 refers to the remission of taxes on goldsmiths. 460 of 1922 mentions the grazing tax of three panams per annum.

to the Jesuit evidence, the king took half of the produce of land as land tax. Payments were generally made in cash. A letter dated 1683 says that Ekōji was receiving money payments as revenue. Vijayarāghava's grant of a charter to the Dutch at Negapatam bears evidence to the existence of a mint at Tanjore. The Dutch, who were also permitted to issue coins of their own were asked to mint coins of the same weight and fineness as was done at the capital. However, sufficient details are wanting to explain in full the working of the revenue system, the nature of the taxes and their incidence. Another source of income was the rent paid by foreigners who had settled on the coast. The epigraphs mention a number of miscellaneous taxes as forming a source of the state revenue; but nothing is known about their character. Some of these taxes were made over to corporations and individuals in recognition of their meritorious services and also to temples and public charities. Lands also were gifted away to temples and charitable institutions free of taxes. The taxes were collected from the people by the village officials and remitted to the royal treasury.[9] The first item of expenditure was the remittance of the tribute due to the suzerain power. It is not known for certain, how much Tanjore paid as tribute; and Father Vico in his letter dated A.D. 1611 says that Tanjore had to pay an annual tribute of six to ten million francs.[10] The ordinary items of expenditure other than the tribute, included the maintenance of the army, public works and charities of public utility and welfare. As the Nayaks had not many poligars under them, they had to maintain a large army at a considerable cost. Large sums of money were spent towards the maintenance, construction and renovation of temples as the State had to look after the spiritual needs of the people. Much was also spent on public charities such as the maintenance of feeding institutions, also on public works like digging of tanks and canals for purposes of irrigation and also in building flights of steps leading to the bathing ghats at many places, on the banks of the Cauvery. Though the irrigational system of the land was fairly well laid by the Chōlas, yet the Nayaks seem to have added more irrigational facilities to the agriculturists by spending large sums of money on such projects. The epigraphs and the literary evidence refer to the construction of a dam across the Cauvery by Achyutappa Nayaka. Likewise numerous tanks were dug up for storing up water against the possible failure of monsoons.

9. 194 of 1922. Refers to the amount payable to the palace by the people (Ūravar) of the Nodiyūr village.

10. *La Mission du Madure*, Vol. II, p. 124.

Commerce was carried on mainly by foreign merchants and the Nayaks did not seem to have generally encouraged trade enterprise on the part of their subjects. The reference in inscriptions to the export and import duties shows that there was foreign trade but it was not conducted by the natives. There was however, a large volume of internal trade carried on by the native merchants. Large quantities of articles were transported from one place to another. Men and pack-animals were employed in the transportation of goods from place to place and the internal means of communication were not at all suitable for the rapid transport of commodities. As the highways were infested with robbers, the merchants generally travelled in groups. The English Factory Records speak of the foreign trade carried on by the Portuguese and the Danes on the Coromandel Coast. Reference is also made to the excellent quality of the Coromandel cloth. 'The goods made in the Naick's country far exceeds Pulicat in colours, goodness and cheapness.' Negapatam was the most important trading centre under the Portuguese merchants. Although Caesar Federike speaks of it 'as a country of small trade,' Barbosa gives a good account of the trade carried on there and also its importance. He says that "a large number of ships from Malabar sail hither every year, most of them to take cargoes of rice by which they make great profits, and they bring hither abundance of goods from Cambaya, copper, quick-silver, vermillion, pepper and goods of other kinds. In this province of Charamandel are also found many sorts of spices and drugs which come from the kingdom of Malacca, China and Bengal.' He also refers to the native Hindu merchants called Chettis, (the common caste title of the trading classes) and says that they were very cunning in every kind of traffic in goods. The English Records speak of pepper, calicoes, indigo used in Europe for dying, saltpetre, raw cotton yarn and fine cotton clothes as chief articles of export while the imports were broad clothes and other woollen stuffs chiefly of English manufacture, tin, lead, quicksilver, ivory from Africa, coral from the Mediterranean, gold and silver embroideries, sword blades, knives and glass. The foreign merchants are said to have made large profits.

Agriculture was the most important industry of the land and it flourished under the careful patronage and protection of the state. The state gave encouragement to this industry by providing irrigational facilities. Sugarcane also was grown on a large scale and the cultivation of cane fostered the manufacture of jaggery and sugar. However these industries were run only on a small scale. Fruit growing and gardening were other supplementary occupations of the people; and the Portuguese writers refer to the abundance of fruit that were available in the land. The most important of the textile industries was the weaving of cotton cloth and the dyeing industry must have been highly developed, since the foreign evidence speaks in glowing terms, about the coloured and the painted cloth of the Coromandel Coast. Another industry that flourished under the Nayaks was the making of salt not only by those who lived near the coast, but also by inland people. The Nayaks fostered these industries as they were a source of revenue to the state. It may be said in passing that most of the articles needed for consumption were locally produced except a few luxuries like silk and glass, which were imported from outside.

The Nayaks continued the traditional Hindu attitude of religious toleration and impartial patronage by extending their patronage to all religious sects. Even though they were the followers of Vaishnavism yet, they supported all the Hindu sects. Śevappa Nayak's grant of lands in favour of a Muhammadan mosque at Tanjore, his permitting the Christians to come and settle in his country, his gifts to Siva temples and his grant of lands to the Madhwa teacher, Vijayīndra Tīrtha, all these show the general attitude of the Nayaks and his religious catholicity. His successors also were great patrons of all these institutions like him. The reference in the chronicles to the mass feeding of Brahmans done by the Nayaks, again stands testimony to their high regard and respect with which they left undisturbed the traditional classes and castes of society. The Brahmans seem to have enjoyed special privileges and their services were utilised for the good of the administration and for the welfare of the people. The three important religious faiths that received royal patronage were, Saivism, Vaishnavism and the Dwaita cult of Madhwa. The Nayaks were close adherents of their faith and as enjoined in the scriptures, they made pilgrimages to holy places. Both the *Raghunāthābhyudayam* and the *Sāhityaratnākara* speak of the austere lives led by the Nayaks. The social institutions of *Sati* and *purdah* were confined mostly to the royal and noble families. The Nayaks were all polygamists and the prevalence of *Sati* in the ruling family is proved by the foreign evidence of Jesuit letters. Both Rāmabhadrāmba and Yagnanārāyana Dīkṣhita refer to the presence of courtesans, who formed part of the society.

The Nayaks were great patrons of learning and it is said that about fifty four poets and men of letters lived and flourished during their time.[11] In spite of all this, yet it appears that the state did not take an active interest in imparting education to the public. There are no ins-

11. P. P. S. Sastri: Introduction to The Descriptive Catalogue of the Mss. in the Tanjore Serfoji Maharaja's Saraswathi Mahal Library at Tanjore.

criptions to show that they founded a public school, but at the same time it cannot be said that they were indifferent to the promotion of learning. Education was largely left to private enterprise but patronage was extended to them by grant of lands and other gifts. The numerous *agraharas* which they founded were all centres of learning but it was not open to all communities. Besides Sanskrit, Tamil and Telugu were also encouraged by them. They made liberal grants to *mathas* and temples which were also centres of learning. The presence of numerous poetesses shows the high level of culture and learning attained by women. The Nayaks attracted learned men from other parts by holding literary durbars frequently. It is said that the Ṭelugu drama known as *Yakshagāna* had its origin during their time. The internal evidence bears ample testimony to the great interest evinced by the rulers in theatrical and other amusements such as the *Bommalātta* or figurine play.[12] The *Yakshagāna* is a dramatic composition 'set to music and sung and acted upon the stage accompanied by instrumental music.' Rāmabhadrāmba also mentions skilled women artists, who were past-masters in the art of dancing. Raghunātha is said to have witnessed such dance recitals and the palace itself contained a stage. There were also women, who could play on the musical instruments such as the *Veena* and the *Mridanga* and to the accompaniment of which the palace dancers danced in the presence of the king. Fine arts such as painting, sculpture and music reached a high level of perfection and excellence under them. The *Raghunāthābhyudaya Nātakam* of Vijayarāghava refers to the decoration of the palace walls with portrait paintings depicting historical events and the coronation durbars. The Nayaks' patronage of music and their high appreciation of it are all recorded in the chronicles. Raghunātha himself was a great lover of music and he was an accomplished *Veena* player. He wrote the *Sangītasudhāniḍhi* which was soon followed by the *Chaturdaṇdiprakāsika* of Vēṇkatamakhi. The latter is called the rejuvenator of *Carnatic Music,* while the former enriched the science of music by his original contributions such as the discovery of new *ragas* like Jayantasēna and *talas* called Rāmānaṇḍa.

The Nayaks of Tanjore thus largely contributed to the advance and progress of the material welfare of their subjects and even though they were not able to make any substantial contribution either to the science of politics or administration, yet they occupy an honourable place among great patrons, for their deep love of learning, encouragement and patronage of learned men, music and painting. The most notable contributions of their benevolent rule are still discernible in the field of lite-

12. *Raghunāthābhyudayam,* Chapter XII, Sloka 10.

rature and music. The present magnificent Tanjore Palace Library is said to have been enlarged from the nucleus left by the Nayaks. The important results of their rule were the migration of a large number of Telugu speaking people into the Tamil land and the evolving of a colloquial form of Telugu with a large admixture of Tamil words. Though they were Telugus by birth, they soon endeared themselves to the Tamil people by their benevolence, justice and love. Their rule was equally noted for its moderation as for its equity and though they were foreigners in the Tamil country at the time of their advent, they made Tanjore their home and became quickly an integral element of the country and continued the traditional policy of protection of the subjects and patronage of religion, arts and letters. Thus the Nayak rule in Tanjore forms, from the cultural point of view, a most pleasing epoch in the history of the South Indian people.

APPENDIX (1)

INSCRIPTIONS BEARING ON THE NAYAKS OF TANJORE CHRONOLOGICALLY ARRANGED.

(Dates calculated on the basis of the Cyclic years are given within brackets. The others are those supplied by the Madras Department of Epigraphy.)

1 A. D. 1511. Nedungunram (North Arcot District). Krishnadeva Raya. Vikrama; Tai. (A.D. 1511). Gift of the income from the lease of fishery in the tank at Kodungalur for deepening the tank, by Dalavay S'evappa Nayaka for the merit of Tirumalai Nayak, the agent of the king. (145 of 1924.)

2 A. D. 1516. Manamadura (Ramnad District). Saka 1438. Dhatu. Mentions Bhuvanaikaviran *panam* and Rāyarvas'il Timmappa Nayaka, the administrator of Madura and Sundaratholudaiyar *alias* Mavali Vanadirayar, who revived the past. (447 of 1924).

3 A. D. 1519. Ânaimalai. Krishnadeva Raya. Saka 1441, Pramadi. Mentions Timmabhupa as the king's door-keeper and a certain Madura - Ramanatha, as his agent, (455 of 1906).

4 A. D. 1521. Kalahasti. Krishnadeva Raya. S. 1443. Gift of a village called Sangarapaḷḷi in Chandragiri rajya by Vās'al Timmappa Nayakar to God for the merit of the king. (182 of 1922).

5 A. D. 1531. Kilianur. (South Arcot District). Achyuta Raya. S. 1453 Khara. Gift of land for the merit of the king and Timmappa Nayaka. (167 of 1919).

6 A. D. 1541. Devikapuram. Ṣarvari; Masi. (1541). Records that Mallappa and S'evappa Nayaka appointed certain shepherds to supply ghee for lamps to the temple for the merit of Achyutaraya. (376 of 1912).

7 A. D. 1549. Māndai. (Tanjore District). Sadasivaraya. Sadharana. (1549). Provision for the celebration of festivals on

the Rathasapthami and Ashtami days by S'evappa Nayakkaraiyan of Nedungunram for the merit of the king. (72 of 1925).

8 Bapurajapuram. (Tanjore District). No date. S'evappa Nayaka. Damaged. Relates to some gifts of land made by Kalattinatha Mudaliar in Malavarayanallur on behalf of S'evappa Nayaka. (245 of 1927).

9 A. D. 1550. Tanjore. Samasarupalli Mosque. S'evappa Nayaka. Sadharana; Margali (1550). Gift of seven *veli* of lands to the Faqirs of Samasarupalli by five Mannaiyars of Nanjikkottai at the instance of the king, (425 of 1924).

10 A. D. 1560. Tiruvarur. S. 1482, expired. Rudhirodgari mistake for Raudri. Achyutappa son of S'evappa. Damaged. (536 of 1904)..

11 A. D. 1566. Tiruvētkalam. (South Arcot District). S. 1488. Akshaya. Gift of the above village to the shrines of Chidambarēs'wara and Sivakāmasundari Amman of the Tirumūlasthāna temple by Achyutappa Nayaka, son of Siru S'evappa Nayaka for the merit of Tirumalarajayyan (Tirumala I). (259 of 1913).

12 A. D. 1566. Ramnad District. S. 1488. Akshaya. Margali. Sadasivaraya. Gift of land called Vannārvayal to the temple for curd and rice to god by a certain Timmaras'ar, son of Kannarasar of Mattur, for the merit of Achyutappa Nayakkaraiyan. (307 of 1923).

13 A. D. 1567. Vallala Gopura. Tiruvannamalai. S. 1489. Prabhava. Sadasivaraya. Remission of certain taxes in the villages belonging to the temple by order of Achyutappa Nayakar.

14. A.D. 1567. Tiruvannamalai. S. 1489. Prabhava. Sadasivaraya. Refers to a gift of taxes in lieu of services by the dancing girls residing in the East and West Streets of the locality. Also refers to the same privilege which they were enjoying previously and to the exaction of taxes by Rayapparasar. The order was now issued by Achyutappa Nayaka and his ooliya karans. (567 of 1902).

15 A. D. 1569. Tiruvannamalai. S. 1491, Vibava. Sadasiva Raya. Records that S'evappa Nayaka reduced the taxes on certain articles of merchandise and remitted those on others, in the markets on Tuesdays and Wednesdays. (427 of 1918).

16 Tiruvannamalai. No Date. Damaged. Verses in praise of the Gopura constructed by S'evappa at Tiruvannamalai. (428 of 1928).

17 A. D. 1570. Tiruvannamalai. S. 1492. Pramōduta. Makara. Tirumalaideva, who was pleased to take all countries. Registers an assignment by S'evappa Nayaka of several villages in Pakkapparru, surrounded by the Nilagiri parvata in Uttamasola valanadu, a subdivision of Palkunrakottam which was a district of Jayangondachola mandalam to the temple of Annamalai Udaiyar. (421 of 1928).

18 A. D. 1571. Elandurai. (Tanjore District). S. 1493. Prajotpatti; Mesha. Achyutappa Nayaka. Grant by the king of the village Mudalkattalai to the Tiruvadamarudur temple for the car festival of the goddess Perunilamamulai Ammai, conducted in the asterism Puram in Adi. (239 of 1927).

19 A. D. 1571. Little Conjeevaram. S. 1493. Angirasa. Srirangadeva Maharaya. Gift of five villages by the temple authorities for conducting the festival in *Vaikasi* for the merit of Achyutappa Nayaka, son of S'iṇṇa S'evappa Nayakar. (380 of 1919).

20 A. D. 1571. Muvalur. (Tanjore District). S. 1493. Prajotpatti. Achyutappa Nayaka. *Sarvamānya* grant of nine *velis* to the temple for lamps by the king. (28 of 1925).

21 A. D. 1572. Tiruvannamalai. S. 1494. (Vēdābhōgya). Verses of Srinivasa Dikshita of S'aktimangalam, Ellappa Nayanar, Kalingarayar, Unnamalai Nayanar, Ellappar and Kalamadutta Mudaliar in praise of the Gopura of eleven storeys built by Timmayya Chinna S'eva, at S'onachala at the request of the brothers S'ivanesa and Lokanatha. (419 of 1928).

22 A. D. 1572. Tiruvannamalai. Angirasa. Krittika Paurnami. 1572, S'evappa Nayaka. Verses by S'onadrinatha record-

ing the setting up of the golden pinnacles on the gopura at S'onadri, by the king. (425 of 1928).

23 A. D. 1573. Swamimalai. (Tanjore District). S. 1495. expired. Built in the middle. Refers to the son of Timmappa Nayakkar of the *Chaturtha gotra*, who was a native of Nedungunram in Thondaimandalam. (497 of 1907).

24 A. D. 1574. Tiruvannamalai. S. 1496. Khara. Srirangaraya. Registers an assignment of taxes to the temple for the merit of S'evappa Nayaka. (423 of 1928).

25 No date. Slightly damaged. Records the construction of the gopura at Arunagiri by Chinna S'eva of the family of Timmabhūpa. (424 of 1928).

26 A. D. 1575. Mūvalur. (Tanjore District). S. 1497. Bhava. S'evappa Nayaka. A *Sarvamanya* gift of 13 *velis* of land by the king for the maintenance of a *chatram* attached to the temple of Margasahayar. (27 of 1925).

27 A. D. 1577. Tanjore. S. 1499. expired Bahudanya. Achyutappa Nayaka, son of S'evappa Nayaka. Grant of exemption from taxes to the goldsmiths of Tanjore. (22 of 1897).

28 A. D. 1579-80. Kumbhakonam. Vikrama; Adi. (1579-80) S'evappa Nayaka. Gift of land in the Brahman village of Tirumalairajapuram by its residents to the temple of Buddha at Tiruvilandurai for the land acquired by them for opening a water channel, (292 of 1927).

29 A. D. 1583. Perumangalam. (Tanjore District). S. 1505. Subanu; Masi. Achyutappa Nayaka. Gift of land and taxes accruing from the above village for the bathing of God Chidambareswara by Aḷagaperumal for the merit of the king. (416 of 1918).

30 A. D, 1583. Vaithīswarankoil. S. 1505. Subanu; Masi. Achyutappa Nayaka. Gift as above. Registers gift of taxes accruing from Mannipaḷḷam in Tiruvāḷiparru. (423 of 1918).

31 A. D. 1583, Tiru-uttarakosamangai. (Sivaganga Zamindari). S. 1505. expired Chitrabanu. S'evappa Nayaka Achyutappa Nayaka. Records the gift at Ramas'etu by the king,

of a village in the Chola country to the temple of this place situated in Sridēs'am, a subdivision of S'embinādu. (84 of 1905).

32 A. D. 1585. Viḷanagar. (Tanjore District). Parthiva (1585). Achyutappa Nayaka. Records that the central shrine, the *ardha* and the *maha mantapas* were built of stone partly out of the palace funds and partly with private donations. (163 of 1925).

33 A. D. 1588. Panaippākkam. (Arkonam Taluk). S. 1515; mistake for 1510. Damaged. Venkatapatidevaraya. Registers a *sarvamanya* gift of land to god Tiruppuliyappar at Panaippākkam. Mentions S'eshagiri Ayyan son of Giriappar, the agent of Achyutappa Nayakkaraiyan. (389 of 1928).

34 A. D. 1588. Tiruppundurutti. (Tanjore District). S. 1540 (Wrong). Sarvadhari; Adi (1588). Achyutappa Nayaka. Records an assignment of taxes on certain articles of merchandise to the Pushpavananatha temple, for the merit of Gōvinda Dikshitaraiyan. (119 of 1930).

35 A. D. 1590. Tiruvannamalai. S. 1512. Vikriti. Venkatadeva Raya. Details the Magamai taxes to be collected in the regime of Achyutappa Nayakkaraiyan of Tiruvannamalai, an independent village in Pennai Vadagarai, Vanagoppadi in Sengunra Kottam, a district of Jayangondacholamandalam. (426 of 1928).

36 A. D. 1596. Nedungunram. (North Arcot District). S. 1518. expired Durmuki. Vira Venkatapati Raya. Gift of money by Achyutappa Nayakaraiyan for the merit of Dikshitaraiyan. (710 of 1904).

37 A. D. 1596. Tiruvādi. Manmatha (1596). Achyuta, son of S'evappa. Eulogises the king and states that he made several gifts to the temple of Rangesa at Srirangam, constructed a dam across the Kaveri, which had been breached and that he made the *Hiranyagarbha* gift. (426 of 1924).

38 Mēlur. (Trichinopoly District). No date. States that this garden (*tōppu*) was the gift of Achyutappa Nayaka to the temple of Srirangam. The Inscription is found on a slab to the north of *Sāvkār Tōppu*.

39 A. D. 1600. Achyutamangalam. (Tanjore District). Sarvaṛi (1600). Fragment. Mentions a certain Ellappa (Nayaka) son of Madaiya Nayakkar, the agent of Raghunātha Nayaka. (412 of 1925).

40 A. D. 1600. Lalgudi. Sarvari (1600). Damaged. Refers to a donation made for the merit of Raghunātha Nayaka and Gōvinda Dīkshita and for offerings to God. (151 of 1928).

41 A. D. 1600. Gōvindavadi. (Chingleput District). Sarvari (1600). Incomplete. Mentions Tittapillai, the agent of Raghunātha Nayaka; grant of land ṭo a lady at Puḷvelur by the *sthanattar* of the Ekambaranātha temple at Kanchi. (57 of 1923).

42 A. D. 1601. Srivānjiyam. (Tanjore District). Sarvari (1601). Raghunātha Nayaka. Gift of certain taxes to the dancing girls of Tiruvānjiyam, for the merit of the king's agent, Madaiya Nayaka son of Mallappa Nayaka. (77 of 1911).

43 A. D. 1604. Narattampundi. (North Arcot District), S. 1526, Krōdi. Venkatapati Raya. A *sarvamanya* gift of the village Kailasapuram for worship for the merit of Raghunātha Nayaka and another person. (379 of 1925).

44 A. D. 1606. Gōvindavadi. Pilavanga (1606). Gift of a few *Kuli* of land by an agent of Raghunātha Nayakaraiyan to the priest, Ekambara Bhattar for special worship during the festival in the month of Panguni. (40 of 1923).

45 A. D. 1607. Tirukkoshtiyur. S. 1529. Pilavanga; Tai. Raghunātha Nayaka. Gift of money by Kolundappar, agent of Raghunātha, for the expenses of some festivals in *Sankramana* and for feeding Brahmans once a day in the *Ramanujakūtam* in the temple of *S'okka Narayana Perumal* for the merit of his master. (308 of 1923).

46 A. D. 1608. Viḷanagar. (Tanjore District). Kilaka (1608). Turaikattuvar mantapa in the temple was the gift of Dīkshitaraiyan. (164 of 1925).

47 A. D. 1611. Papanasam. (Tanjore District). Virodhikrit (1611). Raghunātha Nayaka. Gift of three *panam* which was the annual grazing fee due from a certain

Nallānkōn of Papanasam, for lamp as per orders of Dīkshitaraiyan. Mentions Vengatta Nayaka. (460 of 1922).

48 A. D. 1614. Narattampundi. S. 1536. Pramādicha. Venkatapati Raya. Gift of certain taxes by the treasurers of the temple for offerings. Mentions Narasinga Dīkshita, the agent of Raghunātha Nayakkaraiyan. (381 of 1925).

49 A. D. 1615. Nedungunram. Rākshasa (1615). Mentions a certain S'ōnadri Aiyan, the agent of Raghunātha Nayakkaraiyan. (705 of 1904).

50 A. D. 1615. Tirukkoshtiyur. Ânanda (1615). Raghunātha Nayaka. Gift of land by Gōvinda Dīkshitaraiyan, the agent of the king. (331 of 1923).

51 A. D. 1618. Nāchchiarkoil. (Tanjore District). S. 1540. Kālayukti. Raghunātha Nayaka. The mantapa was built by Aṭṭavaṇai Rangappayyan for the merit of Raghunātha Nayakaraiyan. (286 of 1926).

52 A. D. 1619. Kōttūr. (Tanjore District). Siddhārti (1619). Gift of ten *velis* of land by Raghunātha Nayaka (of Tanjore). (465 of 1912).

53 A. D. 1622. Nodiyur. (Tanjore District). Dundubi (1622). Raghunātha Nayaka. An assignment of 30 *pon* from the amount payable to the palace by the *uravar* of Nodiyur for the worship and sacred bath of the copper images of the God and goddess, newly set up in the temple by Narayana Raja, the agent of the king.

54 A. D. 1631. Kumbakonam. S. 1551 wrong for 1553. Prajōtpatti. Tai. Ragunātha Nayaka. Gōvinda Dīkshita, the *pradhani* of the Nayaka built the *Acharavās'al* and the *Ananta Kalyana mantapa* of the Mahamatha which S'arangaswamiyar, the agent of the Kumbakonam Perianatha was occupying. (290 of 1927).

55 A. D. 1634. Pattiswaram. (Tanjore District). Bava (1634). Refers to Dīkshitaswami and records the settlement of a dispute (Vaḷakkumurai) between the weavers and the chettis of the locality. (Madras Report of South Indian Epigraphy (1927). (257 of 1927),

56 A. D. 1642. Mudigondanallur. (Tanjore District). Chitrabānu (1642). Vijayarāghava Nayaka. Records the order of the king's agent Nayiniappa Nayanar providing for the maintenance of the daily worship and festivals in the temple of Amman in lieu of the temple's right of collecting donations from the villages for that purpose. (166 of 1925).

57 A. D. 1643. Nedungunram. Vishu (1643). Gift of land by the agent of Achyuta Vijaiyarāghava Nayakaraiyan. (709 of 1904).

58 A. D. 1644. Tirukkoshtiyur. S. 1466. Tarana. Vijayarāghava Nayaka. Records the provision made by Dalavay Venkatadri Nayakar, the agent of the king, for the daily offerings during a service in the temple and for feeding in the *Ramanujakutam* for the merit of his master. (309 of 1923).

59 A. D. 1644. Nedungunram. Tarana; Masi. Vijayarāghava Nayaka. Gift of 150 *kuli* of land to the temple of Dharmaputtirar by the villagers and Tiruvambala Pillai, the deputy of Timma Nayaka, who was the agent of the king. (112 of 1924).

60 A. D. 1648. Olayamputtur. (Tanjore District). Sarvadāri; Avani. (1648). Records a '*parivartana*' given by Vaidyanatha Annagal, the agent of Vijayarāghava Nayakkaraiyan to the *Mahajanas* of the Olaiyamangalam. (543 of 1918).

61 A. D. 1654. Papanasam. (Tanjore District). Vijaya; Tai (1654). Achyuta Vijayarāghava Nayaka. Grant of an annual contribution of 15 *panam* to the temple by a certain Vira Perumal Chetty, during the management of Thiagappa Mudaliar. (461 of 1922).

62 A. D. 1656. Copper plate. S. 1578 expired. Manmatha; Mina. Gift of a village called Alamēlumangapuram, an agrahara to Vaishnava Brahmans learned in the Vedas. (10 of Appendix A 1921-22).

APPENDIX (2)

VIJAYARĀGHAVA NAYAK'S GRANT TO THE DUTCH *

The Telugu bears the date S. 15. Margasira of the cyclic year Vilambi. Achyuta Sri Vijayarāghava Nayānayya Volanda Rikulappangusu amaralukku yiccina kaula Nammikka Sasanam. (Deed of agreement given to Rijkloff Van Goens, the Admiral of Holland by Achyuta Vijayarāghava).

Mr. Chinnana Chetti had earnestly submitted to us by means of petitions that your company was desirous of carrying on trade operations in the port of Negapatam and that for that purpose we should grant you an ordinance of agreement laying down rules and regulations. Therefore, as desired by him, you are permitted to come to Negapatam and carry on trade. We have commanded that the port, the houses, and the yards that were in the possession of the Portuguese, should be handed over to you; further, we have assigned to you the total (number of) ten villages, viz., Putur, Muttam, Poruvalacheri, Antonipet, Karuveppangadu, Alinjjilamangalam, Sangamangalam, Niruttamangalam, Manjakollai and Nariyangudi, which were formerly in the enjoyment of the Portuguese Captain and of their Church as well as their gardens. So, you should pay to the state an annual tribute as tax due thereon, every year. Besides, we have decreed that the commodities cloth and corn exported from and the commodities imported into the port of Negapatam should be free from all export and import duties. We have also ordained that the (stranded) ships belonging to your company should be your own with being liable to the state's right of wreckage. If the merchants or other men belonging to your company having appropriated the (cash) balances and (other) properties (of the

---

* Proceedings of the Indian Historical Records Commission, Vol. XIV P. 39: Two Negapatam grants from the Batavia Museum by Prof. K. A. Nilakanta Sastri, M.A.

The importance of these two grants has been very carefully and critically studied by the learned Professor, who has also given the results of his study of the other valuable foreign sources bearing on the subject. As regards the Nayak's grant to the Dutch his English translation of the Telugu Original is reproduced here; but Ekoji's Tamil grant of which he has given the English transliteration, is reproduced in the language of the charter itself following his English version.

company) should take shelter in the villages of (our) state, we undertake to hand them over to you together with their property. We have also commanded that you should be exempted from the payment of minor duties while carrying on trade in our country in a manner acceptable to you. We have also arranged that no minor duties should be collected either from the ryots of the Portuguese villages made over to you or from your merchants residing at Negapatam; nor tolls from your men who go out with (your) passes in different directions. Since, we have issued an ordinance of agreement in these terms, we have pledged our faith to Mr. Chinnana Chetti, that we shall regulate our relations for all time (lit. for our sons and grandsons etc.) with you without the slightest infringement (of these concessions). In these circumstances you are also required to entertain feelings of friendship and loyalty to our state and carry on trade operations in happiness as long as the Sun and the Moon last, remitting the taxes due to our state and placing faith in this deed of agreement.

SRI VIJAYARAGHAVA.

APPENDIX (3)

EKOJI'S GRANT TO THE DUTCH

1676-ம் ஆண்டு நள வருஷம் மார்கழி மீ 30உ விசாபுரம் சாயபு பாத்ஷா[1] அவர்கள் காரியத்துக்கு கருத்தருமாயி சேனுபதியுமாகிய தஞ்சாவூர் சீர்மையாகி(ய) நாட்டுக்கு வந்திருக்கிற, ஸ்ரீ(ம)து ராஜா ஸ்ரீ எகோஜி மகாராஜா அவர்கள் ஒரு பிறமும், உளாந்தா[2] உத்தம. கும்பினிவின் பேரால் இந்தியா வென்ற மலங்கரைக்கு சின்ன ஜெனராலுமாய்[2a] உசிர்த்துணை தலைவனுமாய் இலங்கைக்கும் சோழமண்டலக்கரை சாலக்கரைக்கும் மதுரைக்கும் கடலுக்கும் கரைக்கும் குவற்னதோரும்[3] ஆகிய சினர் அமரேல்[4] மகாராஜா ரிக்கோல்ப் வான் குன்சு[5] அவர்கள் இடமாக, நாகப்பட்டிணம் பெரிய கர்ப்பித்தார் சினர் பிடர் வேர்வேர்[6] அவர்களும், சின்ன கர்ப்பித்தார் சினர் தோமாசு வான்திரோ[7] அவர்கள் முதலான உயிர்த்துணை தலைவ(ர்)மார் ஒரு பிறமும், வார்த்தைப்பாடு முகி(டி)த்து சமர்பாகம் பண்ணிக் கொண்ட வகைக்கு விபாம்.

முதலாவது, உத்தம கும்பினிக்கும் எகோசி மகாராஜா அவர்களுக்கும் உண்டான பகையும் படைப்பும் முறிவும் தவிர்த்து, இன்று முதல் என்னென்னைக்கும் முறியாத ஒரு உறுதியான உறவு ஒன்றுபட்டு சிநேகம் நடந்துகொள்ளுகிறது. இந்தக்கொண்டிராக்டு[8] துடங்கின முதல் இருவகையிலும் அ(டை)டந்திருக்கிற மனுசர் இந்தக்கவில்[9] பிரகாரம் துடந்து வருகிற சட்டப்படிக்கு பலன் கிடைத்து நடந்துகொள்ளுகிறது. கிழக்கு திக்கில் இந்தியக்கரை உலாந்த உத்தம கும்பினிவுக்கு இனுங்க, எகோசி மகாராஜா அவர்கள் சம்மதித்து, விசயபுரத்து சாயபு பாத்ஷா அவர்கள்பேரால் விட்டு நடப்பிக்கிறது.

இரண்டாவது, முந்தின காரியம் உத்தம கும்பினிவுக்கு கிடைக்கும் வர்த்தகப் பலன், தஞ்சாவூர்ச் சிமையிலே எல்லாம் ஒரு விக்கினமும் அன்றியே சுயமாக உத்தம கும்பினிவின் பணிவிடைக்காறரும் வர்த்தகரும் கொண்டுபோய் விற்கிற சரக்குகளுக்கும், மறுபடி கொண்டுவருகிற சரக்குகளுக்கெல்லாம் அரைத்தீர்வை கொடுக்கிறது. இந்தப்படிக்கு விசயபுரத்து பாதிஷா அவர்கள் காரியத்துக்கு க(ர்)த்தரான

---

[1] Padshah Sahib of Bijapur *viz* the Bijapur Sultan.

[2] The Dutch East India Company of Holland.

[2a] Lieutenant-General.

[3] Governor

[4] Signor Admiral.

[5] Rijkloff Van Goens.

[6] Captain Signor Peter.

[7] Captain Signor Thomas.

[8] Contract.

[9] Cowle.

முல்லா[10] அவர்களும் இந்தப்படி நடப்பிவித்தார்கள். அதிப்(ன்)பிறகு காலம் கூடிப் போன தஞ்சாவூர் விஜயராகவ நாயக்கர் அவர்களும் 1661 ஆண்டிலேயும் சம்மதித்து ஒரு வெள்ளிப்பட்டயமும்[11] எழுதித்தந்து அப்படியே நடப்பித்துவந்தார்கள். அந்தச் சுயமான வர்த்தகமும் அரைந் தீர்வைக்கும், எகோசி மகாராஜா அவர்கள் உள்பட்டு இந்த ஒப்பந்தக் கவுலிலேலே சம்மதித்து அவர்கள் நித்தமும் விட்டும் மன்னிமையாக[12] நடப்பித்தாப்போலே உத்தம கும்பினிக்கு நடப்பிக்கிறது. இதுவும் உத்தம கும்பினி வர்த்தகருக்கு தஞ்சாவூருடனே சேர்ந்த சீமையிலே எல்லாம் உத்தம கும்பினி இடமாக இருக்கிற கவுலிலே எழுதியிருக்கிறபடிக்கு அந்தப்படியே எகோசி மகாராஜா அவர்களும் களங்கமர இந்தக்கவில் பிரகாரப்படிக்கு புதுப்பிச்சு உறுதியாக்கி, எகோசி மகாராஜா அவர்கள் சம்மதித்து உத்தம கும்பினிவுக்கு கட்டளையிட்டாப்போலே நடப்பிக்கிறது.

மூன்றாவது, உத்தம கும்பினிக்கு நடந்த பழய கிராமம் பத்தும் அந்தபபடியே உத்தம கும்பினிக்கு நடக்கிறது. இதுவன்றியில் நாகப்பட்டணத்துக் கோட்டைக்குத் தென் புறமாயிருக்கிற பொய்யூர்த் தோட்டமும் புதிய வெளிக்கோபுரத்துக்கு மேல்புறமாயிருக்கிற தோட்டமும், தஞ்சாவூர் விஜயராகவ நாயக்கர் அவர்கள் தந்த கவுலிலே எழுதியிருக்கிறப்போலே, அப்படியே எகோசி மகாராஜா அவர்களும் சம்மதித்து உத்தம கும்பினிக்கு நடப்பிக்கிறது. பழய கிராமம் பத்துக்கும் வருஷம் 1-க்கு பொன் ஆயிரத்து இருநூறு உத்தம கும்பினியில் கொடுத்துவருகிறது.

நாலாவது, இந்த ஒப்பந்தப் பிரகாரத்துக்கு விசயபுரம் சாயபு பாத்ஷா அவர்களுக்கும் எகோசி மகாராஜா அவர்களுக்கும், நாகப்பட்டிணத்தின் பேரிலேயும் கும்பினி பழய கிராமம் பத்தும் பேரிலேயும் இப்போதைக்கும் இனிமேலுக்கும் உள்ள தீனேவும், கவ்வையும் மத்துமுண்டான காரியமும் விட்டு, அப்படியே நாகப்பட்டிணமும் கும்பினி பழய கிராமம் பத்தும் பொய்யூரும் புதிய வெளித்தோட்டமும் கும்பினியின் கீழாக நடக்கும்படி கைவசமாக்கி எகோசி மகாராஜா அவர்கள் ஒப்புவிக்கிறது. உத்தம சினர் அமரேல் மகாராஜா அவர்கள், இப்போ இந்தியக் கரைக்கு சின்ன ஜெனரலாக இருக்கிற ரிக்கோலுப்பு வான்கூசு அவர்கள் மதுரைச் சொக்கநாத நாயக்கர் அவர்கள் காரியத்துக்கு கர்த்தரான காவேட்டி நாயக்கருடனே 1674-ம் ஆண்டு ஆனந்த வருஷம் புரட்டாசி மீ 13 தியதியிலே இந்த ஊருகளுக்கு ஒப்பந்தம்பண்ணித் திருமலை ராசாவின் பட்டணம்,[13] காரைக்கால்கூட கும்பினி கைவசமாக்கி நடந்துவந்த மான்னிமைப்படிக்கு ஆட்சியாக அனுபவித்துக்கொண்டு வந்தது அப்படியே கும்பினிவுக்கும் எகோசி மகாராஜா அவர்களும் நடப்பிக்கிறது. இந்த நன்னிக்காக எகோசி மகாராஜா அவர்களுக்கு, கும்பினி ஒரு கொம்பன்

---

[10] 'Mulla' the Bijapur General.

[11] Silver plate grant.

[12] 'Manyam,' tax free gift held in perpetuity.

[13] Tirumalairajanpattanam, the Triminipatam of the Dutch and the English Records and situated on the coast of the Nannilam Taluk, Tanjore District.

யானையும்[14] ரொக்கமும் கொடுக்கிறோம் என்று இப்போ சொல்லுகிற வார்த்தைப் பாடு; இதுக்கு விபரம் மூன்றைமாத்து முனையிலே பொன் ஒன்றுக்கு பணம் பத்தாக வருஷம் ஒன்றுக்கு கும்பினி பழய கிராமம் பத்துக்கும் பொன் 1200. நாகப்பட்டிணத்துக்கு பொன் மூவாயிரமா(3000)கப் பொன் 4200-ம் ஒரு கொம்பன் யானையும் வருஷம் முடிவிலே எகோசி மகாராஜா அவர்களுக்கு ஆகிலும் அவர்கள் தத்துவமுள்ள பேர்களுக்காகிலும் கும்பினி கொடுக்கிறது.

ஐந்தாவது, நாகப்பட்டணத்திலே பணக்கம்பத்தமும் வீராகன் கம்பத்தமு[15]ம் உத்தம கும்பினி நடக்கும்படிக்கு, எகோசி மகாராஜா அவர்கள் சம்மதித்து தத்துவம் கொடுத்து நடப்பிக்கிறது. அது எதன்றால் தஞ்சாவூர் சீமையிலே வழங்குகிற படிக்கு மூனரைமாத்துப் பணமாகவும் பவழக்காட்டிலே[16] சேர்க்கிற வராகன்படிக்கு வராகன் ஒனறுக்கு எட்டரையே அரைக்கால் மாத்து ஆகவும் சினர் அமரேல் மகாராசா அவர்களும் காவேட்டி நாயக்கரும் ஒத்துப் பேசிக்கொண்ட ஒப்பந்தப் படிக்கு இந்த நாணயம் அடிக்கிற கம்பத்தத்தில் கண்ட ஆதாயத்திலே சிலவு தள்ளி நின்ற ஆதாயம், உத்தம கும்பினிவுக்கு பாதியும் எகோசி மகாராஜா அவர்களுக்கு பாதியும் பெறுகிறது. இந்த கம்பட்டத்திலே (வரு)கிற ஆதாயத்துக்கு எகோசி மகாராஜா அவர்சள் மனுசர் ஒருந்தர் இருந்து கணக்கு எழுதிக்கொள்ளலாம்.

ஆறுவது, இந்த ஒப்பந்த பிரகாரத்துக்கு எகோசி மகாராஜா அவர்கள் சம்மதித்துச் சொல்லுகிற வார்த்தைப்பாடு. இந்த ஊருகளின்பேரிலே ஏதோ ஒரு காரியம் வந்தாலும் எகோசி மகாராஜா அவர்கள் காற்பாத்திக்கொடுக்கிறது. அப்படியே காப்பாற்றிக்கொடாமல் கும்பினியே காப்பாற்றிக்கொள்ள வேண்டியிருந்தால் காப்பாற்றிக்கொண்டு அது நிமித்தமாய்ச் சென்ற சிலவு, வருஷாந்தம் கொடுக்கிற பொன்னிலே ஒத்துக்கொள்ளுகிறது.

ஏழாவது, நாகப்பட்டணத்திலேயுள்ள தேவதாயம்,[17] விரும்தாயம்,[18] மானிபம், மடப்பிரம்[19] முன்பின் ஆண்ட பிரகாரம் நடப்பித்துக்கொள்ளுகிறது.

எட்டாவது, உத்தம சினர் அமரல் மகாராஜா அவர்கள் மதுரையில் சொக்கநாத நாயக்கர் அவர்களுடனே 1674-ம் ஆண்டு ஆனந்த வருஷத்திலே பேசிக்கொண்ட ஒப்பந்தப்பிரகாரப்படிக்கு, முன்னாலே இந்த ஒப்பந்தத்திலே எழுதியிருக்கிறபடியே கரைத்துறையான காரைக்கால் திருமலை ராஜாவின் பட்டணம் இரண்டும் தனதாக கும்பினி வசமாக நடந்தது. அப்படியிருக்க அந்த இரண்டு ஊரையும் ஒன்பது மாதமாய் எகோசி மகாராஜா அவர்கள் கையாடி வருகிறார்கள். இதுவும் தஞ்சாவூர் சீமை எகோசி மகாராஜா அவர்கள் கட்டிக்கொண்டபடியினாலே காரைக்கால்

---

[14] Tusker elephant.

[15] Mint.

[16] Pulicat, north of Madras.

[17] Devadayam, a tax free gift made in favour of temples.

[18] Brahmadayam, a tax free gift made to the learned brahmans.

[19] Madapuram also a gift, in favour of mathas.

திருமலே ராஜாவின் பட்டணமும் தங்களே அடைய வேணுமென்று நினைக்கிருர்கள். இந்த வின்ஞசத்தினுலே இத்தை வரைக்கும் உத்தம கும்பினிக்கும் எகோசி மகாராஜா அவர்களுககும், இருவகைக்கும் வியாபாரத்திலே வெகு தாழ்வு நடக்குது. ஆனபடியினுலே கும்பினிக்கும் எகோசி மகாராஜா அவர்களுக்கும் பெட்டமறச் சீக்கிரத்திலே சமாதானம் முடியவும், உறவு உத்திரகோத்திரமாக நடக்கவும், இருவகையும் சினேகம் நடக்கத்தக்கதாகவும் சரசமாய் வர்த்தகம் நடக்கத்தக்கதாகவும் சம்மதப்பட்டு, ஒப்பந்தமாய் பேசிக்கொண்டது. காரைக்கால் திருமலே ராஜாவின் பட்டணம் பேரிலே கும்பினிவுக்கு உள்ள வழக்கும் நாயமும் இந்நேரத்தைக்கு திருத்தி இலங்கை கரைக்கு கர்த்தரான சீனர் குவர்ணர் துரை அவர்களுக்கு அறிக்கைபண்ணி, அதின்பிறகு அவர்கள் நாகப்பட்டிணத்துக்கு வந்தவுடனே சிநேகமாய் எகோசி மகாராஜா அவர்களுடனே பேசி ஒத்துக்கொள்ளுவார்கள். ஆனபடியினுலே சீனர் குவர்ணர் துரை அவர்கள் வருமளவும், திருமலே ராஜாவின் பட்டணம் காரைக்காலும் இப்போ எகோசி மகாராஜா அவர்கள் கையாடிக்கொண்டு வருகிறது போல, கையாடி வருகிறது. சமாதானம் முடிந்து இந்த ஒப்பந்தத்திலே எகோசி மகாராஜா அவர்கள் கையொப்பம் எழுதின பிற்பாடு உத்தம கும்பினிக்கும் உத்தம கும்பினியினுடைய வர்த்தகத்துக்கும் கிடைக்கும் பலன், தஞ்சாவூர் சீர்மையிலே எல்லாம் சுயமாக செய்யும் வர்த்தகத்துக்கெல்லாம் அரைத் தீர்வையும் மன்னிமையும் இந்த ஒப்பந்தத்திலே இரண்டாவது எழுதியிருக்கிற அதிகாரப்படிக்கு நடப்பித்துக்கொள்ளுகிறது. இதுவும் காரைக்காலிலே உத்தம கும்பினி முன் கட்டியிருந்த பெத்திரி வீடு[20] விழுந்து இருக்கிறபடியினுலே உத்தம கும்பினிக்கு வேண்டியபோது அந்த பெத்திரி வீடும் அதற்கு சேர்ந்த கிடங்குகளும் முன் சதிரமாக இருந்த எல்லேப்படிக்கு கட்டி கும்பினி வெள்ளே மனுசரையும் பணிவிடைக்காறரையும் வைத்து முன் நடந்த மன்னிமைபடிக்கு எகோசி மகாராஜா அவர்கள் பாதுகாத்து யாதொரு விக்கினமன்றியே வர்த்தகமும் நடப்பித்துக்கொள்ளுகிறது.

ஒன்பதாவது, இந்த ஒப்பந்தப்படிக்கு எல்லாம் எகோசி மகாராஜா அவர்கள் சம்மதித்து கையொப்பம் எழுதின பிற்பாடு ....1676 ஆண்டு .... ராட்சத வருஷம் தை மீ முதல் 1677 ஆண்டு பிங்கள வருஷம் ஆனி மீ வரைக்கு வருஷம் ஒன்றறைக்கு இந்த ஒப்பந்தத்திலே எழுதியிருக்கிறபடிக்கு நாகப்பட்டணத்துக்கும்

(Second side of the plate)

பழய கிராமம் 10-க்கும் கூடின பொன் 6300-ம் கொம்பன் யானே ஒன்றும் இது கொடுக்கும் வகைக்கு விபரம்.

1677 ஆண்டு நள வருஷம் தை மீ முடிவிலே கொடுக்கும் பொன் 3150-ம் கொம்பன் யானே ஒன்று ; இதுவும் பிங்கள ஷு ஆனி மீ முடிவிலே கொடுக்கும் பொன் 3150. இந்த ஒப்பந்த பிரகாரத்துக்கு நடப்பித்துக்கொள்ளக்கடவராகவும்.

---

[20] The Factory House.

SELECT BIBLIOGRAPHY

LIST OF AUTHORITIES QUOTED OR REFERRED TO.

Annual Reports on South Indian Epigraphy, Madras.

Archæological Report, Southern Circle, Madras.

Archæological Survey of India, Annual Reports, 1908-1912.

Archæological Report, Mysore.

Archæological Series, The Travancore, Vol. I.

Bertrand, Fr. J. La Mission du Madure, Vols. III and IV. (Extracts given in the Nayaks of Madura).

Burgess and Natesa Sastri Pandit, S. M. Tamil and Sanskrit Inscriptions, Archæological Survey of India.

Burnell, A. C. A Classified index to Sanskrit Manuscripts of the Tanjore Palace Library.

Caldwell, R. History of Tinnevelly.

Cambridge History of India, Vol. V.

Chintamani, Dr. T. R. Sahityaratnakara by Yagnanarayana Dikshita (Madras University).

do Raghunathabhyudayam of Ramabhadramba (Madras University).

Codrington, H. W., A Short History of Ceylon.

Danvers, F. C. The Portuguese Power in India, 2 volumes.

do Report on the Portuguese Records relating to the East Indies, 1892.

Elliot and Dowen. History of India as told by her own Historians. 8 volumes.

Fenger. History of the Tranquebar Mission.

Foster, Sir M. The English Factories in India, 12 volumes.

Gnanaprakasar, Rev., S. History of Jaffna under the Portuguese.

Hemingway, F. W. The Tanjore District Gazetteer.

Heras, Rev. H. The Aravidu Dynasty of Vijayanagara.

Hickey. The Maratha Principality of Tanjore.

Krishnaswamy Aiyangar, Dr. S. Sources of Vijayanagar History. Madras.

Kuppuswami Sastri, T. S. A Short History of the Tanjore Nayak Princes (Tamil) 1903.

Lakshman Sarup. The Varadambika Parinayam.

Lockman, John. Travels of the Jesuits, 2 volumes.

Moothoothambi Pillai. The History of Jaffna (Tamil).

Nelson, J. H. The Madura Manual.

Nieuhoff, John. Voyages and Travels into Brasil and the East Indies, Vol. II.

Nilakanta Sastri, K. A. The Pandyan Kingdom.

Olaganatha Pillai. A Descriptive Catalogue of the Tamil Mss. in the Tanjore Library (Tamil).

Orme, Robert. Historical Fragments of the Mogul Empire.

Peiris, Dr., P. E. Ceylon and the Portuguese.

do Ceylon and the Portuguese Era.

do History of the Jaffna Peninsula.

do The Dutch Power in Ceylon.

Prabhakara Sastri, Veturi. Tanjavuri Andhra Rajula Charitamu (Telugu) (Vavilla Edition).

Purchas, Samuel. His Pilgrims, 20 Volumes.

Rajachudamani Dikshita. Rukmani Parinayam. (Vani Vilas Edition).

Rangajamma. The Mannarudasa Vilasam (Telugu). Andhra Sahitya Parishad. Coconada.

Radhakrishna Aiyar, S. A General History of the Pudukkotta State.

Rangacharya, V. Inscriptions of the Madras Presidency, 3 Volumes.

Rasanayagam, C. Ancient Jaffna.

do The History of Jaffna (Tamil).

Sambamurti Rao, T. Inscriptions of the Marathas.

Sathianatha Aiyar, R. The Nayaks of Madura.

do Sriranga III of Vijayanagar. Third Oriental Conference.

do The Climacteric of Talikota. (Journal of Indian History, Madras).

Sewell, Robert. A Forgotton Empire.

do List of Antiquities, Madras, 2 Vols.

Sewell, Robert. Historical Inscriptions of Southern India, Edited by Dr. S. K. Aiyangar.

Sitaramayya, K. The Tanjavur Andhra Nayaka Charitam. (Telugu).

Srinivasachari, C. S. The History of Gingee.

Subrahmanyan, Dr. K. R. The Maratha Rajas of Tanjore.

Tennent. The Progress of Christianity in Ceylon.

Thevenot, M. Travels, 1687.

The Indian Historical Records Commission, Vol. XIV.

The Journal of the Royal Asiatic Society. (J. R. A. S.)

The Journal of the Ceylon Branch of the Royal Asiatic Society (J. C. B. R. A. S.)

The Journal of the Andhra Historical Research Society.

The Journal of the Music Academy, Vol. I. Madras.

The Indian Antiquary, 1914-1917.

The Tirumalai Tirupati Devasthanam Epigraphical Report.

Taylor, William. The Oriental Historical Mss. 2 Volumes.

do Catalogue Raisonne, 3 Volumes. 1835.

Venkasami Rao, T. The Tanjore Manual.

Venkatakavi, Ch. The Vijayavilasam (Telugu).

Venkataramanayya, Dr. N. Studies in the Third Dynasty of Vijayanagara. (Madras University).

Wilks, Mark. History of Mysoor, 2 Volumes.

Wilson, H. H. The Historical Sketch of the Kingdom of Pandya, 1838.

Whiteaway, R. S. The Rise of the Portuguese Power in India.

INDEX

References are to pages and foot-notes

A

B

C

D

E

F

G

H

I

J

K

L

M

N

O

P

T

Y

Z

THE END.

ERRATA

Page	Line	For	Read
1	28	Madura District: A Manual	Madura Country : A Manual
2	29	and in the sequence of events	and the sequence of events.
	33	La Mission de Madurē	La Mission du Madurē
	36	of the letters of of	of the letters of
6	22	coromandel coast	Coromandel Coast
11	30	accession to Madura	accession at Madura
13	10	Kuppuswami Sastri in the Tanjore Gazetteer and accepted.	Kuppuswami Sastri and accepted in the Tanjore Gazetteer.
16	Note 23 Line 2	honorary affix	honorary suffix
	,, Line 12	neither more or less	neither more nor less
19	Line 16	,,	,,
20	Note 31 Line 13	ननु शजलक्षणम्	ननु राजलक्षणम्
21	Line 26	Besides, there was the Chola ruler	Besides, there was no Chola ruler
22	,, 19	Achyutarayabhyudayam gives no dates	Akyutarayabhyudayam gives us no dates
23	,, 22	probabilty	probability
	,, 30	Also, Prof. Sathianathaier has fixed	Prof. Sathianathaier has also fixed
24	,, 15	Raghunāthabhyudayam,	Raghunāthabhyudayam ;
26	,, 28	(Vijaraghava)	(Vijayaraghava)
27	,, 15	One of Krishnadevaraya's epigraphs mention	One of Krishnadevaraya's epigraphs mentions
55	Note 6	कल्याणसिन्धोस्स्तटे	कल्याणसिन्धोस्तटे
67	,, 18	सयाचमहिप:	सयाचमहिप:
118	,, 12	धर्थसमर्थश्च	धर्थंसमर्थश्च
127	Line 11	Raghunathabhuyudayam	Raghunathabhyudayam
	Note 11	शश्यामाकार्मुक	श्यामाकार्मुक
142	Line 16	admist,	amidst.
145	Note 51	severly	severely
154	Line 20	Gao	Goa
160	,, 8	and man of letters	and a man of letters
165	,, 8	begin to heal	began to heal
166	Note line 17	suceeding	succeeding
173	Line 31	John Neiuhoff	John Nieuhoff
174	,, 13	trail	trial
176	,, 17	Cæsar Federike	Cæsar Frederike
177	,, 18	Nayaks and his religious Catholicity	Nayaks and their religious catholicity

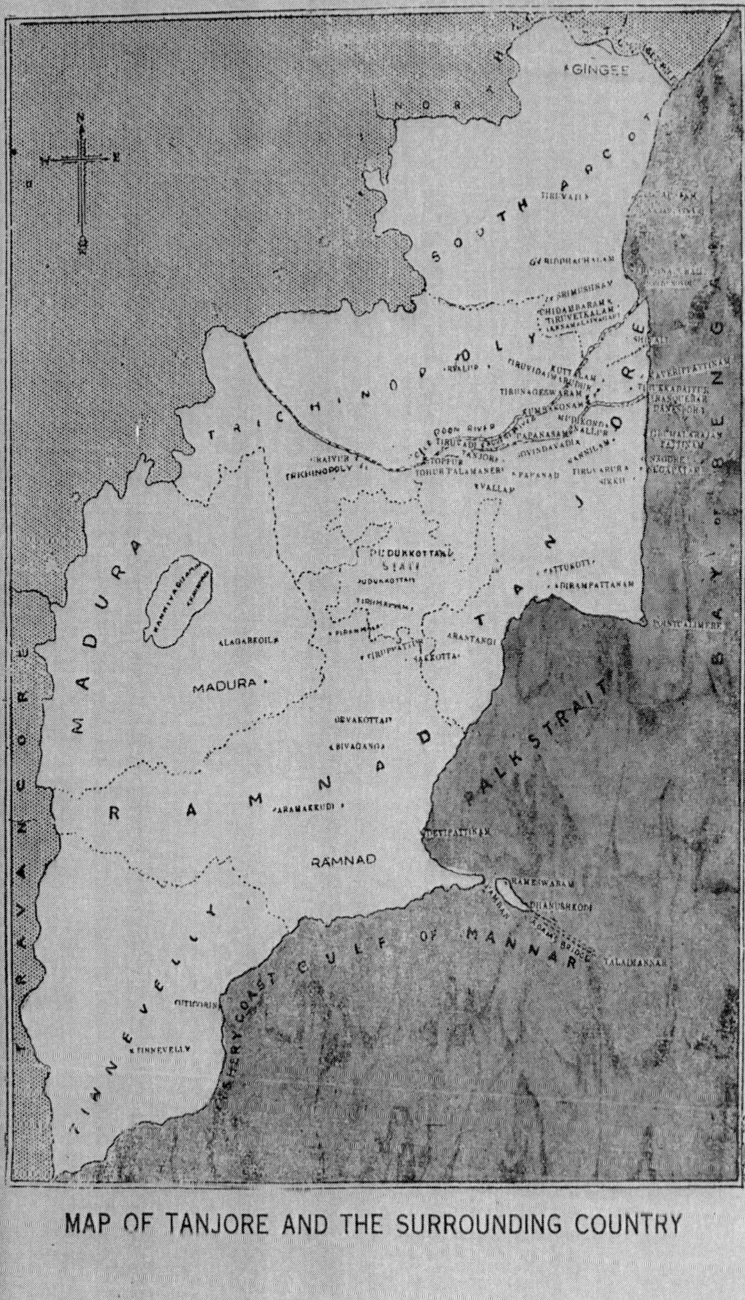

MAP OF TANJORE AND THE SURROUNDING COUNTRY